GW00787346

Migration, Diasporas and Citizenship

Series Editors: **Robin Cohen**, Former Director of the International Migration Institute and Professor of Development Studies, University of Oxford, UK, and **Zig Layton-Henry**, Professor of Politics, University of Warwick, UK

Editorial Board: **Rainer Baubock**, European University Institute, Italy; **James F. Hollifield**, Southern Methodist University, USA; **Jan Rath**, University of Amsterdam, The Netherlands

The *Migration, Diasporas and Citizenship* series covers three important aspects of the migration progress: firstly, the determinants, dynamics and characteristics of international migration; secondly, the continuing attachment of many contemporary migrants to their places of origin, signified by the word 'diaspora'; and thirdly the attempt, by contrast, to belong and gain acceptance in places of settlement, signified by the word 'citizenship'. The series publishes work that shows engagement with and a lively appreciation of the wider social and political issues that are influenced by international migration.

Titles include:

Bridget Anderson and Isabel Shutes *(editors)*
MIGRATION AND CARE LABOUR
Theory, Policy and Politics

Floya Anthias and Mojca Pajnik *(editors)*
CONTESTING INTEGRATION, ENGENDERING MIGRATION
Theory and Practice

Fiona Barker
NATIONALISM, IDENTITY AND THE GOVERNANCE OF DIVERSITY
Old Politics, New Arrivals

Loretta Bass
AFRICAN IMMIGRANT FAMILIES IN ANOTHER FRANCE

Harald Bauder and Christian Matheis
MIGRATION POLICY AND PRACTICE
Interventions and Solutions

Michaela Benson and Nick Osbaldiston
UNDERSTANDING LIFESTYLE MIGRATION
Theoretical Approaches to Migration and the Quest for a Better Way of Life

Glenda Bonifacio and Maria Kontos
MIGRANT DOMESTIC WORKERS AND FAMILY LIFE
International Perspectives

Michael Collyer
EMIGRATION NATIONS
Policies and Ideologies of Emigrant Engagement

Daniel Conway and Pauline Leonard
MIGRATION, SPACE AND TRANSNATIONAL IDENTITIES
The British in South Africa

Rosie Cox *(editor)*
SISTERS OR SERVANTS
Au Pairs' Lives in Global Context

Saniye Dedeoglu
MIGRANTS, WORK AND SOCIAL INTEGRATION
Women's Labour in the Turkish Ethnic Economy

Asuncion Fresnoza-Flot and Itaru Nagasaka *(editors)*
MOBILE CHILDHOODS IN FILIPINO TRANSNATIONAL FAMILIES
Migrant Children with Similar Roots in Different Routes

Jane Garnett and Sondra L. Hausner
RELIGION IN DIASPORA
Cultures of Citizenship

Majella Kilkey, Diane Perrons and Ania Plomien
GENDER, MIGRATION AND DOMESTIC WORK
Masculinities, Male Labour and Fathering in the UK and USA

Amanda Klekowski von Koppenfels
MIGRANTS OR EXPATRIATES?
Americans in Europe

Eleonore Kofman and Parvati Raghuram
GENDERED MIGRATIONS AND GLOBAL SOCIAL REPRODUCTION

Catrin Lundström
WHITE MIGRATIONS
Gender, Whiteness and Privilege in Transnational Migration

Dominic Pasura
AFRICAN TRANSNATIONAL DIASPORAS
Fractured Communities and Plural Identities of Zimbabweans in Britain

Shanthi Robertson
TRANSNATIONAL STUDENT-MIGRANTS AND THE STATE
The Education–Migration Nexus

Helen Schwenken and Sabine Ruß-Sattar
NEW BORDER AND CITIZENSHIP POLITICS

Olivia Sheringham
TRANSNATIONAL RELIGIOUS SPACES
Faith and the Brazilian Migration Experience

Evan Smith and Marinella Marmo
RACE, GENDER AND THE BODY IN BRITISH IMMIGRATION CONTROL
Subject to Examination

Holly Thorpe
TRANSNATIONAL MOBILITIES IN ACTION SPORT CULTURES

Louise Waite, Gary Craig, Hannah Lewis and Klara Skrivankova (editors)
VULNERABILITY, EXPLOITATION AND MIGRANTS
Insecure Work in a Globalised Economy

Vron Ware
MILITARY MIGRANTS
Fighting for YOUR Country

Migration, Diasporas and Citizenship
Series Standing Order ISBN 978–0–230–30078–1 (hardback) and
978–0–230–30079–8 (paperback)
(*outside North America only*)

You can receive future titles in this series as they are published by placing a standing order. Please contact your bookseller or, in case of difficulty, write to us at the address below with your name and address, the title of the series and the ISBN quoted above.

Customer Services Department, Macmillan Distribution Ltd, Houndmills, Basingstoke, Hampshire RG21 6XS, England

Vulnerability, Exploitation and Migrants

Insecure Work in a Globalised Economy

Edited by

Louise Waite
Associate Professor of Human Geography, University of Leeds, UK

Gary Craig
Professor of Social Justice, University of Durham, UK

Hannah Lewis
Vice Chancellor's Fellow, University of Sheffield, UK

Klara Skrivankova
Europe Programme and Advocacy Coordinator, Anti-Slavery International, UK

First published 2015 by
PALGRAVE MACMILLAN

Palgrave Macmillan in the UK is an imprint of Macmillan Publishers Limited, registered in England, company number 785998, of Houndmills, Basingstoke, Hampshire RG21 6XS.

Palgrave Macmillan in the US is a division of St Martin's Press LLC, 175 Fifth Avenue, New York, NY 10010.

Palgrave Macmillan is the global academic imprint of the above companies and has companies and representatives throughout the world.

Palgrave® and Macmillan® are registered trademarks in the United States, the United Kingdom, Europe and other countries.

ISBN 978–1–137–46040–0

This book is printed on paper suitable for recycling and made from fully managed and sustained forest sources. Logging, pulping and manufacturing processes are expected to conform to the environmental regulations of the country of origin.

A catalogue record for this book is available from the British Library.

Library of Congress Cataloging-in-Publication Data
Vulnerability, exploitation and migrants : insecure work in a globalised economy / Louise Waite, Gary Craig, Hannah Lewis, Klara Skrivankova.
    pages   cm. — (Migration, diasporas and citizenship)
    ISBN 978–1–137–46040–0 (hardback)
    1. Immigrants—Employment.   2. Illegal aliens—Employment.
    3. Foreign workers.   4. Labor market—Moral and ethical aspects.
    5. Emigration and immigration—Economic aspects.   6. Emigration
    and immigration—Social aspects.   I. Waite, Louise, 1975– editor.
    HD8488.A2V85 2015
    331.5'44—dc23   2015019743

Contents

List of Figures and Tables   xii

Acknowledgements   xiii

Notes on Contributors   xiv

List of Abbreviations   xxi

Introduction   1
Louise Waite, Gary Craig, Hannah Lewis and Klara Skrivankova

     Vulnerability and exploitation at work: Precarious
         migrant lives   2
     The globalisation of vulnerability   4
     Migrant workers, unfreedom and forced labour   5
     The vulnerability of asylum seekers   6
     Hidden from view: The most exploited workers   7
     Interventions: Tackling labour exploitation   8

Part I   The Globalisation of Vulnerability

1 **Private Governance and the Problem of Trafficking and
   Slavery in Global Supply Chains**   15
   Nicola Phillips

   The limits of corporate self-regulation   16
   The limits of consumer-driven change   20
   The limited reach of public regulation   22

2 **The Political Economy of Outsourcing**   28
   John Smith

   Introduction   28
   The globalisation of production ... and of the producers   29
   Export-oriented industrialisation: Widely spread
         or narrowly concentrated?   30
   The southwards shift of the industrial working class   32

'Global labour arbitrage': Key driver of the globalisation
of production   33
The GDP illusion   36
Growing wage inequality   37
Falling labour share of national income   38
Global wage differentials   40
Conclusion   41

3   **Labour, Exploitation and Migration in Western**
Europe: An International Political
Economy Perspective   **44**
Lucia Pradella and Rossana Cillo

Introduction   44
IWP research, migration and migrant workers   45
Neoliberal globalisation, migration and impoverishment   48
Labour market effects of the economic crisis   49
Trade union responses   51
Conclusion   53

Part II   Migrant Workers, Unfreedom and Forced
Labour

4   **Social Reproduction and Migrant Domestic Labour in**
Canada and the UK: Towards a Multi-Dimensional
Concept of Subordination   **59**
Kendra Strauss

Introduction   59
The political economy of migrant domestic labour   60
(Re)producing precarity: The state, migration and
regimes of social reproduction   63
Conclusion: The subordination of the social   67

5   **Labour Exploitation of Non-EU Migrants in Slovakia:**
Patterns, Implications and Structural Violence   **72**
Matej Blazek

Introduction   72
Migration in Slovakia: Migrant workers, migration policy
and politics   73
Migration to Slovakia   73

Non-EU migrants and work   74
Migration policy and politics   76
Migrants in Slovakia and labour exploitation   77
    Background to labour exploitation: Institutions, policies
        and law   77
    Extent of labour exploitation   79
    Intersections of violence, abuse and exploitation: Migrants
        and structural violence   81
Conclusions   82
Acknowledgements   83

6 **Understanding and Evaluating UK Efforts to Tackle
   Forced Labour**   86
   Alex Balch

   Introduction   86
   Forced labour in the UK: What we know   86
   UK policy and practice to tackle forced labour   87
       Policy framing   88
       Implementation   91
   The Modern Slavery Bill: Leading 'the global fight'?   92
   Conclusions: Addicted to cheap labour?   94

Part III   The Vulnerability of Asylum Seekers

7 **The Contribution of UK Asylum Policy 1999–2010 to
   Conditions for the Exploitation of Migrant Labour**   101
   Tom Vickers

   Introduction   101
   British capitalism and the international reserve army
       of labour   103
       The 'New Migration' from Eastern and Central Europe   105
   Refugees in Britain and the management of migration   106
   Conclusions   110

8 **Precarity at Work: Asylum Rights and Paradoxes of
   Labour in Sweden**   115
   Maja Sager

   Introduction   115
   Asylum rights and paradoxes of labour: Mira's story   116

Precarity at work   117
Work as a strategy against precarity   119
Institutionalised precarity   120
Precarity between neoliberalism and protectionism   123
Conclusion   126

 9 **Bangladeshi Fruit Vendors in the Streets of Paris:**
    Vulnerable Asylum Seekers or Self-Imposed Victims of
    Exploitation?   129
    Donghyuk Park

    Introduction   129
    Being an asylum seeker in France: Constrained access to
        legal rights to work   130
    The methodology of the research   132
    Bangladeshi in France: Increasing asylum migration   132
    Street fruit vending as constrained livelihood strategies 134
    Fruit vending work and organisation   136
    Contested presence of fruit vendors in public space   138
    Conclusion   139

10 **Refused Asylum Seekers as the Hyper-Exploited**   143
    Louise Waite, Hannah Lewis, Stuart Hodkinson and Peter
    Dwyer

    Introduction   143
    Destitution and survival   145
    Pushed into the labour market   147
    The interaction between risk of destitution, 'illegality'
        and labour market position   148
    Contesting exploitation   151
    Conclusions   154

Part IV   Hidden from View: The Most Exploited
Workers

11 **Sweatshop Workers in Buenos Aires: The Political**
    Economy of Human Trafficking in a Peripheral
    Country   161
    Jerónimo Montero Bressán and Eliana Ferradás Abalo

    Introduction   161
    Local sweatshops in Buenos Aires   163

From Fordism to neoliberalism in garment manufacturing 164
Widespread precarity as the prelude to forced labour 166
Progress and retreat: The anti-trafficking struggle and
   the State 167
Open borders, isolated workers: The atypical case of
   Argentina's progressive immigration legislation 169
Conclusions 170

12 **Experiences of Forced Labour among UK-Based Chinese**
   Migrant Workers: Exploring Vulnerability and
   Protection in Times of Empire **174**
   Rebecca Lawthom, Carolyn Kagan, Sue Baines, Sandy Lo,
   Sylvia Sham, Lisa Mok, Mark Greenwood and Scott Gaule

   Introduction 174
   The research 175
   Empire, Multitude and *Commonwealth* 175
   Family networks 178
   Travel networks 181
   Work networks 184
   Conclusion 184

13 **The Working Lives of Undocumented Migrants: Social**
   Capital, Individual Agency and Mobility **187**
   Alice Bloch, Leena Kumarappan and Sonia McKay

   Sectors of work and terms and conditions 188
   Job search within the context of being an undocumented
      migrant 190
      Using networks of friendship and acquaintances 190
      Family support in locating jobs 192
      Job search through job agencies 193
   A case study: The working life of an undocumented
      migrant in Britain 194
   Conclusion 197

14 **Slavery in the Twenty-First Century: A Review of**
   Domestic Work in the UK **200**
   Ismail Idowu Salih

   Introduction 200
   Context 202

International and national policies on domestic workers 202
Employee/employer relationship 204
The invisibility of domestic workers 206
Conclusion 207

Part V Interventions: Tackling Labour Exploitation

15 Global Citizenship: The Need for Dignity and Respect for Migrants 215
Domenica Urzi

Introduction 215
Dignity in the workplace 217
Methodology 218
The stratification of farm workers 218
Romanian workers 219
Regular Tunisian migrants 221
Refugee workers 223
Irregular migrants 224
Conclusion 226

16 Winning a Living Wage: The Legacy of Living Wage Campaigns 230
Ana Lopes and Tim Hall

Introduction 230
The living wage campaign at the UEL 231
The living wage: Impact and problems 232
Methods 235
Data analysis and findings 236
Benefits from the introduction of the living wage 236
'Evening things out': Negative consequences of living wage introduction 237
Discussion 240
Conclusion 241

17 Forced Labour and Ethical Trade in the Indian Garment Industry 244
Annie Delaney and Jane Tate

Forced labour and labour exploitation 246
The textile and garment sector in Tamil Nadu, India 247

Interventions on forced labour   249
   Indian campaigns   249
International campaigns   250
Ethical Trading Initiative   251
Using the exploitation continuum to inform policy,
   ethical trade and campaign responses   252

18 The Staff Wanted Initiative: Preventing Exploitation,
    Forced Labour and Trafficking in the UK Hospitality
    Industry   256
    Joanna Ewart-James and Neill Wilkins

    Introduction   256
    Nature of the hotel industry   257
       Use of third parties   258
       Low-wage, low-value business model   258
    The London 2012 Olympic Games and Glasgow 2014
       Commonwealth Games   260
    Staff Wanted Initiative at the government level   260
    Staff Wanted Initiative's work on business responsibility to
       respect human rights   263
    Conclusions   266

Index   269

Figures and Tables

Figures

2.1   Developing nations' trade in manufactures   30
2.2   Developing nations' share of developed nations'
      manufactured imports   31
2.3   Global Industrial Workforce   33
2.4   Share of labour in world gross output (1980–2011)   39

Tables

5.1   Key groups of non-EU migrants in Slovakia according to
       the country of origin (Data as on 30 June 2014)   76
6.1   Competing or complementary? A comparison of
       international frameworks for tackling forced labour   89
7.1   UK asylum applications and refusal rates 1999–2010   103
16.1   Living wage cleaner profiles, one year on   236

Acknowledgements

The authors who have contributed to this book participated in the conference 'Vulnerable Workers, Forced Labour, Migration and Ethical Trading' held at the University of Leeds, UK, in December 2012. This international event was coordinated by Dr Stuart Hodkinson, Dr Hannah Lewis, Dr Louise Waite and Calum Carson, University of Leeds; Professor Peter Dwyer, University of York; and Professor Gary Craig, University of Durham. The conference was organised on behalf of the ESRC-funded project 'Precarious Lives: Asylum Seekers and Refugees' Experiences of Forced Labour' (RES-062-23-2895), with additional financial support from the Joseph Rowntree Charitable Trust. We would like to thank the above and also the 200+ participants of the conference for the vibrant discussions that helped develop the chapters within this book.

Contributors

Sue Baines has many years of experience working in multi-disciplinary environments to deliver applied social research. She has researched and published extensively on social enterprise, innovation and collaboration across sectors, as well as on 'enterprise' in public and voluntary services. Since 2012, she has been based at the Centre for Enterprise, Manchester Metropolitan University, UK.

Alex Balch works with a range of government and non-government organisations on research on immigration, forced labour and human trafficking. His research is particularly focused on the role of ideas in political and policy processes. Recent work has included analysis of the changing nature of press coverage over immigration in the UK and the parliamentary process around the Modern Slavery Bill. He is a member of the steering group of the Forced Labour Monitoring Group (FLMG; www.forcedlabour.org), which is a network of people and organisations interested in research and policy on forced labour.

Matej Blazek is Lecturer in Human Geography at Loughborough University, UK. He is a social geographer with interest in the formation of agency, geography of marginalisation and community development, particularly in relation to children and migrants. Most of his work throughout his career has been done with, for, or as a practitioner.

Alice Bloch is Professor of Sociology at the University of Manchester, UK. She has researched and published widely in the area of forced migration. Her recent books are *Sans Papiers: The Social and Economic Lives of Young Undocumented Migrants* (with Sigona, N. and Zetter, R., 2014) and *Race, Multiculture and Social Policy* (with Neal, S. and Solomos, J., Palgrave Macmillan, 2013).

Rossana Cillo is a Research Fellow at the University of Venice Ca' Foscari, Italy, and a member of staff of the MA programme in Migration and Social Transformations. Since 2005, she has been a member of the Venice Laboratory for Social Research. She conducts research into various aspects of immigrant workers' labour conditions, racial discriminations at work, immigrant workers and trade unions, labour exploitation in agriculture and precarious work of young generations.

Gary Craig is Professor of Community Development and Social Justice at Durham University and Emeritus professor of Social Justice at the Wilberforce Institute for the study of Slavery and Emancipation, University of Hull, which he helped to found. His main research interests lie in 'race' ethnicity, modern slavery and community development and he is co-convenor of the Forced Labour Monitoring Group.

Annie Delaney is a Lecturer at the College of Business, Victoria University, Australia. Her research interests include informal and home-based work, gender and global garment production networks. She has published in highly ranked international journals in these areas. She is currently engaged in two research projects: non-judicial redress mechanisms exploring worker redress in relation to the garments, mining and agribusiness sectors in India and Indonesia; and corporate denial in the garment sector in India and Bangladesh.

Peter Dwyer is Professor of Social Policy at the University of York, UK. His research focuses on issues related to social citizenship, inclusion/exclusion and welfare and migration. He currently leads a large, collaborative, ESRC-funded project on welfare conditionality (see www.welfareconditionality.ac.uk) and is also working on a EU-funded project on Roma inclusion in Europe (see http://www.migrationyorkshire.org.uk).

Joanna Ewart-James, a human rights professional, is Director of Walk Free Partner Network, UK, which builds the power of anti-slavery organisations around the world to campaign effectively. She developed and implemented Staff Wanted Initiative while working at Anti-Slavery International. There she led business engagement and lobbied for the adoption of a new criminal offence of slavery in UK law. She built upon this success by launching joint campaigns on corporate action, child trafficking and domestic workers, to secure a strong Modern Slavery Act.

Eliana Ferradás Abalo is Academic Coordinator of the programme 'Argentina: Social Movements and Human Rights' of the US-based School for International Training. Her research focuses on Argentinean history and human rights, especially on the period of Argentina's last dictatorship (1976–1983). For several years, she volunteered in La Alameda Foundation, a Buenos Aires-based NGO that fights human trafficking.

Scott Gaule is a cultural anthropologist and works as a research associate at the Research Institute for Health and Social Change, Manchester Metropolitan University, UK. He has a background in community engagement, diversity and public involvement and worked for several years in the National Health Service. His recent research focuses on the possibilities of play literacy and game design to inform social change processes.

Mark Greenwood is Health and Social Care Manager at Wai Yin Chinese Women Society, UK, and has been working there since 2002. He is a qualified psychiatric nurse with nearly 30 years of experience in both the NHS and voluntary sectors. He has previously worked as a senior lecturer in Nursing at Manchester Metropolitan University and currently manages the SEVA Team, a partnership project with the Pakistani Resource Centre and the African and Caribbean Mental Health Service.

Tim Hall teaches politics at the University of East London, UK. He is interested in new forms of political activism and researches and campaigns on the issues of debt and low wages. He is currently writing a book on the sources of common life in contemporary society.

Stuart Hodkinson is Lecturer in Critical Urban Geography at the University of Leeds, UK. His research focuses on 'new urban enclosures', such as the privatisation of public housing estates, the gentrification of cities and the displacement of low-income groups from central urban areas. He is interested in how urban enclosures are produced through neoliberal urban and welfare policies, who benefits from them and how they are contested by people on the ground. His most recent research was an ESRC-funded project exploring residents' experiences of public housing regeneration in England under the Private Finance Initiative.

Ismail Idowu Salih is a non-practising Barrister of the Honourable Society of Lincoln's Inn and a law lecturer at the Middlesex University School of Law, London, UK. His research interests include employment law, migration and international protection of human rights.

Carolyn Kagan is Professor Emeritus of Community Social Psychology at the Research Institute for Health and Social Change, Manchester Metropolitan University, UK. She has vast experience working on participative community projects in partnership with local people. She is particularly interested in finding creative ways to evaluate community projects and to facilitate change in human services. She collaborates closely with colleagues working in Latin America and Australia and sits on the steering groups of a number of community projects. Her more recent work has involved researching arts for health initiatives, higher education-community engagement, urban regeneration and the development of intergenerational practice.

Leena Kumarappan is a senior Research Fellow at the Working Lives Research Institute, London Metropolitan University, UK, whose primary research focus is on discrimination in the labour market. She has researched and published in areas of employee representation and inequalities in the workplace based on class, 'race', gender and immigration status.

Rebecca Lawthom is Professor of Community Psychology at Manchester Metropolitan University, UK, and leads the Centre on Social Change and Community Well-Being. Her work engages with participative and collaborative research with those marginalised by the social system. She has written on disability, feminism and migrant literature, working qualitatively and in solidarity.

Hannah Lewis is Vice Chancellor's Fellow at the University of Sheffield, UK, with research interests in forced migration, citizenship, immigration and asylum policy, forced labour, integration, multiculturalism and community. She has co-authored *Precarious Lives* (2014) with Professor Peter Dwyer, Dr Stuart Hodkinson and Dr Louise Waite, the first academic study of forced labour experiences of refugees and asylum seekers. Her work has been published in *Progress in Human Geography*, *Policy & Politics*, *Refugee Studies*, *Poverty and Social Justice*, *Social and Cultural Geography* and *Leisure Studies*.

Sandy Lo is a researcher at the Wai Yin Chinese Women Society, UK, and an associate of the Research Institute for Health and Social Change, Manchester Metropolitan University, UK.

Ana Lopes is a Senior Lecturer at the University of the West of England, UK, and a member of the Centre for Employment Studies Research. She was previously a lecturer at the University of East London, UK. She has written on a variety of topics, including sex work, migrant labour and community organising. Her current research focuses on casualisation in higher education, gendered employment, and women professionals and managers who are employed in male-dominated industries and organisations. She is on the Executive Board of the British Universities Industrial Relations Association (BUIRA).

Sonia McKay is a visiting Professor in the Faculty of Business and Law at the University of the West of England, UK, and previously Professor of European Socio-Legal Studies at the Working Lives Research Institute, London Metropolitan University, UK. Her recent books are *Statutory Regulation and Employment Relations* (with S. Moore, 2013), *Refugees, Recent Migrants and Employment* (ed., 2009), *Undocumented Workers' Transitions* (with E. Markova and A. Paraskevolopoulou, 2011) and *Workplace Equality in Europe* (with A. Paraskevolopoulou, 2015).

Lisa Mok is Assistant Director of Wai Yin Chinese Women Society, UK. She has a passion for providing services to support asylum seekers and refugees. Among numerous partnerships forged, she has been responsible for Wai Yin's partnership with Barnados, which led to the setting up of support services for trafficked children in the UK.

Jerónimo Montero Bressán is a researcher at the Labour Studies division of the Ministry of Labour, Argentina. He is currently coordinating a research on the organisation of garment production, seeking to advance policy recommendations for stopping sweatshop abuses. He is the Latin American editor of *Human Geography*.

Donghyuk Park is a PhD candidate in Sociology of Migration at the University of Paris Diderot, France. His research focuses on rural–urban migration, irregular migration and migration business (smuggling) and EU migration/asylum policies. His current research investigates processes of international rural–urban migration of Bangladeshi migrants to European countries and their working experiences in street vending.

Nicola Phillips is Professor of Political Economy and the Head of the Department of Politics at the University of Sheffield, UK. She is also the Chair of the British International Studies Association (BISA). Her research and teaching interests focus on global economic governance, labour in global production networks, and migration and development, and she has published widely on all of these topics. Between 2010 and 2013, she held a prestigious Major Research Fellowship from the Leverhulme Trust, for research on forced labour and human trafficking for labour exploitation in the global economy.

Lucia Pradella works at the University of Venice Ca' Foscari, Italy, and is a Research Associate in the SOAS Department of Development Studies, University of London, UK. She conducts research on the working poor in Western Europe, globalisation, the history of political economy, and alternatives to neoliberalism and the crisis. She is the author of *L'Attualità del Capitale* (2010) and *Globalization and the Critique of Political Economy* (2014) and co-editor of *Polarizing Development* (2014).

Maja Sager is a post-doctoral researcher at the Department of Gender Studies, Lund University, Sweden. Her post-doctoral project is a comparative study of Sweden, Denmark and the UK which will further explore how irregular migrants with support from civil society challenge the exclusion from social rights and create alternative forms of belonging and inclusion.

Sylvia Sham has been Director of Wai Yin Chinese Women Society, UK, since 1998. She contributes to many national, regional and local advisory groups, and health and social care organisations for BME business issues. She has published in a number of areas related to Chinese communities, including drug misuse, identity and adolescence and emotional labour.

Klara Skrivankova is a recognised expert on human trafficking and forced labour in supply chains in the UK and internationally. She has been working in the field since 2000, with La Strada Czech Republic, and Anti-Slavery International in London where she leads its work programme and advocacy work in Europe managing research, advocacy and projects on human trafficking and forced labour in supply chains. Since 2009 she has been the programme adviser for the Joseph Rowntree Foundation Forced Labour Programme. She was also a specialist contributor of *Human Trafficking Handbook* and is on the board of editors for a forthcoming book on migrant worker exploitation in Europe.

John Smith is a researcher and hourly paid lecturer based in Sheffield. He is currently employed by Kingston University, UK.

Kendra Strauss is Assistant Professor of Labour Studies at Simon Fraser University, Canada, and an associate member in the Department of Geography. She is a feminist economic and labour geographer with research interests in the areas of unfree labour, social reproduction and migration.

Jane Tate is a coordinator of Homeworkers Worldwide, an international NGO based in Leeds, UK, which supports homeworkers and other informal women workers in organising and advocacy work for their rights. She has been working on issues around homeworking and international supply chains since the 1990s. She coordinated the campaign for the adoption of the ILO Convention on Home Work and an international action-research project supporting organising of homeworkers in 13 countries.

Domenica Urzi completed her PhD at the School of Sociology and Social Policy at the University of Nottingham, UK, where she graduated in the summer of 2015.

Tom Vickers is a social scientist at Northumbria University and activist with a keen commitment to social justice and anti-oppressive interventions. A related set of themes run through his research across different projects, concerning the relationships between imperialism, the capitalist crisis, migration and community action. He published his first book *Refugees, Capitalism and the British State* in 2012.

Louise Waite is Associate Professor of Human Geography at the University of Leeds, UK. Her research interests span migration, citizenship and belonging, with a particular focus on unfree/forced labour and exploitative work among asylum seekers and refugees. She has published on these themes in a range of peer-reviewed journals and in recent books: *Precarious Lives: Forced Labour, Exploitation and Asylum* (with H. Lewis, S. Hodkinson and P. Dwyer, 2014) and *Citizenship, Belonging and Intergenerational Relations in African Migration* (with C. Attias-Donfut, J. Cook and J. Hoffman, Palgrave Macmillan, 2012).

Neill Wilkins is the project manager for Migrant Workers and Work with Dignity at the Institute for Human Rights and Business, UK, where he helped oversee the development of The Dhaka Principles for Migration with Dignity. The Dhaka Principles provide a key framework for addressing the challenges facing migrant workers and those who recruit and employ them worldwide; they are used and referenced by business and civil society organisations worldwide. He also manages the Staff Wanted Initiative, which seeks to prevent the exploitation of staff working in the UK hospitality industry.

Abbreviations

BME	Black and Minority Ethnic
CBI	Confederation of British Industry
COE	Council of Europe
CSR	Corporate Social Responsibility
EOI	Export-Oriented Industrialisation
ETI	Ethical Trading Initiative
EU	European Union (bear in mind that EU15 indicates EU member states prior to 2004, EU25 from 2004 to 2007, EU27 from 2007 to 2014 and EU28 at the time of writing)
EU-SILC	European Statistics on Income and Living Conditions
FDI	Foreign Direct Investment
FOI	Freedom of Information
GDP	Gross Domestic Product (of a single country)
GLA	Gangmasters Licensing Authority
GPN	Global Production Networks
ILO	International Labour Organization
IMF	International Monetary Fund
IND	Immigration and Nationality Directorate
IOM	International Organization for Migration
IWP	In-Work Poverty
JRF	Joseph Rowntree Foundation
LCP	Live-in Caregiver Programme
MAC	Migration Advisory Committee
MDWs	Migrant Domestic Workers
NASS	National Asylum Support Service
NGO	Non-Governmental Organisation
NINos	National Insurance Numbers
NMW	National Minimum Wage
NRM	National Referral Mechanism
ODW	Overseas Domestic Worker
TELCO	The East London Communities Organisation
TFWP	Temporary Foreign Worker Programme
TNC	Transnational Corporation

TPF	Tirupur People's Forum for Protection of Environment and Labour Rights
TISC	Transparency in Supply Chains
TUC	Trades Union Congress (UK)
UEL	University of East London
UN	United Nations
UNCTAD	United Nations Conference on Trade and Development
UNODC	UN Office on Drugs and Crime
WRS	Workers Registration Scheme

Introduction

*Louise Waite, Gary Craig, Hannah Lewis and
Klara Skrivankova*

> Precarity is something that isn't reserved for a small specialised
> group of people – the precariat or whoever. It spreads, it affects
> us all. The whip of insecurity disciplines even those who were
> recently comfortable.... We are all zero hours.
>
> (Richard Seymour, *Guardian*, 1 May 2014)

> One in five workers in this country have no idea what days they
> will work or even if they will work from week to week...zero
> hours are not a rarity, they are a trap of low wages, anxiety and
> utter uncertainty.
>
> (Len McCluskey, Unite Union, BBC News,
> 9 September 2013)

> Firms are almost obliged to treat workers on zero hours con-
> tracts badly – for example, avoiding making offers of work on a
> regular basis – if they want to make sure that the employment
> status of the individual remains that of a worker [rather than
> an employee].
>
> (Ian Brinkley, The Work Foundation, August 2013)

As evoked through the above quotes, this edited book explores issues
of vulnerability and exploitation in the labour market, drawing on
material from across the world. It does this through a broad-reaching
analysis of the lived experiences of exploitation in different geographical contexts. In cataloguing these experiences, we range across global
neoliberalised economies and emergent supply chains, states' management of migrants' mobility and the structural production of immigration statuses, characteristics of enclave economies for migrants and their
co-ethnic/co-language networks, and national/international responses
and interventions designed to tackle migrant exploitation.

1

Vulnerability and exploitation at work: Precarious migrant lives

Exploitation at work is a topic garnering significant attention throughout history (e.g. Marx, 1976 [1867]). Yet there is a sense and a growing body of evidence that exploitation is on the rise across the world today (TUC, 2008; Holgate, 2011; Sargeant and Ori, 2013). Often presented by governments and the media in the Global North as mainly a problem for poor countries and marginal workers in the Global South, over the past two decades the prevalence of extreme exploitation and what some have called 'unfree labour' has become undeniably globalised. More recently, it has been suggested that the ongoing global financial and economic crisis is deepening exploitation, having negative consequences for vulnerable workers, who may lose their jobs in the current downturn or may remain in work facing worsening conditions and reductions in pay (IOM, 2009). Recent revelations in the UK of rising numbers of 'zero hours' contracts are symptomatic of such deepening exploitation.

The term 'precarity' is often used when attempting to describe these growing global levels of vulnerability and exploitation (Standing, 2011; Lewis et al., 2014). In a literal sense, precarity refers to those who experience precariousness and is generally used to invoke lives characterised by uncertainty and instability. Three important dimensions of precarity can be identified within the literature. First, a rise in insecure employment emerging from the globally prevailing neoliberal labour market model that renders certain groups vulnerable to exploitative and insecure working conditions, particularly in the context of a move towards deregulation of markets (e.g. Bourdieu, 1998, 1999; Dorre et al., 2006; Fantone, 2007). Those who work in the unprotected and precarious lower echelons of the labour market are said routinely to face uncertainty over continuity of employment, a lack of individual and collective control over wages and conditions, limited or no social protection against unemployment, discrimination and insufficient income or economic vulnerability (Rodgers and Rodgers, 1989). Secondly, wider feelings and experiences of insecurity beyond the labour market are experienced, indicative of a generalised societal malaise (e.g. Neilson and Rossiter, 2005). Thirdly, precarity has been politicised and identified as a potential platform for collective action to challenge both exploitative labour processes and a wider insecurity (Foti, 2005; Waite, 2009). This is supported by global institutions, such as the International Labour Organization (ILO) and the European

Trade Union Confederation, which are gathering data to underpin such action.

This book is an exploration of how and why *migrants in particular* are implicated in these precarious labourscapes. In recent decades, many receiving countries have faced increasingly diversified and complex migration streams and are encountering highly disparate groups of international migrants, driven by differing processes, within their borders. These include high- and low-skilled labour migrants, refugees, trafficked persons, students, undocumented persons and migrants moving for family reunion, marriage or lifestyle changes. In focusing on experiences of vulnerability and exploitation, this book is concerned, however, with the mass of migrant workers who find themselves working at the bottom of labour markets in low-paid precarious work, rather than transnational labour elites.

Although migrants have long underpinned low-wage economies in, particularly, the 'Global North', this dependency is thought to have grown dramatically in recent years (Burnett and Whyte, 2010; McLaughlin and Hennebry, 2010; Wills et al., 2010). For many employers looking to cut labour costs and to establish or maintain a competitive advantage, migrant workers offer a cheaper and more compliant alternative to local workers (MacKenzie and Forde, 2009), especially for those looking to employ people to do the 'dirty, dangerous and dull' (Favell, 2008) jobs at the bottom of the labour market. Migrants, especially new arrivals, are presented as being harder workers, more loyal and reliable and prepared to work longer hours due to their lack of choice and frequently limited understanding of their rights. This therefore intensifies competition and offers employers the pick of the 'best' migrant workers (McDowell, 2008; McDowell et al., 2009). As such, a growing body of work details the clear connections between migrants and exploitation in its various – and sometimes extreme – forms (Anderson and Rogaly, 2005; Craig et al., 2007; van den Anker, 2009).

The five parts of this book (described in the following) all spring from our key argument that vulnerable migrant workers experience commonplace exploitation within labour markets that are mediated and structured by the interplay of broader political, economic, social and gendered processes. Understanding the structural production of vulnerability through a political economy lens is a central theme of this book, alongside considering how the very process of defining certain workers as vulnerable can reinforce the segmentation of labour markets and global and national divisions of labour.

The globalisation of vulnerability

The chapters in Part 1 are rooted within the global political economy perspective. Phillips, Smith and Pradella and Cillo together explore how the organisation of production and trade in the contemporary global economy generates or accentuates vulnerability and extreme exploitation in different contexts. Central here is the context of globalisation, the advance of neoliberalism and the resulting erosion of working-class power, widely held to have underpinned the rise of insecure and casualised employment relations over the past 30 years. Arguably, these processes have combined to structure two-tier labour markets in many countries, in which well-paid, skilled and highly protected employment is contrasted with flexible, low-skilled work routinely undertaken by marginalised groups such as migrants, young people and women (Barbieri, 2009). Global supply chains and the mushrooming of subcontracted agency labour (Fudge and Strauss, 2014) enable corporations to organise production across borders, generating an enormous supply of labour in competition for jobs and a 'race to the bottom' in wages and conditions – a phenomenon also apparent in national supply chains.

In Chapter 1, Nicola Phillips focuses on global trade and production and considers emerging private governance initiatives which aim to address the problems of forced labour and trafficking in global supply chains. She swiftly draws our attention to a recent initiative in California, USA – the Transparency in Supply Chains Act. This legislation – recently informing a clause in the UK government's Modern Slavery Act – is designed to deal with forced labour and trafficking and places firms as the agents of primary importance in this endeavour. As such, Phillips explains that this is an ostensibly new approach to governing supply chains in relation to labour exploitation and arguably serves as a 'world leader' worthy of emulation in other places. However, the chapter problematises the effectiveness of the Act in relation to corporate conduct and accountability in the global economy and broader public governance strategies.

Continuing the focus on the globalisation of production, in Chapter 2, John Smith considers the central place of outsourcing in the neoliberal era through firms' substitution of relatively high-wage Global 'North' labour with low-wage Global 'South' labour in countries such as China and Mexico. He charts a picture of increasing vulnerabilities and deteriorating social conditions for a growing majority of the South's industrial working class. The chapter argues that such neoliberal globalisation can be seen as a new imperialist stage of capitalist development characterised by the persistent economic exploitation of southern labour by northern capitalists.

The final chapter in Part 1 from Lucia Pradella and Rossana Cillo (Chapter 3) illustrates Smith's focus on industrial workers in Global South countries by examining the phenomenon of the working poor in Western Europe, with a focus on the UK, Germany and Italy. Again we see the deployment of a global political economy lens as Pradella and Cillo speculate on the relationship between impoverishment and neoliberal globalisation in their case-study countries. The chapter contributes to debates on in-work poverty and asks whether enhanced worker protection can ever return under the aegis of the 'European social model' or if this is incompatible with the growth of casualised neoliberal labour markets.

Migrant workers, unfreedom and forced labour

The chapters in Part II ask how and why particular migrant socio-legal statuses contribute to processes and continuums of unfreedom and forced labour, focusing particularly on the governance and legal regulatory processes at play when attempting to tackle such issues. With different foci, Kendra Strauss (Chapter 4), Matej Blazek (Chapter 5) and Alex Balch (Chapter 6) explore experiences of, and responses to, the particularly severe end of the exploitation spectrum (Skřivánková, 2010): forced labour/unfreedom. Although forced labour is typically understood as occurring primarily in the so-called slavery super-centres of India, Pakistan and Brazil (Craig, 2009), a recent surge of literature together with high-profile media cases have revealed the widespread occurrence of forced labour outside these geographical regions (e.g. Andrees, 2008; Geddes et al., 2013). Discussions of forced labour further overlap with the concept of 'unfree labour'. Argued to be a more expansive, and hence useful, concept compared to the more rigid definition of forced labour (which leans on fixed binaries such as free/forced), unfree labour situates 'unfreedoms' in opposition to 'free' labour, characterised by agreement, or 'free' contractual relationships (Phillips, 2013).

In the first chapter of this part, Strauss probes the intersection of migration and care-work to consider issues of commodification, privatisation and extreme exploitation in the 'private' realm. She focuses on Canada and the UK to explore domestic workers' experiences of unfreedom which often arise as a consequence of a sought-after settlement route. Strauss moves our understanding of the structural subordination of migrant workers' rights towards a political economy construction of gendered domestic work.

Blazek shines an analytical light on a lesser-explored group of migrants in his chapter: non-EU migrants working in East Central Europe. In exposing the voices of, particularly, Ukrainian and East Asian migrants, he draws on the concept of structural violence to illustrate the intractable links between workplace exploitation and other forms of abuse at home and in public spaces. He further problematises the assumption that small migrant communities always give rise to homogenous experiences, for he finds diversity and differentiation among non-EU migrants working in Slovakia.

Balch brings Part II to a close with a rigorous evaluation of the UK's efforts to tackle forced labour. He charts the incidents involving migrant workers that have significantly raised public awareness of forced labour in the UK, arguing that these have shaped the emerging political discourse (reflected in a new Act of Parliament) around 'modern slavery'. The 'gaps' in regulation and enforcement are critically commented upon with a critique of early drafts of the Modern Slavery Bill,[1] together with a distillation of the reaction to this new legislation that highlights underlying political calculations and divisions.

The vulnerability of asylum seekers

Part III illuminates the experiences of a particular migrant category by exploring the lives of refugees seeking asylum in different parts of the world. The chapters by Tom Vickers (Chapter 7), Maja Sager (Chapter 8), Donghyuk Park (Chapter 9) and Louise Waite and collaborators (Chapter 10), each analyses the interplay between asylum, broader migration policy and labour exploitation. Much recent research on migrant exploitation has concentrated on the constrained position of certain groups of migrants categorised by, for example, nationality (Pai, 2008; Kagan et al., 2011) or sector (Anderson et al., 2006). Yet immigration policy and insecure immigration status in particular are known to provide an environment conducive to exploitation by employers (Dwyer et al., 2011). The lack of, or highly conditional, access to legal work and/or welfare for asylum seekers therefore often renders them susceptible to severe exploitation.

In the first chapter of this part, Vickers catalogues asylum policies in the UK between 1999 and 2010. He argues that an increasingly repressive and punitive policy environment exists for asylum seekers and that this is likely to continue, despite vociferous resistance from civil society groups and asylum seekers themselves. He links the position of asylum seekers to the broader role of migrant labour in the British economy and the pervasive dominance of a neoliberal system that implicitly champions the exploitation of labour for the benefit of the owners of capital.

Sager's chapter explicitly deploys the concept of precarity in the course of her analysis. In her exploration of the lives of 'refused' asylum seekers in Sweden, she traces the meanings of migrant irregularity for working experiences. She suggests that the concept of precarity is instructive, in that it allows an understanding of how exploitative work can potentially offer moments of security and inclusion, albeit temporarily.

The chapter by Park, in a similar way to Blazek's, focuses on an empirically lesser-explored group of migrants: Bangladeshi asylum seekers in Paris. Park closely describes their work in the informal economy of street fruit vending as a constrained livelihood strategy. He further indicates an increasingly unfavourable political atmosphere towards asylum seekers in France and documents their exposure to risky practices of police control and detention.

To close Part III, the chapter by Waite and collaborators argues that refused asylum seekers in the UK form a hyper-exploited pool of 'illegalised' and unprotected workers. A political economy perspective allows the authors to understand the construction of enforced destitution for 'refused' asylum seekers through sets of draconian asylum and immigration controls. Resulting strategies of individuals are frequently survival oriented, traversing both for-cash labouring and also labour that is transactionally exchanged for lodgings or food, operating in or close to an enforced situation of 'illegality'.

Hidden from view: The most exploited workers

Part IV urges continued attention to heterogeneity within the 'migrant worker' category as it focuses on another socio-legal group of migrants – that of irregular or undocumented migrants, often portrayed as paradigmatic precarious workers. The four chapters from Jerónimo Montero Bressán and Eliana Ferradás Abalo (Chapter 11), Rebecca Lawthom and colleagues (Chapter 12), Alice Bloch and collaborators (Chapter 13), and Ismail Idowu Salih (Chapter 14) dwell on different experiences and constructions of irregularity and insecure work in migrants' lives.

Montero and Ferradás open Part IV by addressing the exploitation of migrant workers in the garment industry in Buenos Aires. The overwhelming majority of these workers are undocumented workers from Bolivia – some having been trafficked into the industry. The authors turn their attention to the seemingly contradictory state action in this area – relatively progressive immigration and anti-trafficking legislation on the one hand but an implicit tolerance of the lucrative garment industry on the other, with associated compromising of migrant workers' rights.

The theme of fully or partially 'hidden' lives continues with Lawthom et al.'s chapter and their discussion of Chinese migrant workers in the UK. Many such workers enter the UK irregularly and lack understanding of the UK's complex immigration system. The chapter digs beneath the surface of this hidden community to reveal the networks mobilised to enable Chinese workers travel to the UK in pursuit of work – work that frequently becomes severely exploited.

In the penultimate chapter of this part, Bloch and colleagues continue this interest in how networks facilitate undocumented migrants' lives. They draw on research with undocumented migrants working in London and discuss how networks are particularly crucial for workers to secure jobs and switch jobs, yet they can also bind workers to exploitative labour. The nature of hidden lives means that these networks often remain within ethnic enclaves, and the authors discuss, importantly, how workers' agency can be deployed in these contexts to make gradual changes in working lives.

The chapter from Salih closes this part by focusing on the situation of domestic workers in the UK, who, he argues, can experience conditions of slavery. Although there is a particular 'regular' visa category for overseas domestic workers in the UK,[2] Salih suggests that factors such as the hidden nature of domestic workplaces and a lack of legal protection combine to heighten concealed experiences of exploitation and servitude. He also considers the transition from a highly constrained immigration category to an 'escape' into irregularity.

Interventions: Tackling labour exploitation

The chapters in the book's final part consider the multi-scalar steps that might be taken to combat exploitation of the most vulnerable workers. Taken together, the chapters from Domenica Urzi (Chapter 15), Ana Lopes and Tim Hall (Chapter 16), Annie Delaney and Jane Tate (Chapter 17), and Joanna Ewart-James and Neill Wilkins (Chapter 18) highlight innovative intervention strategies in particular sectors and spheres and argue for strong concerted action from a range of key local, national and international actors and agencies.

In the opening chapter of the part, Urzi explores the experiences of migrant workers labouring in the agricultural sector of southern Sicily. She incorporates the idea of pursuing 'dignity in the workplace' as a strategy for exploitation reduction. As with the work of Waite and colleagues, she argues that citizenship categories matter and shows how the immigration status of new European citizens and non-European citizens affects their relationship with the local labour market. The policy response should be a new form of European citizenship.

Lopes and Hall focus on a much-lauded strategy to improve workplace conditions, both for migrants and other vulnerable categories of workers: the 'living wage'. Despite living wage campaigns growing in prominence in civil society and political circles, there remains a lack of rigorous analysis of the impact of such strategies. The authors set about to make their contribution in this area, through an analysis of the impact and legacy of a living wage campaign among cleaning workers in a London university.

The chapter by Delaney and Tate takes us back to the context of globalised supply chains raised in Part I and focuses our attention on initiatives to ameliorate exploitative employment practices. They examine the Indian textile industry, introducing the lives of young women working in highly exploitative conditions and producing garments for export to European retailers. Delaney and Tate explore the approaches taken at different scales in order to apply pressure on global corporations to improve workers' conditions in garment supply chains.[3]

The final chapter of this part similarly shines a light on an initiative designed to tackle exploitation in a specific industrial sector. Ewart-James and Wilkins introduce us to the low-wage, low-value business model of the UK hospitality sector and describe the 'Staff Wanted' initiative, designed to highlight the compatibility of business ethics with respect for human rights. The chapter in particular encourages any similar intervention and advocacy work to engage industry leaders and employers to incorporate effective redress mechanisms for workers subject to exploitative employment practices.

Overall, the book both provides a perspective on vulnerability, exploitation and precariousness from across the world, informed both by global analyses and by local case studies, and reflects the perspectives of many migrants whose labour market incorporation is structured by constrained citizenship status. The book challenges the notion of precarity as a condition affecting a relatively small number of workers in unusual situations: this kind of vulnerability affects hundreds of millions of workers for reasons which are driven by global structural economic changes and require global responses in which governments, transnational organisations, such as the ILO, and trade unions have to take active and high-profile leadership roles. Without this countervailing action, precarity will indeed eventually affect us all.

Notes

1. The Bill received its Royal Assent to become an Act on 26 March 2015.
2. This visa status became a focus of campaigning during the passage of the UK Modern Slavery Bill as the removal of the right to change employer means that overseas domestic workers protesting their working conditions (which may include violence, abuse and rape) by leaving their employment are liable to be deported.
3. These conditions came to prominence with the collapse of the Rana Plaza building in Bangladesh in 2014 in which hundreds of workers died: it transpired that factories within it produced clothing for a range of well-known high-street brands across the world.

References

Anderson B and Rogaly B (2005) *Forced Labour and Migration to the UK*. London: Trades Union Congress.
Anderson B, Ruhs M, Rogaly B and Spencer S (2006) *Fair Enough? Central and East European Migrants in Low-Wage Employment in the UK*. York: JRF.
Andrees B (2008) Forced Labour and Trafficking in Europe: How People Are Trapped in, Live through and Come Out. *ILO Working Paper*: Geneva: International Labour Office.
Barbieri P (2009) Flexible Employment and Inequality in Europe. *European Sociological Review* 25: 621–628.
Brinkley I (2013) Flexibility or insecurity? Exploring the rise in zero hours contracts. *The Work Foundation*, August 2013. Available at: http://www.theworkfoundation.com/DownloadPublication/Report/339 _Flexibility%20or%20Insecurity%20-%20final.pdf
Bourdieu P (1998) *La précarité est aujourd'hui partout*. *Contrefeux*. Paris: Liber Raisons d'agir, 95–101.
Bourdieu P (1999) Job Insecurity Is Everywhere Now. *Acts of Resistance: Against the Tyranny of the Market*. New York: New Press.
Burnett J and Whyte D (2010) *The Wages of Fear: Risk, Safety and Undocumented Work*. Leeds: PAFRAS and the University of Liverpool.
Craig G (ed.) (2009) *Child Slavery*. Bristol: Policy Press.
Craig G, Gaus A, Wilkinson M, McQuade, A and Skrivankova, K (2007) *Contemporary Slavery in the UK: Overview and Key Issues*. York: Joseph Rowntree Foundation.
Dorre K, Kraemer K and Speidel F (2006) The Increasing Precariousness of the Employment Society – Driving Force for a New Right-Wing Populism? *15th Conference of Europeanists*. Chicago, IL.
Dwyer P, Lewis H, Scullion L and Waite L (2011) *Forced Labour and UK Immigration Policy: Status Matters?* York: Joseph Rowntree Foundation.

Fantone L (2007) Precarious Changes: Gender and Generational Politics in Contemporary Italy. *Feminist Review* 87: 5–20.

Favell A (2008) The New Face of East-West Migration in Europe. *Journal of Ethnic and Migration Studies* 34: 701–716.

Foti A (2005) Mayday Mayday! Euro Flex Workers, Time to Get a Move on! *European Institute for Progressive Politics.* Available at: http://eipcp.net/transversal/0704/foti/en (accessed 15 November 2013).

Fudge J and Strauss K (2014) *Temporary Work, Agencies, and Unfree Labour: Insecurity in the New World of Work.* London: Routledge.

Geddes A, Craig G, Scott S, with Scullion D, Ackers L and Robinson O (2013) *Forced Labour in the UK.* York: Joseph Rowntree Foundation.

Holgate J (2011) Temporary Migrant Workers and Labor Organization. *Working USA: The Journal of Labor and Society* 14: 191–199.

IOM (2009) The Impact of the Global Financial Crisis on Migrants and Migration. Policy Brief March 2009. IOM.

Kagan C, Lo S, Mok L, Lawthom R, Sham S, Greenwood M and Baines S (2011) *Experiences of Forced Labour among Chinese Migrant Workers.* York: Joseph Rowntree Foundation.

Lewis H, Dwyer P, Hodkinson S and Waite L (2014) *Precarious Lives: Forced Labour, Exploitation and Asylum.* Bristol: The Policy Press.

MacKenzie R and Forde C (2009) The Rhetoric of the 'Good Worker' versus the Realities of Employers' Use and the Experiences of Migrant Workers. *Work, Employment & Society* 23: 142–159.

Marx K (1976 [1867]) *Capital, Volume 1.* Harmondsworth: Penguin.

McCluskey, L. (2013) Viewpoints: Are zero-hours contracts exploitative? *BBC News,* 9 September 2013. Available at: http://www.bbc.co.uk/news/uk-24017011

McDowell L (2008) Thinking through Work: Complex Inequalities, Constructions of Difference and Trans-National Migrants. *Progress in Human Geography* 32: 491–507.

McDowell L, Batnitzky A and Dyer S (2009) Precarious Work and Economic Migration: Emerging Immigrant Divisions of Labour in Greater London's Service Sector. *International Journal of Urban and Regional Research* 33: 3–25.

McLaughlin J and Hennebry J (2010) Pathways to Precarity: Structural Vulnerabilities and Lived Consequences for Migrant Farmworkers in Canada. In Goldring L and Landolt P (eds), *Producing and Negotiating Non-Citizenship: Precarious Legal Status in Canada.* Toronto: University of Toronto Press, 175–194.

Neilson B and Rossiter N (2005) *From Precarity to Precariousness and Back Again: Labour, Life and Unstable Networks.* Available at: http://five.fibreculturejournal.org/fcj-022-from-precarity-to-precariousness-and-back-again-labour-life-and-unstable-networks/.

Pai HH (2008) *Chinese Whispers.* Harmondsworth: Penguin.

Phillips N (2013) Unfree Labour and Adverse Incorporation in the Global Economy: Comparative Perspectives on Brazil and India. *Economy and Society* 42: 171–196.

Rodgers G and Rodgers J (1989) *Precarious Jobs in Labour Market Regulation: The Growth of a Typical Employment in Western Europe.* Brussels: International Labour Organization (International Institute for Labour Studies).

Sargeant M and Ori M (2013) *Vulnerable Workers and Precarious Working.* Cambridge: Cambridge Scholars Publishing.

Seymour R (2014) Zero-hours contracts, and the sharp whip of insecurity that controls us all. *The Guardian*, Thursday 1 May 2014. Available at: http://www.theguardian.com/commentisfree/2014/may/01/zero-hours-contracts-insecurity-work

Skřivánková K (2010) *Between Decent Work and Forced Labour: Examining the Continuum of Exploitation.* York: Joseph Rowntree Foundation.

Standing G (2011) *The Precariat: The New Dangerous Class.* London, New York: Bloomsbury Academic.

TUC (2008) *Hard Work, Hidden Lives. The Full Report of the Commission on Vulnerable Employment.* Available at: http://www.vulnerableworkers.org.uk/files/CoVE_full_report.pdf.

van den Anker C (2009) Rights and Responsibilities in Trafficking for Forced Labour: Migration Regimes, Labour Law and Welfare States. *Web Journal of Current Legal Issues*, 1. Available at: http://eprints.uwe.ac.uk/12725/1/vandenan kerlegalissues.pdf (accessed 25 January 2010).

Waite L (2009) A Place and Space for a Critical Geography of Precarity?. *Geography Compass* 3: 412–433.

Wills J, Datta K, Evans Y, Herbert J, May J and McIlwaine C (2010) *Global Cities at Work: New Migrant Divisions of Labour.* London: Pluto Press.

Part I
The Globalisation of Vulnerability

1
Private Governance and the Problem of Trafficking and Slavery in Global Supply Chains

Nicola Phillips

On 1 January 2012, innovative legislation came into force in the US state of California. The Transparency in Supply Chains (TISC) Act focuses attention on the problem of human trafficking in global supply chains,[1] seeking to encourage large firms doing business in California to take the issue of trafficking seriously and obliging them to report on the steps that they are taking in this direction. The focus on supply chains was also central to US President Barack Obama's major statement on trafficking in September 2012, in which he announced a series of measures which aimed to 'eradicate' these worst forms of labour exploitation from the global economy, both by encouraging action on the part of firms and by putting in place rules relating to government procurement processes. In 2014, a Bill which aimed to transpose the substance of this legislation to the federal level was introduced in Congress.[2]

Interestingly, this initiative has generated momentum across the Atlantic, spurring parallel activity in the UK. In October 2011, Prime Minister Cameron stated in Parliament his ambition for the UK to 'lead the world in eradicating modern-day slavery'.[3] Introduced as a Private Members' Bill first by Fiona McTaggart MP in February 2012, and then by Michael Connarty MP in June 2012, the Transparency in UK Company Supply Chains (Eradication of Slavery) Bill effectively constituted a replica of the California TISC legislation. It began to attract attention and support from a variety of quarters, but ultimately it was blocked by government before the end of the 2012–13 session of Parliament and consequently was not passed. The Home Secretary's Modern Slavery Bill – elaborated over the course of 2013 and 2014 and gaining Royal Assent in March 2015 – was equivocal on the subject of provisions on

supply chains, but latterly it came to include disclosure provisions modelled on the California legislation. These were much more minimalist
than many had hoped, but their inclusion was broadly welcomed as an
important step in integrating supply chains into anti-slavery strategies.

It is striking that in debates about this issue in the UK, reference has
often been made to 'successful' legislation in California, and indeed the
case for a UK equivalent has usually been made in those terms. Given
that it came into force only in early 2012, it is still difficult to know
whether the California legislation has been successful or not, if success
is defined as achieving concrete outcomes relating to a reduction in the
incidence of slavery and trafficking in firms' supply chains, or improvements in the conditions in which millions of people work in the global
economy. Indeed, there is no attempt contained within the legislation
or any of the emerging corporate responses to it to measure or document
outcomes of that nature. What reference to the 'successful' California
legislation can only mean, then, is that it was successfully passed, and
that some companies are ostensibly engaging with the agenda that it
embodies. Indeed, while TISC initiatives are unquestionably a worthy
innovation in an arena characterised by gaping deficits of appropriate
governance, I argue in this chapter that, as a means of addressing the
persistent, hidden, highly complex and global problems of trafficking
and slavery in supply chains, they contain important limitations and
contradictions which impose considerable constraints on their potential
effectiveness. What follows explores some of the reasons for this.

The limits of corporate self-regulation

Ostensibly, the reach of the California TISC Act is significant. The
California Franchise Tax Board estimated at the time the Act was passed
that it would directly affect some 3200 companies and indirectly the
many more thousands of suppliers and vendors incorporated into their
supply chains (Verité, 2011: 3). It applies to larger firms with worldwide
gross receipts in excess of US$1 million. Those companies are required
by law to engage in verification of their supply chains to evaluate and
address the risk of human trafficking, perform audits to enforce compliance with firm standards, obtain certification from direct suppliers
that materials they use comply with national legislation on slavery and
human trafficking, maintain internal accountability standards and procedures for employees or contractors that contravene firm standards and
train relevant employees and management on human trafficking and
slavery (Verité, 2011: 2; Pickles and Zhu, 2013).

Yet, despite these stipulations, the Act in fact requires very little of its target actors. It provides no more than a requirement for companies to disclose the nature of their efforts to deal with trafficking and forced labour in their supply chains, relative to the company's *own* standards for ensuring adequate labour conditions. It imposes no direct penalty for non-compliance, relying instead on large firms' concerns about protecting their brand. Firms which encounter problems of trafficking and forced labour in their supply chain are required only to provide assistance to the 'victims' as and when they are identified. In other words, the legislation requires little attention – much less alteration – to prevailing business models, the ways in which supply chains are organised and monitored, or a shift in corporate cultures to move towards more robust corporate social responsibility (CSR) or accountability strategies. Equally, there is no stipulation by the state or other agents of public governance of a set of standards for labour or other social conditions in supply chains, with which firms are expected to work towards complying. Instead, firms are expected to act solely within the parameters of their own standards, typically established through internally designed codes of conduct which are not externally or independently monitored, and whose shortcomings as a platform for CSR strategies have amply been exposed both in academic literatures and by CSR-related organisations (e.g. O'Rourke, 2006; Barrientos, 2008; Lund-Thomsen, 2008; Stohl et al., 2009; Taylor, 2011; Verité, 2011).

TISC initiatives thus put in place a model which is fully consistent with the prevailing drift of contemporary global governance, which is towards the primacy of private governance and corporate self-regulation (Appelbaum, 2012). They articulate a mode of governance which relies on a contract not between firms and government, nor between firms and workers, but between firms and consumers. It reflects an ongoing process through which the rise of buyer-driven value chains and the primacy of brand name loyalty in contemporary retailing have shifted the power to negotiate terms with companies from governments and workers decisively to consumers (Esbenshade, 2004, 2012). The reporting process demanded by TISC legislation is conceived as a process by which a firm reports not to government but to consumers (and shareholders), in order to enable them to make informed decisions about the provenance and credentials of the goods and services they are purchasing. The idea is that the fear of displeasing consumers will lead to a generalised disposition among large firms to improve labour standards and ensure compliance among suppliers.

However, it is far from clear that the incentives for firms to engage in energetic self-regulation are robustly embedded in contemporary global supply chains. Such incentives are weakened by the core tension which exists between the CSR-related aspects of a firm's activities and its commercial operations. A large body of research indicates, with extensive data, that despite several waves of CSR, the vast majority of global corporations remains concerned first and foremost with the relationship with direct stockholders, based on returns on investment and the generation of profit for those stockholders, and indeed that they frame their concerns in that language (Stohl et al., 2009: 618). Notwithstanding the appeal of CSR and the ability of civil society actors (and possibly states) to coerce or cajole companies into more active and responsible governance of their supply chains, the uncomfortable reality is that the 'heart and soul of corporate ethics will remain "business as usual"' (Stohl et al., 2009: 619).

The disincentives to effective self-regulation and to driving tangible improvements in supply chain conditions are especially pronounced in those sectors which are price-sensitive and labour-intensive and demand relatively low skill inputs, where competitive advantage accrues primarily from the maintenance of flexibility in relation to labour supply and labour costs. Indeed, it seems often to be forgotten that governance 'deficits' exist for a reason – that they have purposefully been constructed and are actively maintained by firms and private actors, especially in these kinds of sectors, which seek competitive advantage from more permissive legal and regulatory environments and associated supply conditions for abundant, cheap and unprotected labour. Indeed, many arenas of global production, and specific supply chains, rely heavily on a workforce with such characteristics, a large proportion of which is made up of migrant, contract and informal workers (Bauder, 2006; Barrientos, 2008; Phillips, 2011). It has been shown that firms in price-sensitive and labour-intensive sectors, such as the global clothing industry, as well as firms which rely on retail strategies, prefer less stringent regulation and will go to some lengths to secure those conditions (Fransen and Burgoon, 2012). Likewise, the huge numbers of 'invisible' firms and entrepreneurs in the informal economy (even if they are subcontractors to registered firms) generally lack incentives imposed by external stakeholders to go 'against the tide' and seek to boost their 'social legitimacy' profile; to the contrary, the incentives they face point in the opposite direction, particularly as their share of the consumer market rests on cut-throat price competition (Knorringa, 2014).

In these contexts, pressures on firms to engage in self-regulation, whether from states, consumers or non-governmental organisations (NGOs), often lead to one of two outcomes, and usually in combination. The first is that the 'bare minimum' becomes the norm, where a firm gives the appearance of an active programme of social responsibility but only genuinely acts when the threat or fact of exposure becomes real. This was the story with Nike and Gap as two early cases, in which sustained pressure led to far-reaching change. It has also been the case with a handful of examples since, most notably the pressure on Apple and Foxconn in the early 2010s, exposed as using companies dependent on slave labour, which led, eventually, to an ostensibly energetic programme of remedial action (Arthur, 2012; Barboza and Duhigg, 2012; Mayer, 2014). Even then, there have been concerns that Apple and Foxconn's response has been partial and cosmetic, driven not by a fulsome desire to improve standards in supply chains but by a concern to do what is necessary to protect brand reputation and profits (Bader and Morrison, 2012; Nova and Shapiro, 2012; SACOM, 2012).

The second common scenario is that the case for CSR and greater self-regulation is accepted more wholeheartedly but the costs of social compliance are not absorbed by the lead firm, but rather they are pushed down the value chain so that they are required to be absorbed by suppliers, producers and, most of all, workers. A good deal of research has shown how the act of passing the costs of compliance down the value chain has the effect of squeezing smaller participants out of the production process and otherwise intensifying the commercial pressures on suppliers and vendors. The consequences are felt in heightened levels of precarity, exploitation and adversity for workers in those supply chains, a large proportion of which are often migrant workers, with all of the social ramifications created by those conditions (e.g. Gibbon and Ponte, 2005; Kaplinsky, 2005; Ponte, 2008).

Taken together, these scenarios indicate that a reliance on firms as agents of self-regulation is unlikely to provide a robust foundation for the governance of global supply chains. Indeed, it rarely has provided such a foundation in the past. CSR strategies provide very few checks and balances in relation to 'irresponsible' firms in the global economy; their impact is felt largely in encouraging already responsible firms to go 'beyond compliance' (Newell, 2005: 542). So it is that, despite the passing of a substantial period of time since company codes of conduct and the 'compliance industry' came to dominate the governance of global supply chains, even violations of the International Labour Organization's (ILO) Fundamental Principles continue to be significant problems.

Indeed, many of the critiques of private governance and CSR in relation to labour standards attain particular relevance in the case of the worst violations associated with human trafficking and slavery. Like other violations of workers' rights, slavery and trafficking are much more likely to occur in arenas characterised by high levels of outsourcing, price sensitivity and labour intensity, which, as we saw above, are also those in which incentives for compliance, self-regulation and energetic programmes of improvement in labour standards are least likely to prevail (Phillips, 2013b). Such sectors are also those which rely heavily on unregistered, unprotected migrant and contract labour that are not covered by company codes of conduct or auditing systems, are systematically hidden from sight and as such are least likely to be scrutinised for associated problems of slavery and trafficking. Equally, auditing systems tend to be limited in their purview to first-tier suppliers and the workers that are employed directly by those suppliers, whereas often the problems of trafficking and slavery tend to be concentrated in tiers of activity further down the supply chain. Most firms tend to resist including such areas in their definition of supply chain for CSR purposes by suggesting such areas are beyond their direct control and hence difficult to audit.

The limits of consumer-driven change

We have seen that TISC initiatives articulate and harness a notion of private governance as a conversation between firms and consumers, identifying the latter as the key agents of change. As one observer put it, the California TISC Act 'requires rather little from the business community, yet much from the consuming public' (Mattos, 2012). The classic 'brand reputation' logic raises a number of problems. In the first instance, the evidence is still very mixed on the extent of consumer concern about labour standards, and interpretations vary as to the extent to which consumers can constitute a reliable and effective driving force for change (see Esbenshade, 2012: 547–548). Some of these interpretations draw attention to the self-interest of consumers driven by price considerations, some to the obstacles consumers face in obtaining or verifying the necessary information (Seidman, 2007, 2008). The uncomfortable truth is that only in exceptional cases have we seen concrete changes in consumer behaviour of an order that would concern a large firm, certainly in comparison with changes occasioned by other kinds of supply chain 'scandals' relating to product quality and/or a risk affecting consumers themselves – the discovery of horsemeat in UK food supply chains in 2013 being a case in point (Phillips, 2013c). More than 100 workers perished in a fire in a garments factory in Dhaka, Bangladesh, in late 2012, which was supplying household-name retailers in the US and Europe, including Wal-Mart and Primark (the outsourcing of textile manufacture to Bangladesh is discussed further in Smith's chapter (Chapter 2), this volume). A newspaper report a short time after the fire offered anecdotal detail about how shoppers at Wal-Mart, when asked, either did not know anything about it, which is in itself revealing although not surprising, or did know but indicated that it would not deter them from shopping at Wal-Mart, as it sold what they wanted at the price they wanted (Mayerowitz, 2012). Following the collapse of the Rana Plaza garments factory in the same city in April 2013, which killed 1,135 workers, a significant number of retailers, including the giants Gap, Primark and Wal-Mart, held back for some time from signing an agreement to improve safety conditions which other retailers had endorsed, apparently not feeling that such a step was unequivocally necessary in order to protect their brand integrity or consumer base (Morrison, 2013).

The second key problem is that the notion of consumer power holding sway over business is based on a consumer market concentrated in Europe and North America, where ethical concerns among consumers are most established. Yet the focus on the 'Western' consumer increasingly no longer captures the reality of how global production is organised. In the first place, the assumption that global value chains are essentially 'south–north', where the end market is in Europe or North America, is no longer valid. Trends in global industrial organisation have been characterised by an increasing regionalisation of value chains, such that both dominant lead firms and end consumer markets are no longer predominantly North American, European or 'Western' (Kaplinsky and Farooki, 2010; Gereffi, 2013; Gereffi and Sturgeon, 2013; Milberg et al., 2013; Yeung, 2013; Guarin and Knorringa, 2014). This has significant implications for standards in global production. Detailed research on dominant South African supermarkets, for instance, shows clearly that there is some monitoring of *product* standards by South African retailers but very little monitoring of *social* standards (Barrientos and Visser, 2012), the same applying elsewhere. Concerns about social and environmental ethics in production and trade have far less of a foothold in the 'newer' consumer markets of Asia and Africa, for instance, than they do in Europe. Consequently, as global value chains are being reconfigured in this way, we can be much less confident in solely using an appeal to European or North American consumers to pressure Western lead firms to improve labour standards as a strategy for eliminating slavery and human trafficking in supply chains.

The limited reach of public regulation

Ostensibly, TISC initiatives bring public, state-based authority back into the realms of private, firm-based governance. Yet appearances are deceptive: as indicated earlier, TISC initiatives do not deviate – in intention or in outcome – from the central principles of this mode of private governance. We have seen that they entrench the ideas of corporate self-regulation and consumer-driven regulation of production, lacking clear sanctions for non-compliance and with scarcely any regulatory or enforcement role for the governments enacting this legislation. The role of the state here is legalistic and rhetorical. Yet it is equally not a move towards 'legally mandated private standards' (Henson and Humphrey, 2010) but rather only a move towards mandatory *disclosure* – a model which in previous incarnations has an undistinguished record of commanding compliance with its requirements (Graham and Woods, 2006: 878). In February 2014, two years since the legislation had come into force, it was reported that almost 400 companies had complied with the disclosure requirements of the California legislation, but 85 had failed to do so.[4] Similarly, in June 2014, ten companies were challenged by a civil society organisation for 'complying' with the disclosure legislation merely by posting minimal statements dismissing the issue and stating that no policies were in place.[5]

This situation has strongly ideological and political roots in the market fundamentalism that is entrenched in the global political economy, and which remains essentially unchallenged by political elites, perhaps most especially in the UK and US. The key problem is that challenging the orthodoxy of private governance in relation to labour standards would take considerable political courage – a willingness to demand significant change from powerful business interests and a readiness to re-insert the state and public regulation into the governance arena. It is striking that there was initial opposition from business even to the limited provisions of the California TISC Act, and also that parliamentary consideration of the proposed TISC legislation in the UK in 2012–13 was mired in anxiety about the need to avoid any kind of restraining regulation of private sector activity.[6] In the same vein, the authors of a highly influential report issued by the centre-right Centre for Social Justice were almost apologetic in expressing their support for TISC legislation. They signalled that they 'understood' the government's aversion to 'over-regulating', suggested that the 'TISC bill could be included as part of wide-ranging *de*-regulatory reforms should this be more politically agreeable' and reassured the government that the legislation would leave undisturbed the principle of self-regulation by business and 'would not demand any direct government involvement' (CSJ, 2013: 12, emphases added). All of these points provide the clearest illustration that it would be erroneous to see TISC initiatives as advocating any kind of consequential 're-entry' by the state into the arena of regulation or indeed as representing an emerging challenge to the primacy of voluntary corporate self-regulation.

We have already explored the limits of firm-led governance as a means of 'ratcheting up' labour standards in general and dealing with human trafficking and slavery in particular. Yet we also have strong evidence to suggest that public governance remains of critical importance. The most successful initiatives that have yet emerged for dealing with slavery in supply chains have been driven by states' mobilisation of public authority alongside corporate responsibility initiatives. Such a situation has prevailed most clearly in Brazil, where, since the early 2000s, a robust national legislative framework has been in operation which uses public authority to both regulate and enforce compliance. Under the National Pact for the Eradication of Slavery, firms found to be using what under Brazilian law is termed 'slave labour' are cited on a so-called dirty list, which functions to name and shame but also to cut off federal funds to those companies for a period of two years. An additional 2014 law permits the confiscation by the state of property where slave labour is found. In 2012, in the state of São Paulo new legislation was passed to put such firms out of business and prevent them from operating in the same economic sector for ten years. The federal labour inspection system developed to enforce the legal provisions of the National Pact is among the most extensive and robust in the world, even though under-resourced and its work complicated by extreme geographical inaccessibility in large parts of the country. From 1995 to mid-2010, 37,205 workers in Brazil were 'freed' by these labour inspection teams from 'conditions analogous to slavery' (Phillips and Sakamoto, 2012).

Efforts in the direction of public governance mechanisms are unquestionably difficult, politically and logistically. Most of all, these initiatives are national, when the structures and processes that stand in need of governing are global in their scope. It is precisely this disjuncture which poses the key problem for governance in (and of) a global economy (Phillips and Mieres, 2014: 13). It is evident in the under-development of mechanisms of global public governance capable of regulating conditions in relation to the activities of transnational business and in the shortcomings of global private governance that we have discussed here. The point for present purposes is that the evidence suggests strongly the need for an appropriate *combination* of public and private governance strategies – at national, regional and global levels – in dealing with slavery and trafficking in global supply chains, as well as in efforts to promote labour standards in general (Locke, 2013). In TISC initiatives, as they have been articulated thus far, there is little evidence of such a combination and instead a reliance on a limited (national) state intervention to reinforce the global primacy of firm-led governance.

Notes

1. Global supply chains are the structures associated with a pattern of production in which the various stages and functions of production are fragmented and geographically dispersed across international borders.
2. http://www.iccr.org/investors-welcome-federal-bill-calling-corporate-disclosures-trafficking-and-slavery-risks
3. http://www.humantraffickingfoundation.org/02/parliamentary-questions-full-list-chronological/. The terminology favoured in the US tends to be 'human trafficking', while the UK legislation refers to 'slavery'.
4. http://www.csrwire.com/press_releases/36712-85-firms-still-silent-on-California-Transparency-in-Supply-Chains-Act
5. http://blog.knowthechain.org/when-sb-657-compliance-is-transparent-but-indifferent/
6. http://www.theyworkforyou.com/debates/?id=2012-10-19b.662.0

References

Appelbaum R (2012) Making Blue the Next Green: Can CSR Help Improve Working Conditions in Global Supply Chains?, Paper Presented to the Annual Convention of the International Studies Association, San Diego CA, 1–4 April.
Arthur C (2012) Apple Faces Its 'Nike Moment' Over Working Conditions in Chinese Factories. *The Guardian*, 20 February.
Bader C and Morrison J (2012) Is the Organization Investigating Apple's Factories Good Enough? *Forbes Leadership Forum*, 3 May, Available at: http://www.forbes.com/sites/forbesleadershipforum/2012/03/05/is-the-organization-investigating-apples-factories-good-enough/
Barboza D and Duhigg C (2012) Pressure, Chinese and Foreign, Drives Changes at Foxconn. *The New York Times*, 19 February.
Barrientos S (2008) Contract Labour: The Achilles Heel of Corporate Codes in Commercial Value Chains. *Development and Change* 39(6): 977–990.
Barrientos S and Visser M (2012) South African Horticulture: Opportunities and Challenges for Economic and Social Upgrading in Value Chains. Capturing the Gains Working Paper 12, University of Manchester, September.

Bauder H (2006) *Labor Movement: How Migration Regulates Labor Markets.* New York: Oxford University Press.

CSJ (Centre for Social Justice) (2013) *It Happens Here: Equipping the United Kingdom to Fight Modern Slavery.* London: Centre for Social Justice.

Esbenshade J (2004) *Monitoring Sweatshops: Workers, Consumers, and the Global Apparel Industry.* Philadelphia, PA: Temple University Press.

—— (2012) A Review of Private Regulation: Codes and Monitoring in the Apparel Industry. *Sociology Compass* 6(7): 541–556.

Fransen L and Burgoon B (2012) A Market for Worker Rights: Explaining Business Support for International Private Labour Regulation. *Review of International Political Economy* 19(2): 236–266.

Gereffi G (2013) Global Value Chains in a Post-Washington Consensus World. *Review of International Political Economy*, DOI: 10.1080/09692290.2012.756414.

Gereffi G and Sturgeon T (2013) Global Value Chain-Oriented Industrial Policy: The Role of Emerging Economies. In Deborah Elms and Patrick Low (eds.), *Global Value Chains in a Changing World.* Geneva: World Trade Organization, 329–360.

Gibbon P and Ponte S (2005) *Trading Down: Africa, Value Chains and the Global Economy.* Philadelphia, PA: Temple University Press.

Graham D and Woods N (2006) Making Corporate Self-Regulation Effective in Developing Countries. *World Development* 34(5): 868–883.

Guarin A and Knorringa P (2014) 'New' Middle Class Consumers in Rising Powers: Responsible Consumption and Private Standards. *Oxford Development Studies* 42(2): 151–171.

Henson S and Humphrey J (2010) Understanding the Complexities of Private Standards in Global Agri-Food Chains. *Journal of Development Studies* 46(9): 1628–1646.

Kaplinsky R (2005) *Globalization, Poverty and Inequality.* Cambridge: Polity.

Kaplinsky R and Farooki M (2010) Global Value Chains, the Crisis, and the Shift of Markets from North to South. In Olivier Cattaneo, Gary Gereffi and Cornelia Staritz (eds), *Global Value Chains in a Postcrisis World: A Development Perspective.* Washington, DC: World Bank, 125–153.

Knorringa P (2014) Private Governance and Social Legitimacy in Production. In Anthony Payne and Nicola Phillips (eds), *The Handbook of the International Political Economy of Governance.* Cheltenham: Edward Elgar, 361–378.

Locke R (2013) *The Promise and Limits of Private Power: Promoting Labor Standards in a Global Economy.* Cambridge: Cambridge University Press.

Lund-Thomsen P (2008) The Global Sourcing and Codes of Conduct Debate: Five Myths and Five Recommendations. *Development and Change* 39(6): 1005–1018.

Mattos E (2012) New California Law Takes Aim at Forced Labor, Labor Is Not a Commodity Blog, 19 March, Available at: http://laborrightsblog.typepad.com/international_labor_right/2012/03/new-california-law-takes-aim-at-forced-labor.html

Mayer FW (2014) Leveraging Private Governance for Public Purpose: Evolving Roles for Business, Civil Society and the State in Labour Regulation. In Anthony Payne and Nicola Phillips (eds), *The Handbook of the International Political Economy of Governance.* Cheltenham: Edward Elgar, 343–360.

Mayerowitz S (2012) Shoppers' Habits Not Changed in Bangledeshi Factory Fire. *Business Report*, 2 December, Available at: http://www.iol.co.za/business/shoppers-habits-not-changed-in-bangladeshi-factory-fire-1.1434148#.UVWTG pNwquo

Milberg W, Jiang X and Gereffi G (2013) Industrial Policy in an Era of Vertically Specialized Industrialization. Paper presented at the workshop on 'Governance in a GVC World', Duke University, Durham NC, 11–13 April.

Morrison S (2013) Bangladesh Factory Collapse: Gap Refuses to Back Safety Deal. *The Independent*, 14 May, Available at: http://www.independent.co.uk/news/world/asia/bangladesh-factory-collapse-gap-refuses-to-back-safety-deal-8615599.html

Newell P (2005) Citizenship, Accountability and Community: The Limits of the CSR Agenda. *International Affairs* 81(3): 541–557.

Nova S and Shapiro I (2012) Polishing Apple: Fair Labor Association Gives Foxconn and Apple Undue Credit for Labor Rights Progress. EPI Briefing Paper #352, Economic Policy Institute.

O'Rourke D (2006) Multi-Stakeholder Regulation: Privatizing or Socializing Global Labor Standards? *World Development* 34(5): 899–918.

Phillips N (2011) Informality, Global Production Networks and the Dynamics of 'Adverse Incorporation'. *Global Networks* 11(3): 380–397.

—— (2013a) The Failures and Failings of Governance: Slavery and Human Trafficking in Global Production Networks. Presented at the workshop on 'Governance in a "GVC" World', Duke University, Durham NC, USA, 11–13 April 2013.

—— (2013b) Unfree Labour and Adverse Incorporation in the Global Economy: Comparative Perspectives from Brazil and India. *Economy and Society* 42(2): 171–196.

—— (2013c) Horsemeat, Tax, Human Labour Conditions – in That Order? *SPERI Comment Blog*, 3 April.

Phillips N and Mieres F (2014) The Governance of Forced Labour in the Global Economy. *Globalizations* DOI: 10.1080/14747731.2014.932507:1–17.

Phillips N and Sakamoto L (2012) Global Production Networks, Chronic Poverty and 'Slave Labor' in Brazil. *Studies in Comparative International Development* 47(3): 287–315.

Pickles J and Zhu S (2013) The California Transparency in Supply Chains Act. Capturing the Gains Working Paper 15, University of Manchester, February.

Ponte S (2008) Developing a 'Vertical' Dimension to Chronic Poverty Research: Some Lessons from Global Value Chain Analysis. *Chronic Poverty Research Centre Working Paper series*, no. 111, University of Manchester.

SACOM (Students and Scholars Against Corporate Misbehaviour) (2012) FLA Waters Down Rights Violations at Apple Suppliers, Hong Kong, 18 February, Available at: http://sacom.hk/archives/931

Seidman GW (2007) *Beyond the Boycott: Labor Rights, Human Rights, and Transnational Activism*. New York: Russell Sage Foundation.

—— (2008) Transnational Labour Campaigns: Can the Logic of the Market Be Turned against Itself? *Development and Change* 39(6): 991–1003.

Stohl C, Stohl M and Popova L (2009) A New Generation of Corporate Codes of Ethics. *Journal of Business Ethics* 90: 607–22.

Taylor M (2011) Race You to the Bottom...and Back Again? The Uneven Development of Corporate Codes of Conduct. *New Political Economy* 16(4): 445–462.

Verité (2011) Compliance Is Not Enough: Best Practices in Responding to the California Transparency in Supply Chains Act. White Paper, Amherst MA, November.

Yeung H and Wai-Chung (2013) Governing the Market in a Globalizing Era: Developmental States, Global Production Networks and Interfirm Dynamics in East Asia. *Review of International Political Economy* DOI: 10.1080/09692290.2012.756415.

2
The Political Economy of Outsourcing

John Smith

Introduction

The globalisation of production is the most significant, dynamic and transformative development of the neoliberal era. Its fundamental driving force is what some economists call 'global labour arbitrage': efforts by firms in Europe, North America and Japan to cut costs and boost profits by replacing higher-waged domestic labour with cheaper foreign labour, achieved either through emigration of production to low-wage countries ('outsourcing', otherwise known as 'offshoring') or through immigration of workers from those countries. Reduction in tariffs, removal of barriers to capital flows and advances in telecommunications and transport technology have facilitated the migration of production to low-wage countries, but militarisation of borders and rising xenophobia have had the opposite effect on this migration – not stopping migrants altogether, but inhibiting their flow and reinforcing their vulnerable, second-class status. As a result, factories freely cross the US–Mexican border and pass with ease through the walls of Fortress Europe, as do the commodities produced in them and the capitalists who own them, but the human beings who work in them have no right of passage. This is not globalisation but a travesty of globalisation: a world without borders to everything and everyone – except for workers.

Global wage differentials, largely resulting from suppression of the free movement of labour, provide a distorted reflection of global differences in the rate of exploitation (simply, the difference between the value workers generate and their wages). The southwards shift of production processes signifies that the profits of firms headquartered in

Europe, North America and Japan, the value of all manner of financial assets derived from these profits and the living standards of their citizens have become highly dependent on higher rates of exploitation of workers in so-called emerging nations. Neoliberal globalisation must therefore be recognised as *a new, imperialist stage of capitalist development*, where 'imperialism' is defined not by its territorial form but by its economic essence: the exploitation of southern living labour by northern capitalists.

The chapter begins with a panoramic view of the global shift of production and the accompanying transformation of the international working class, arguing that migratory flows from low-wage countries to Europe and North America, and class stratification within countries, must be understood within this broader context. It then identifies and analyses the prime driver of these processes – global wage differentials – and singles out two of their most important features and trends for special attention: labour's falling share of national income and increasingly unequal distributions of this share. As a result, widely touted statistics on per capita GDP and average wages obscure the reality of increasing vulnerability and deteriorating social conditions endured by a growing majority of working people on both sides of the North–South divide. The concluding section considers what this means for workers, farmers and youth in the new era of chronic economic crisis and political disorder.

The globalisation of production ... and of the producers

The globalisation of production is reflected in an enormous expansion of the power and reach of transnational corporations (TNCs), predominantly owned and controlled by capitalists resident in imperialist countries. The United Nations Conference on Trade and Development (UNCTAD) estimates (2013: 135) that 'about 80 per cent of global trade (in terms of gross exports) is linked to the international production networks of TNCs'. This heightened activity takes two basic forms: in-house Foreign Direct Investment (FDI) and 'arm's-length' relations between 'lead firms' and their formally independent suppliers. South–North trade as a whole is not so much 'trade' but a manifestation of the globalisation of production. This in turn should be seen not as a technical rearrangement of machinery and other inputs but as an evolution of capitalism's defining social relation, the relation of exploitation between capital and labour, increasingly between northern capital and southern labour.[1]

Export-oriented industrialisation: Widely spread or narrowly concentrated?

Export-oriented industrialisation (EOI, or 'outsourcing' viewed from a northern perspective) is the only capitalist option for poor countries not blessed – or cursed – with abundant natural resources,[2] yet it is a widely held view that growth in the South's industrial proletariat is highly concentrated in China and a handful of other low-wage countries. Thus Ajit Ghose, a senior International Labour Organization (ILO) economist, argues (2005: 12–14) that 'what appears to be a change in the pattern of North–South trade is in essence a change in the pattern of trade between industrialised countries and a group of 24 developing countries', with the rest facing 'global exclusion'. Yet these 24 developing countries include nine of the ten most populous Southern nations, home to 76 per cent of its total population, while many smaller nations host manufacturing enclaves that exert a powerful and distorting influence on their economies (Figures 2.1 and 2.2).

'Developing nations' share of global manufactured exports began its long ascent in the 1970s (see Figure 2.1, solid line), rising from around 5 per cent in the pre-globalisation period to nearly 30 per cent by the beginning of the millennium. Figure 2.1 also shows (broken line) that

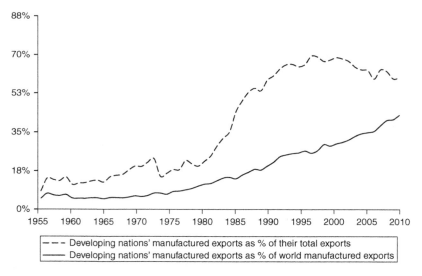

Figure 2.1   Developing nations' trade in manufactures
Source: UNCTAD, *Statistical Handbook*.

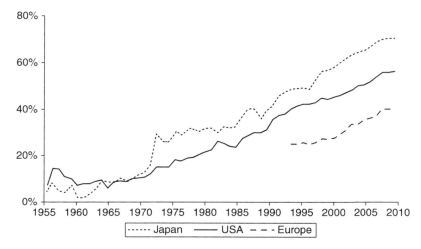

Figure 2.2 Developing nations' share of developed nations' manufactured imports
Source: UNCTAD, *Statistical Handbook*.

the share of manufactured goods in their total exports tripled in barely 10 years, stabilising in the early 1990s at over 60 per cent. Figure 2.2 shows this dramatic transformation from the perspective of imperialist countries. In 1970, barely 10 per cent of their manufactured imports came from what was then called the Third World; by 2000, this share – of a greatly expanded total – had quintupled.[3]

The US auto industry vividly illustrates this – in 1995, it imported four times as much automobile-related value-added from Canada as from Mexico, just 10 per cent more in 2005, and by 2009, the latest year for which data are available, Mexico was the source of 48 per cent more value-added than Canada.[4] The relocation of production processes to low-wage countries has been at least as important to European and Japanese firms as to their North American rivals. A study of EU–Chinese trade concluded that 'offshoring the more labor-intensive production and assembly activities to China provides an opportunity to our own companies to survive and grow in an increasingly competitive environment' (Van Assche et al., 2008: 15–16), while 'Japanese electronics companies continue to flourish in American markets precisely because they have moved their assembly lines to China' (*The Economist*, 2007).

The essential feature of the globalisation of production is therefore its southwards shift, and this has resulted in a highly peculiar structure

of world trade – in which northern firms compete with other northern firms – including a race to outsource labour-intensive production
processes to low-wage countries; meanwhile, firms in low-wage countries fiercely compete with each other, all seeking to exercise the same
'comparative advantage', their surfeit of cheap, unemployed workers
desperate for work – but *northern firms do not compete with southern firms*.
This is obviously true of relations between parent companies and their
wholly owned subsidiaries (i.e. of FDI), but it also applies to increasingly favoured 'arm's-length' relationships between Primark and H&M
and their Bangladeshi suppliers, and between General Motors and the
Mexican firms who manufacture more and more of its components.
The relationship is complementary, not competitive, even if it is highly
unequal. Important exceptions can be identified; indeed, this peculiar
structure is riven with contradictions, but the overall pattern is clear:
there is North–North competition, and cut-throat South–South competition reaching race-to-the-bottom proportions, *but no North–South
competition* – between firms, if not between workers, who face heightened competition across the global divide, facilitating wage repression
and an accelerating decline everywhere in labour's share of GDP.

The southwards shift of the industrial working class

The globalisation of production has transformed not just commodity
production but social relations in general, and especially that which
defines capitalism: *the capital–labour relation*, increasingly dominated by
the relation between northern capital and southern labour. Figure 2.3
shows the enormous growth of the industrial workforce in 'developing'
nations, revealing that a third of the world's industrial workers lived in
'less developed [low-wage] regions' in 1950, rising to a half by 1980, and
four-fifths by 2010. This huge shift reflects an even bigger qualitative
transformation: Southern industrial workers are not only more numerous, but they are now much more integrated into the global economy,
producing for world markets rather than protected domestic markets as
in the pre-neoliberal era.

In absolute terms and as a share of the global industrial proletariat,
the South's industrial workforce has seen spectacular growth since 1980,
but its share of the South's total workforce has been more modest, rising from 14.5 per cent in 1980 to 16.1 per cent in 1990, 19.1 per cent
in 2000 and 23.1 per cent in 2010 (by contrast, industry's share of
total employment in imperialist nations declined from 37.1 per cent
in 1980 to 22.5 per cent in 2010). With the partial exception of China –

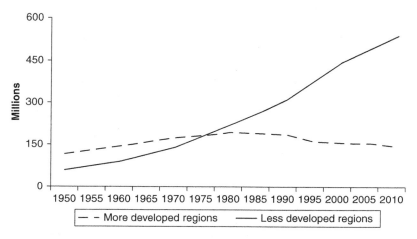

Figure 2.3   Global Industrial Workforce
Sources: ILO, n.d. *Population and Economically Active Population;* KILM (Key Indicators of the Labour Market), various editions.

a special case because of its 'one-child' policy, its extraordinarily rapid GDP growth since 1980 and its as-yet incomplete transition from socialism to capitalism – no economy has grown fast enough to provide jobs to the millions of young people entering the labour market and millions of migrants fleeing rural poverty. Tacitly acknowledging the failure of the EOI development model, senior ILO economist Majid (2005: 3–4) observed that 'the commerce sector [...] is the main employment growth sector in both low and middle-income groups [... this] shows that the expectation on manufacturing leading employment growth is unwarranted' – and this was his verdict on a period of exceptionally robust economic growth in 'low and middle-income' countries. This failure results in structural unemployment, misery and destitution for millions, enormous downward pressure on wages of those able to work and greatly increased migratory pressure.

'Global labour arbitrage': Key driver of the globalisation of production

By uprooting hundreds of millions of workers and farmers in Southern nations from the land and their jobs in protected national industries, neoliberal capitalism has accelerated the expansion of a vast pool of super-exploitable labour. Suppression of the free mobility of labour interacts with this hugely increased supply to produce a dramatic widening of international wage differentials which, according to World Bank researchers, 'exceed any other form of border-induced price gap by an order of magnitude or more' (Clemens et al., 2008: 33). This steep wage gradient provides two different ways for northern capitalists to increase profits – through emigration of production to low-wage countries, or immigration of workers from those countries. The International Monetary Fund (IMF) (2007: 180) makes the precise connection between outsourcing and migration: '[t]he global pool of labor can be accessed by advanced economies through imports and immigration', significantly observing that '[t]rade is the more important and faster-expanding channel, in large part because immigration remains very restricted'.

Bangladesh provides a vivid example of how, during the neoliberal era, outsourcing and migration have become two aspects of the same wage-differential-driven transformation of global production. According to the International Organization for Migration, in 2012, 5.4 million Bangladeshis worked overseas, more than half in India, with the rest spread between Western Europe, North America, Australasia and the Middle East, especially Saudi Arabia. As Siddiqui (2003: 2) notes, 'the continuous outflow of people of working-age [...] has played a major role in keeping the unemployment rate stable'. Some US$14 billion of remittances flowed into households in Bangladesh in 2012, equivalent to 11 per cent of Bangladesh's GDP. In the same year, Bangladesh received US$19 billion for garment exports, including the cost of imported cotton and other fabrics, typically 25 per cent of the production cost (outsourcing of textile industries and low wages are discussed by Montero and Ferradás in Argentina (Chapter 11), and Delaney and Tate in India (Chapter 17), this volume). In other words, net earnings from garment exports in 2012 (80 per cent of Bangladesh's total exports) approximately equalled total remittances from Bangladeshis working abroad. And while only a small fraction of export earnings are paid in wages, remittances flow directly into poor households. The World Bank reports that, in 2013, Britain's 210,000 Bangladeshi migrant workers sent home an average of US$4,058. In comparison, even after a 77 per cent wage rise in November 2013 won by strikes and street protests, average garment workers' wages in Bangladesh were US$1,380 per year.[5] Thus each (largely male) Bangladeshi working in Britain remits in one year what it would take his wife, sister or daughter three years to earn.

What the IMF calls 'accessing the global labour pool' others have dubbed 'global labour arbitrage', whose essential feature, according to Stephen Roach, is the substitution of 'high-wage workers here with like-quality, low-wage workers abroad' (Roach, 2004). Roach, then senior economist at Morgan Stanley responsible for its Asian operations, argued (2003: 5) that 'a unique and powerful confluence of three mega-trends is driving the global arbitrage [...] the maturation of offshore outsourcing platforms [...] E-based connectivity [...and] the new imperatives of cost control'. Of these, 'cost control' – that is, lower wages – is 'the catalyst that brings the global labor arbitrage to life'. The first two mega-trends, in other words, merely provide the necessary conditions for the third – profiting from ultra-low wages – to express itself. Roach elaborates:

> In an era of excess supply, companies lack pricing leverage as never before. As such, businesses must be unrelenting in their search for new efficiencies. Not surprisingly, the primary focus of such efforts is labor, representing the bulk of production costs in the developed world [...] Wage rates in China and India range from 10 per cent to 25 per cent of those for comparable-quality workers in the US and the rest of the developed world. Consequently, offshore outsourcing that extracts product from relatively low-wage workers in the developing world has become an increasingly urgent survival tactic for companies in the developed economies.
>
> (Ibid.: 6, author's emphasis)

This is a much sharper description of neoliberal globalisation's driving force than that offered above by the IMF's technocrats. We might ask, though, why Roach says 'extracting product' instead of 'extracting value' – capitalists, after all, are not interested in the product of labour but in the value contained in it. The answer, we suspect, is that 'extracting value' would make it even more explicit that these low-wage workers create substantially more wealth than they receive in the form of wages; in other words, *they are exploited* – heresy for a mainstream economist.

Nevertheless, Roach's emphasis on the 'extraction of product' from low-wage workers contrasts with the general rule in academic and business literature, which is to obfuscate this most important point, treating labour as just one factor of production among others, while making glancing references to wage differentials as one of many possible factors influencing outsourcing decisions. UNCTAD's 'Inward FDI Potential Index' (2007: 31ff) is a typical example: the index is a composite of 12 variables, including GDP per capita, real GDP growth rate, exports/GDP, inward FDI, telephone lines per 1,000 inhabitants and spending on research and on tertiary education. The criterion most closely related to the price of labour is GDP per capita – but this is included to indicate the size of the potential market for the firms' products, not the cost of hiring labour.

Low wages are the pre-eminent factor affecting outsourcing decisions. Milberg comments,

> [t]he irony is that precisely at the moment computerisation has led to a revolution in the mechanisation of production, the ability to outsource has reasserted the importance of the labour component of production costs. Instead of being inconsequential as the result of technological change, labour costs are now an important determinant in the production location decision. (2004: 10)

What's especially ironic is that instead of replacing labour with machines, capitalists are using new technology to replace labour with cheaper labour, thereby prolonging the life of obsolete production processes. More ironic still, outsourcing is not only an alternative to increasing labour productivity; it allows corporate profits to be diverted into speculation in financial assets, thereby feeding the financialisation of the imperialist economies and deepening their tendency to stagnation and crisis.

The GDP illusion

Roach's observation begs a large question – how do 'companies in the developed economies' 'extract product' from workers in Bangladesh, China and elsewhere? The only visible contribution of these workers to the revenues of firms in 'developed economies' is the flow of repatriated profits associated with FDI. In the case of the increasingly favoured form of outsourcing – 'arm's-length' contractual relations with independent suppliers – there is no sign of any contribution to profits of TNCs. None of H&M's or General Motors' profits can be traced to their Bangladeshi or Mexican suppliers; all of it appears as value-added by their own activities. This conundrum, inexplicable to mainstream economic theory and therefore ignored, can only be resolved by redefining *value-added* as *value captured*; in other words, a firm's value-added does *not* represent the value *it* has produced, but it represents the portion of total, economy-wide value it has succeeded capturing in the (global) marketplace. There is, therefore, no necessary relationship between the value a firm *produces* and the value it *captures* – banks, for example, generate no value but capture a great deal. Since a country's GDP is simply the sum of the value-added of all its firms, the global shift of production to low-wage countries combined with vast mark-ups on production costs means that a significant part of the 'gross domestic product' of imperialist nations is actually generated by super-exploited workers in Bangladesh, China and elsewhere. In this way, GDP data diminish the real contribution of Southern nations to global wealth and exaggerate the real contribution of 'developed' countries, thereby veiling the increasingly parasitic relationship between them. I call this *the GDP illusion* (Smith, 2012).

Growing wage inequality

To bring international wage differentials into focus, two other outstanding features of the neoliberal era need examining: the declining share of wages in national income in both North and South and increasingly unequal distributions of this declining share. The ILO (2008: 29) calls growing intra-national wage inequality 'one of the most important developments in recent years', adding that 'on average, wage inequality is higher in countries with a lower GDP per capita'. Freeman and Oostendorp (2001: 392) also find that the poorer the country, the higher the wage inequality, a fact already 'well known from more limited country comparisons'. This increasing trend is being driven especially by falling wages of the lowest-paid workers, in contrast to rich countries, where the driver is the increasing wages of the highest paid. These represent two distinctly

> different types of increase in wage inequality. The first – the 'collapsing bottom' – refers to the situation where wage inequality is growing as a result of deterioration in the lowest wages. The second – the 'flying top' – is the opposite, where top wages increase faster than in other wage groups.
>
> (ILO, 2008: 26)

Comparing 1995–2000 with 2001–2006, the report added that 'the more developed countries [...] mainly fall into the category of "flying top" wages [...] countries from developing regions are predominantly close to the scenario of "collapsing bottom"'.

Super-wages, bonuses and share options received by employers and managers falsely counted towards labour income partially explain increases in wage inequality, exaggerating labour's share of national income. Anne Krueger, former World Bank chief economist, provides a striking example (2002: 46): '[i]f the owner of the Chicago Bulls, Jerry Reinsdorf, were to pay [basketball star] Michael Jordan an additional US$20 million, and reduce his own salary by an equivalent amount, labor's share would be unchanged because both are counted as employees of the Bulls'. Luckily for Jordan, he didn't rely on Reinsdorf's generosity – in 1998, Nike paid him US$45 million in 'wages' for appearing in adverts, enough to pay the annual wages of 30,000 of the Indonesian workers producing the famous brand's shoes.

Falling labour share of national income

All income can be divided into income to labour – wages and the 'social wage' – and income to capital – profits from financial assets.[6] This provides the basis for an important metric: *labour's share of national income*, defined as the ratio of total employees' compensation (pre-tax wages and salaries plus national insurance and other social contributions) to total national income. Self-employed workers are also considered to be owners of capital; the convention is to split their income into two parts, income to capital and income to labour. The IMF (2007: 182) bravely assumes that these 'categories of workers earn the same average wage as employees', an especially problematic assumption when applied to 'developing' nations, where a much higher proportion of the economically active population is classified as self-employed, often subsisting on small fractions of the paltry wages paid to those in employment. Wages are recorded pre-tax because it is assumed that workers receive benefits in exchange for the taxes they pay to the state. As a result, most of the 'state's share' of GDP is counted towards labour's share, even that part of it spent servicing sovereign debt, waging foreign wars and tooling up police to attack picket lines. It is little surprise, therefore, that '[i]ncreasing government spending is associated with an increase in labor shares, for both rich and poor countries' (Harrison, 2005: 29).

Figure 2.4 dramatically depicts the global decline in labour's share of the wealth it produces. The trajectory of the graph reveals an *accelerating* trend – labour's share declined as much between 2000 and 2007 as in the previous two decades – and the true extent of this is masked by increased wage inequality and by falsely accounting income to capital as labour income.

How much of a distortion the super-wages received by the top decile of wage-earners can make is illustrated by an analysis of US wages by Elsby, Hobijn and Şahın (2013). The results are staggering. A 3.9 per cent

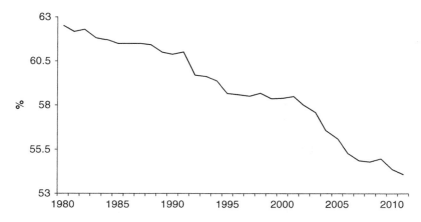

Figure 2.4 Share of labour in world gross output (1980–2011)
Source: UNCTAD (2013), Trade & Development Report, 2013, Chart 1.4.

decline in the share of national income received by all employees becomes a 14 per cent decline when the highest-paid 10 per cent are excluded, their share falling from 42 per cent of national income in 1980 to 28 per cent in 2011. In other words, the share of national income received by the lowest paid 90 per cent of the US workforce during these years fell by a third, explaining how the US grew richer while the majority of its workers didn't.

This is a global trend: in its 2011 *World of Work Report*, the ILO (2011: 58) noted that since the early 1990s 'the share of domestic income that goes to labour [...] declined in nearly three-quarters of the 69 countries with available information. The decline is generally more pronounced in emerging and developing countries than in advanced ones.' Declines in labour's share in low-wage countries were very steep – the wage share in Asia fell by around 20 per cent between 1994 and 2010; moreover, '[t]he pace of the decline accelerated in the past decade [...] with the wage share falling more than 11 percentage points between 2002 and 2006. In China, the wage share declined by close to 10 percentage points since 2000' (Ibid.). Africa's *toilers saw their share of national income decline by* 15 per cent in the two decades from 1990, again 'with most of this decline – 10 per centage points – taking place since 2000. The decline is even more spectacular in North Africa, where the wage share fell by more than 30 per centage points since 2000' (Ibid.). Latin America experienced the smallest decline, its wage share falling by 'only' 10 per cent since 1993. Meanwhile, '[t]he wage share among advanced economies has been trending downward since 1975 [...] [but] at a much more moderate pace than among emerging and developing economies – falling roughly 9 per centage points since 1980' (Ibid.: 56–57). *These estimates take no account of the sharply increasing inequality between skilled/professional and unskilled workers or of income to capital* masquerading as income to labour, effects likely to be at least as large as those reported above for the US.

Global wage differentials

Statistics on wages between nations must be treated with great caution, not only because they count taxes as labour income and ignore growing intra-national wage inequality, but because they often cover only those in the formal sector, because governments and employers have many reasons and opportunities to embroider the facts and because of huge problems of data coverage and comparability. Additionally, the conversion of wages into purchasing power parity dollars – necessary for comparing real wages in different countries – introduces biases and distortions large enough on their own to swamp the weak trends in real wages we are trying to identify.

As noted, average wages veil sharply increased wage dispersal between high-skilled and low-skilled occupations. One way to exclude this effect is to consider international wage differentials *within* occupations, as did Freeman and Oostendorp (2001: 400), who surveyed wages during 'early' and 'late' periods of globalisation (1983–89 and 1992–99) for 137 occupations across 135 countries. The 'key result' of their research was that 'inequality of wages across countries in the same occupation increased over this period despite globalisation, which should have reduced the inequality'. This finding is confirmed by trends in garment workers' wages. Werner International, a management consultancy serving the garment industry, finds no sign of the much-trumpeted convergence in wages between rich and poor countries. On the contrary (2012: 3), '[t]he wage gap between developed and developing countries is increasing and the range from the lowest hourly cost to the highest hourly cost is showing an ever increasing expansion'. This finding was confirmed by the Worker Rights Consortium (2013: 2): 'apparel manufacturing in most leading garment-exporting nations has delivered diminishing returns for its workers. Research conducted [...] on 15 of the world's leading apparel-exporting countries found that between 2001 and 2011, wages for garment workers in the majority of these countries fell in real terms'.

Finally, underlining the vulnerability of all but the most aristocratic layers of the working class in times of crisis, the ILO reports (2008: 15) that 'whereas in times of economic expansion, wages are less than fully responsive to changes in GDP per capita, during the economic downturns wages tend to become overly responsive and fall faster than GDP', adding that 'in many of the countries that suffered from an economic crisis in the late 1990s (in particular some South Asian and Latin American countries) real wages have not fully recovered to pre-crisis levels despite significant economic recovery over recent years'.

Conclusion

During the neoliberal era, racial and national divisions have played an increasingly important economic role, allowing capitalists in imperialist nations to profit from higher rates of exploitation in low-wage countries, from exploitation of their migrant workers and from general downward pressure on wages resulting from heightened competition between workers across the North–South divide. And they have played a no less important political role, undermining solidarity and paralysing the political independence and agency of the working class at national and global levels. This results in increased vulnerability and insecurity for all but the most privileged layers of the international working class.

All these features are intensified by the new era of deflation, stagnation and depression inaugurated by the global economic crisis, a crisis from which there is no peaceful capitalist way out. On the other hand, the southwards shift of the working class and its reinforcement in imperialist countries through immigration, and everywhere through the influx of women into wage labour, mean that the international working class now much more closely resembles the face of humanity at large, strengthening its chances of prevailing in coming battles.

Notes

1. Large companies also of course indirectly exploit workers through the activities of their supply chains, discussed by Phillips (Chapter 1, this volume).
2. The existence of a socialist option is proved by Cuba, whose revolution has survived more than half a century of economic warfare, terrorism and subversion orchestrated by successive US governments. Cubans have paid a high price for their defiance, yet they enjoy a higher life expectancy, lower infant mortality and greater access to education and culture than their US neighbours. For an excellent account of the Cuban revolution's staying-power, see Morris (2014).

3. The trace for Europe, generated by subtracting intra-EU manufactured imports from the EU total, begins in 1995 because data are only continuous since the EU enlargement in that year with the accession of Austria, Finland and Sweden.
4. Mexico's export of value-added to the USA is equal to the gross value of its exports minus the value of imported inputs used in their production. Data from OECD-WTO 'Trade in Value Added' database.
5. This is just 19 per cent of what is needed to provide a worker in Bangladesh, her/his partner and two children with the basic necessities of life (http://www.cleanclothes.org/livingwage/living-wage-versus-minimum-wage).
6. 'The whole annual produce of the labour of every country [...] [is] parcelled out among different inhabitants of the country, either as the wages of their labour, the profits of their stock, or the rent of their land' (Adam Smith, [1776] 1986: 155). 'Land' stands for the feudal aristocracy, which since Adam Smith's day has been absorbed into the capitalist class.

References

Clemens MA, Montenegro CE and Pritchett L (2008) *The Place Premium: Wage Differences for Identical Workers across the US Border*. Background Paper to the 2009 World Development Report. Policy Research Working Paper 4671. New York: World Bank.

The Economist (2007) The Great Unbundling. *The Economist*, 18 January 2007.

Elsby M, Hobijn B and Şahın A (2013) *The Decline of the U.S. Labor Share*. Brookings Papers on Economic Activity. Available at: http://www.brookings.edu/~/media/Projects/BPEA/Fall%202013/2013b_elsby_labor_share.pdf (accessed 12 February 2015).

Freeman R and Oostendorp R (2001) The Occupational Wages around the World Data File. *International Labour Review* 140(4): 379–401.

Ghose AK (2005) *Jobs and Incomes in a Globalizing World*. New Delhi: Bookwell.

Harrison A (2005) *Has Globalization Eroded Labor's Share? Some Cross-Country Evidence*. Munich Personal RePEc Archive. Available at: http://www.iadb.org/res/publications/pubfiles/pubS-FDI-9.pdf (accessed 12 February 2015).

ILO (2008) *Global Wage Report 2008–9*. Geneva: ILO.

ILO (2011) *World of Work Report 2011*. Geneva: ILO.

IMF (2007) *World Economic Outlook 2007*. Washington DC: IMF.

Krueger A (2002) *A New Approach to Sovereign Debt Restructuring*. International Monetary Fund. Available at: http://www.imf.org/external/pubs/ft/exrp/sdrm/eng/ (accessed 12 December 2014).

Majid N (2005) *On the Evolution of Employment Structure in Developing Countries*. Employment Strategy Papers 2005/18. Geneva: ILO.

Milberg W (2004) Globalised Production: Structural Challenges for Developing Country Workers. In William Milberg (ed) *Labour and the Globalisation of Production – Causes and Consequences of Industrial Upgrading*. New York: Palgrave Macmillan, 1–19.

Morris E (2014) Unexpected Cuba. *New Left Review* 88: 5–45. Available at: http://newleftreview.org/II/88/emily-morris-unexpected-cuba (accessed 12 December 2014).

Roach S (2003) *Outsourcing, Protectionism, and the Global Labor Arbitrage*. Morgan Stanley Special Economic Study. Available at: http://www.neogroup.com/PDFs/casestudies/Special-Economic-Study-Outsourcing.pdf (accessed 12 December 2014).

Roach S (2004) More Jobs, Worse Work. *New York Times*, 22 July 2004.

Siddiqui T (2003) *Migration as a Livelihood Strategy of the Poor: The Bangladesh Case*. Refugee and Migratory Movements Research Unit, Dhaka University, Bangladesh. Available at: http://r4d.dfid.gov.uk/PDF/Outputs/MigrationGlobPov/WP-C1.pdf (accessed 12 December 2014).

Smith J (2012) The GDP Illusion. *Monthly Review* 64(3): 86–102. Available at: http://monthlyreview.org/2012/07/01/the-gdp-illusion (accessed 12 December 2014).

Smith A ([1776] 1986) *The Wealth of Nations, Book I*. Harmondsworth: Penguin.

UNCTAD (2007) *World Investment Report 2007 – Transnational Corporations, Extractive Industries and Development*. Geneva: UNCTAD.

UNCTAD (2013) *World Investment Report 2013*. Geneva: UNCTAD.

Van Assche A, Hong C and Slootmaekers V (2008) *China's International Competitiveness: Reassessing the Evidence*. LICOS Discussion Papers #20508. Available at: http://papers.ssrn.com/sol3/papers.cfm?abstract_id=1137560 (accessed 12 December 2014).

Werner International (2012) *International Comparison of the Hourly Labor Cost in the Primary Textile Industry*, Winter 2011. Available at: http://www.ukft.org/documents/industryinformation/04-ASSOC-INDSTRAT-122-2012AI-Werner%20Textile%20Labour%20Costs.doc%5B1%5D.PDF (accessed 12 January 2015).

Worker Rights Consortium (2013) *Global Wage Trends for Apparel Workers, 2001–2011*. Available at: www.americanprogress.org/wp-content/uploads/2013/07/RealWageStudy-3.pdf (accessed 12 December 2014).

3
Labour, Exploitation and Migration in Western Europe: An International Political Economy Perspective

Lucia Pradella and Rossana Cillo

Introduction

In Western Europe (the EU15), the economic crisis erupted in 2007/08 and consequent austerity programmes are leading to a general, but uneven, worsening of labour conditions (Hermann, 2014). Unemployment levels have reached record high inter-country differences: in the second half of 2014, they ranged from 5 per cent in Germany to 6 per cent in the UK, 12 per cent in Italy and around 25 per cent in Spain and Greece (Eurostat). Between 2010 and 2012, real wages declined by more than 3 per cent in Italy and the UK, by almost 7 per cent in Portugal and Spain, and by 23 per cent in Greece (Schulten, 2013). According to the European Statistics on Income and Living Conditions (EU-SILC), between 2007 and 2012, the number of the poor increased by 8.5 millions, reaching nearly 92 millions (almost one-fourth of the population). In 2012, poverty affected 9 per cent of workers (+1 percentage point greater than in 2007), increasing also both in Italy (10 per cent) and the UK (9 per cent). Trends in severe material deprivation are even more dramatic, with an increase by 125 per cent in the first five years of the crisis (from 1.9 per cent in 2007 to 4.3 per cent in 2012).

The increase in the number of ordinary working people who face conditions of poverty and material deprivation undermines the foundations of the 'European social model' and its assumptions that employment protects individuals from poverty. Despite this trend, the uneven effects of the crisis, along with the decline of the organised Left in many countries, have reinforced nationalist political responses, as the European elections in May 2014 and the reactions to the attacks on the French magazine *Charlie Hebdo* have shown. While migration is at the top of the agenda for many governments, institutional racism is also finding a fertile ground in a social context characterised by rising unemployment and job competition. Immigrants are increasingly blamed for the crisis itself.

This chapter develops an international political economy analysis of the effects of the crisis on labour, on immigrant workers in particular. It focuses on Italy and the UK, two countries with different migration histories and positions in EU15 migratory routes. Italy has been chosen as a country of relatively recent immigration exemplifying broader trends in southern states within the Eurozone. The case of Britain – a country with a longer history of immigration and arrival point for immigrants coming, inter alia, from the Mediterranean through Italy itself – is helpful in isolating the effects caused by political economy trends as opposed to the specific institutional complex within the Eurozone. We argue that, because of their focus on welfare regimes analysis, the main comparative studies on in-work poverty (IWP) in Europe are ill-equipped to link labour and poverty studies and are unable to overcome the problem of methodological nationalism: an approach that conflates society with the national territory, considering international production restructuring and migration as external variables of a national developmental path. We then seek to locate the economic crisis in Europe within the processes of international production restructuring that have taken place under neoliberalism. We then examine the differential effects of the crisis on EU member states and on various sections of the workforce. We discuss how trade unions are responding to these challenges.[1] Finally, the 'Conclusion' section closes by making some broader comments about international solidarity.

IWP research, migration and migrant workers

In the EU, working poor individuals are those who are 'in employment' for at least seven months in a year and are members of households with an annual income below the poverty threshold, set at 60 per cent of the average national income (after social transfer) (Peña-Casas and Latta, 2004). Including both a labour market and a household dimension, IWP research lies at the intersection between labour and poverty studies. The main comparative studies on IWP in Europe (e.g. Andreβ and Lohmann, 2008; Fraser, Gutiérrez and Peña-Casas, 2011), however, do not problematise the nature of capitalist working relations, simply assuming that employment protects individuals from poverty, an assumption now widely challenged, including elsewhere in this book. Research focuses on the effects of different welfare regimes, and the degree of de-commodification they allow for, on the size and composition of the working poor. Political economy analysis thus tends to be overlooked for statistical methods in identifying regimes. Despite some attention to union bargaining power, employer and union strategies are not examined (Gazier, 2008). The thrust of the literature – and of policy responses – becomes residual relief rather than socio-economic transformation (Powell and Barrientos, 2011: 74).

Even though comparative IWP studies recognise the importance of processes of neoliberal restructuring and migration for explaining IWP trends in Western Europe, they generally overlook these processes in case studies. The focus on welfare regimes excludes a systematic analysis of capitalist working relations, and of the links between the national and the international dynamics of capital accumulation; it also leads to a lack of analysis of how labour movements relate to evolving economic determinants. The role of Western European states in promoting neoliberal globalisation is ignored, as are the effects of migration restrictions on immigrant workers' labour conditions and collective agency. The questionnaire and sampling methods of the EU-SILC (the main database on IWP in the EU), moreover, do not fully incorporate immigrant populations and ignore the presence of undocumented immigrant workers, both of which have higher rates of unemployment, precarity and poverty than native-born workers (Alvarez-Miranda, 2011: 253–255). Poor immigrants' experience of social exclusion, in addition, is more acute than that of other groups because of anti-immigration and racist discourses, practices and legislation (Wright and Black, 2011: 559).

The limits of IWP comparative literature partially depend on Esping-Andersen's own failure to investigate the 'structural underpinnings for processes such as de-commodification and stratification, and how these give rise to more or less complex outcomes across ideal types' (Fine, 2014: 10). In our view, however, Esping-Andersen's key concept of de-commodification itself reflects an underlying dualism in the analysis of social policy. De-commodification would occur 'when a service is rendered a matter of right, and when a person can maintain a livelihood without reliance on the market' (Esping-Andersen, 1990: 22). By guaranteeing individual independence from the market, state intervention in the field of social policy would follow a different logic from that of capitalist reproduction, external to the commodification of labour power that is its fundamental premise.

Neoliberalism and the global economic crisis, however, are proving that both social policy and labour market transformations have to be examined against the backdrop of the international dynamics of capital accumulation. In capitalist society, production is aimed not at the satisfaction of social needs but at increasing profit, and profit depends on labour exploitation. Exploitation is not a perversion of the system, but it is caused by the sale of labour power in exchange for a quantity of value that is necessarily lower than that which workers produce. In this exchange, workers necessarily impoverish themselves, and this is the case also when their real wages increase.[2] The lack of analysis of capitalist working relations also leads to a separation between the national and international dynamics of accumulation (Pradella, 2014). Labour markets appear to be static containers, limited by national borders, while cross-national movements become an anomaly, an exception to the rule of remaining settled within the boundaries of one nation-state (Wimmer and Glick-Schiller, 2002: 583). International migration, however, is an integral element of the evolving processes of production restructuring and working-class reconfiguration.

Contemporary migratory movements need to be understood against the backdrop of the growth in the global industrial reserve army of labour (which plays a fundamental role in the disciplining of labour) due to the processes of impoverishment, rural dispossession and production restructuring occurring in the Global South in the neoliberal period (Pradella, 2010; Foster et al., 2011). An abundant labour supply, in fact, creates the conditions for the compression of wages and puts pressure on employed workers, limiting their claims, and these workers are forced by the low level of real wages to prolong the working day, reducing the demand for labour power and permitting a greater labour supply in the market – in a vicious circle of impoverishment and exploitation (Marx, 1976: 790; Foster, McChesney and Jonna, 2011). As we shall see in the next section, moreover, in the neoliberal period, immigration in Western Europe has been accompanied by increasingly restrictive and selective policies. By granting a residence permit only to those immigrants who have an employment contract, these policies effectively render immigrants as precarious workers, forced to make every sacrifice to stay in a country. They also promote racial and national labour market stratifications, thus acting as a means to divide the working class, increasing the precarity of labour relations and intensifying the exploitation of virtually all workers (Basso, 2011).

Neoliberal globalisation, migration and impoverishment

As a response to the profitability crisis that erupted in the mid-1970s, the implementation of neoliberal policies internationally determined a drastic increase in global inequalities and poverty (Ferreira and Ravaillon, 2008), leading to an expansion, if not a 'doubling', of the global industrial reserve army of unemployed, 'vulnerably employed' and inactive. In 2010, according to the International Labour Organization (ILO), this comprised about 2.4 billion people, and was 70 per cent bigger than the global workforce. This reserve army of labour is accessed by Western European capital through outsourcing/offshoring, trade and immigration. The integration of the EU and the introduction of the Euro accelerated this process, which determined a relative decline in the role of manufacturing industry in the EU15, paralleled by a growth of industrial workforce in low-wage countries (European Commission, 2012: 51–52). According to the United Nations, between 1990 and 2010 the number of non-EU15 immigrants grew from about 50 to 70 millions; the EU's eastward expansion in 2004 and 2007 further enhanced intra-EU migration (ECB, 2008).

Along with reforms promoting increasing labour market participation (e.g. workfare and pension reforms), relative deindustrialisation and increasing immigration created a growth in labour supply in all EU15 countries. Between 1996 and 2007, labour market participation in the Eurozone increased by 5.6 percentage points, 7.4 percentage points for non-EU immigrants (ECB, 2008: 15). In the neoliberal period, moreover, EU and national immigration policies, coordinated under the umbrella of EU regulations (e.g. Schengen), became increasingly restrictive and selective. These measures, presented as a deterrent for immigration from outside 'Fortress Europe' and justified by securitarian discourses, *created* a discriminatory system of rights and employment structure (Kundnani, 2007: 37; Basso, 2011). Many low-paid semi- or unskilled jobs have been racialised, with immigrant workers being concentrated in the most precarious, unhealthy and dangerous jobs. In most countries, moreover, foreign-born workers are among the least unionised and suffer various forms of workplace discrimination (Ferrero and Perocco, 2011; see also later chapters in this book).

Crucially, this racialised structure of employment does not affect only the most directly penalised by it, but it contributes to a broader process of labour market segmentation and liberalisation. Indeed, in all EU15 countries the neoliberal period has been characterised by a decline of the wage share of GDP, growing wage inequality, low pay and IWP (Andreβ and Lohmann, 2008; Fraser, Gutiérrez and Peña-Casas, 2011; Bengtsson and Ryner, 2014). This trend reflects the greater power of employers in a context in which trade union density and collective bargaining coverage have been significantly eroded. In Britain, the former almost halved from the 1980s and the latter fell even more sharply. In Italy, the decline in union membership has been less severe, but it has been particularly acute in the private sector, in small/medium enterprises and for young and fixed-term workers (Gumbrell-McCormick and Hyman, 2013: 63). The weakening of organised labour resulted in increasing workplace discipline and worsening labour conditions for the *entire* workforce (Vaughan-Whitehead, 2011: 12).

Labour market effects of the economic crisis

The crisis since 2008 has dramatically intensified these trends. While an analysis of its root causes is beyond our scope, the crisis highlighted not only a persisting crisis of profitability (Callinicos, 2010) but also the contradictory effects of the processes of international production restructuring on EU15 economies. At the EU level, between 2008 and 2012, about 4.2 million industrial jobs have been lost, corresponding to 12 per cent of manufacturing employment (Eurofound, 2014). This process is taking place unevenly among sectors and among member states, partially reflecting the existing polarisation of the EU productive structure and the international specialisation of the single member states. While capital-intensive production and 'services' are concentrated in northern states, in fact, southern states have specialised in lower capital-intensive productive sectors, now particularly affected by the competition of emerging countries (Cambridge Econometrics 2011; Felipe and Kumar, 2011).

With China as the second main competitor after Germany and a profitability crisis that started in the early 2000s, between 2008 and 2012 Italy's industrial output declined by 25 per cent and it lost 13 per cent of its industrial capacity (Bank of Italy, 2012: 6–9). Despite a market expansion of some high-capital-intensive export-oriented sectors, in April 2014 British industrial output was 11 per cent below pre-crash levels (Roberts, 2014), while austerity measures put an end to a long-term capacity of public sector employment to compensate job losses in the private sector (Buchanan et al., 2013: 401). In 2010, developing economies absorbed close to half of global FDI flows, with production relocation to Asia gaining relative importance in comparison to relocations to the EU12 (EU Commission, 2012: 64–65; UNCTAD, 2013). The

crisis, moreover, led to a slowdown in economic migration to Organisation for Economic Co-operation and Development (OECD) countries,
but it did not fundamentally change the dynamics of international
migration (OECD, 2013: 18). The absolute number of 'economic' immigrants in the EU15 continues to grow, although more slowly; intra-EU
migration is growing and the increase in the number of asylum seekers is accelerating. The majority of immigrants, moreover, have not
returned to their countries of origin, proving that immigration is a
steadily growing structural process (Castles, 2011: 319–320).

In all European countries, documented and, even more so, undocumented immigrant workers are among the most affected components of
the workforce. The crisis, in fact, hit hardest those sectors (industry, construction and public services, and jobs connected with contracting) in
which the mechanisms of labour market stratification had already concentrated immigrant workers (Grimshaw and Rafferty, 2011: 534–535).[3]
In all EU15 countries, along with austerity measures, immigration
restrictions have also been toughened.

In Italy, job losses are concentrated in sectors like metalworking
and construction, in which immigrant workers – even if placed in
dirty, dangerous and demanding jobs – tend to get equal treatment
in terms of contract and employment stability. This trend thus determined a decrease in most protected and unionised jobs, along with a
drop in the levels of immigrant workers' qualification and remuneration (Caritas-Migrantes, 2012). As a consequence, a growing number
of immigrant women entered the labour market to offset the reduction in family incomes due to the job losses of their male relatives.[4]
This process thus entailed a surge in lower paid and less protected jobs
and an expansion of severely exploitative labour conditions, which now
affect at least 100,000 workers in the agricultural sector alone (Cillo
and Perocco, 2012; Fondazione Placido Rizzotto, 2012). As in other
southern EU member states, moreover, the EU intervened to enhance
the ongoing process of erosion of the Italian system of collective bargaining (Hermann, 2014: 120). The so-called Pacchetto Sicurezza (Law
94/2009), in addition, has introduced the penal crime of 'illegal staying',
enhancing an ongoing process of criminalisation of immigrants.

In Britain, the Coalition government elected in May 2010 focused
its action on debt reduction, implementing half a million public sector job cuts by 2014, a pay freeze, and major reductions in public sector
pensions and in welfare spending (Grimshaw and Rafferty, 2011). Large
numbers of women and ethnic minority workers who had moved into
the public sector with the decline of manufacturing are now seeing

their jobs under threat.[5] In this context, a shift is taking place from relatively protected to less stable, non-unionised and low-paid sectors and contracts (Hermann, 2014: 119). This trend is negatively affecting immigrant and BME (black and minority ethnic) workers[6] employed in low-skilled, precarious jobs and vulnerable sectors of the economy, with an increasing number of women among the working poor (Fawcett Society, 2013). What is more, modifications to the points-based (immigration) system further restricted the entries reserved for low-skilled workers, forcing immigrants to follow more risky and illegal entry routes and making them even more vulnerable to conditions of severe labour exploitation (Geddes et al., 2013: 11). Employers, moreover, are using the Civil Penalty Scheme – which obliges them to check the immigration status of foreign-born workers – to obtain a more disciplined and submissive workforce, discriminating against workers involved in employment disputes or joining unions.

Trade union responses

Immigrant workers, however, are not only victims, but they can be central actors in the new kind of collective response needed to build viable alternatives to the crisis. In the last few decades, we have witnessed significant increases in unionisation rates of immigrant and BME workers. The main unions have promoted forms of active recruitment of immigrant workers and of cooperation with social movements, along with the proliferation of individual services to them. Both in the UK and Italy, trade unions have organised campaigns to raise awareness about and oppose the exploitative conditions to which immigrant workers are subjected. The Trades Union Congress (TUC) Commission on Vulnerable Employment, established in 2007, has launched a number of projects with this goal. Since 2004, moreover, TGWU/Unite has supported the Justice for Cleaners Campaign, which demands better wages and working conditions for janitors employed in the bank sector and universities (Adler et al., 2014: 61–62). In 2009, FLAI-CGIL (Federazione Lavoratori Agro-Industria – Confederazione Generale Italiana del Lavoro), the Italian union of agricultural workers, launched the 'Red Gold – From reality to real life' campaign, sending union representatives to the Puglia countryside (a southern Italian region) to protect and inform workers about their rights.[7] British unions have a much longer experience in this field compared to Italian unions, which witnessed a growth in immigrants' unionisation only from the late 1990s onwards. In Italy, the number of registered immigrant union members increased from

220,000 in 2000 to 1.2 millions in 2011, falling to 1.15 millions in 2012, mainly because of job losses and greater vulnerability of union members in precarious employment (Caritas-Migrantes, 2012: 273; UNAR, 2013: 327).

In both Britain and Italy, however, immigrant and BME workers' unionisation, while having an important impact in numerical terms, had less so in terms of effective participation and decision-making. No British or Italian union as yet has anything remotely close to proportionality of immigrant or minority-origin union officials within their membership. Further, in the wake of the crisis, trade unions have generally adopted a strategy of generic defence of workers' rights, presenting it as a means of coping with a common increase in unemployment and precarity and as a way of addressing the deterioration of relations between native-born and immigrant workers resulting from growing anti-immigrant propaganda and labour market competition. In reality, this position has reduced the importance of the immigration issue on trade union agendas, in some cases aggravated by decreases of company and/or state funding for the social inclusion of immigrant workers and against racial discrimination (see, e.g., the Union Modernisation Fund in Britain) (Cillo et al., 2013; Kumarappan et al., 2013).

Increasing labour market competition between native-born, BME and immigrant workers, moreover, is generating further contradictions. In the UK, these contradictions were brought to the surface by the Lindsey dispute at the beginning of 2009 and by the influence of the then Prime Minister Gordon Brown's ill-judged slogan 'British Jobs for British Workers' during the strikes. The main British unions, moreover, have responded only very late to the rise of the xenophobic party UKIP (United Kingdom Independence Party), and in their campaigns are stressing its anti-labour/Thatcherite elements but are avoiding the main issue, racism itself. In Italy, the ongoing process of institutionalisation of the unions is having negative effects on the relationship between unions and immigrant workers. While in the 1990s and early 2000s the unions supported immigrants' demands and campaigns against restrictive legislation, in 2009 the confederations CISL (Confederazione Italiana Sindacato Lavoratori) and UIL (Unione Italiana Lavoratori) accepted the 'Pacchetto Sicurezza', while the Italian General Confederation of Labour (CGIL) opposed it without mobilising its members against it. The generic principle of defence of all workers, upheld by the union leaderships, was not part of concrete actions of local representation of workers; its application rather depended on the presence and weight of immigrant workers within union structures. Significantly, at the last CGIL national congress the number of immigrant delegates halved (Galieni, 2014). Recent struggles in the logistics industry – so far, the most important mobilisations in Italy against the crisis – have been organised by immigrant workers without any support from the main unions.

Conclusion

The economic crisis of 2007/08 has led to undermining the foundations of the 'European social model', expanding conditions of poverty and exploitation traditionally associated with the Global South to Western Europe. This trend can only be understood by investigating the international political economy roots of social policy and labour market transformations. The neoliberal process of production restructuring has undermined the previous division of labour between Global South and North, generalising industrial competition. The resulting effects on labour markets and social policies are particularly harsh in southern member states like Italy, but they are affecting also northern member states like Britain. In both countries, moreover, immigration is a steadily growing structural process, and immigrant and BME workers have been disproportionally affected by the crisis.

In spite of increasing unionisation levels of immigrant workers, both in Italy and the UK, the crisis has led to a reduction in the importance of the immigration issue in trade union agendas. These limits lead to a dispersion of the potential for struggle of increasingly international working classes. The globalisation of production and international migration, in fact, do not only create vulnerability for workers but provide them with new sources of structural power. Tackling workers' impoverishment and exploitation in a globalised economy requires a strategy that is built on rank-and-file self-confidence, solidarity and organisation. This requires a strengthening of trade union democracy and a defence of immigrant workers' interests as a condition for the defence of the interests of all workers. Such a defence does not only imply a struggle for equal treatment and against discrimination in workplaces, but it also requires a questioning of the broader processes that produce precarity and illegality among immigrant workers. Despite its fragmentation, the working class has never been as numerous and multicultural as it is today. International solidarity is thus not something secondary but a vital necessity in everyday struggles.

Notes

1. We draw on the results of previous research on the topic (Cillo and Perocco, 2012 and Cillo et al., 2013; Pradella and Cillo, 2015). See, in particular, the 2012 TEAM project (*Trade Unions, Economic Change and Active Inclusion of Migrant Workers*) and the 2013 CRAW project (*Challenging Racism at Work*). Reports are available at www.ub.edu and www.workingagainstracism.org
2. For a more systematic analysis of this point, see Pradella (2010).
3. Between 2008 and 2012, EU15 unemployment rate of foreign-born male workers increased from 10.6 to 15.5 per cent, and that of native-born male workers from 6.1 to 9.9 per cent. The unemployment rate of foreign-born women increased from 11.9 to 15.8 per cent, and that of native-born women from 7.1 to 9.9 per cent (Eurostat, 2014).
4. Between 2008 and 2012, in Italy, foreign-born women's unemployment rates rose from 11.8 to 15.6 per cent, less than those of foreign-born men (from 5.9 to 12.4 per cent) (Eurostat, 2014).
5. Between 2008 and 2012, the largest increase in unemployment in Britain occurred among foreign-born women (7.5–10.5 per cent). In the same period, unemployment increased from 6.8 to 8 per cent among foreign-born men; 6.8 to 8.2 per cent among native-born men; and 4.8 to 7 per cent among native-born women (Eurostat, 2014).
6. Black and minority ethnic workers are included in our analysis because they face labour market and workplace discrimination for their visible ethnic origin. Chapters in this volume such as that by Waite et al. reflect on the position of the most vulnerable racialised workers.
7. See www.cgil.it/DettaglioDocumento.aspx?ID=12171

References

Adler LH, Tapia M and Turner L (eds) (2014) *Mobilizing against Inequality: Unions, Immigrant Workers, and the Crisis of Capitalism*, New York: Cornell University Press.

Alvarez-Miranda B (2011) In-Work Poverty among Immigrants. In N. Fraser, R. Gutiérrez and R. Peña-Casas (eds), *Working Poverty in Europe: A Comparative Approach*. Basingstoke and New York: Palgrave Macmillan, 250–277.

Andreβ H-J and Lohmann H (eds) (2008) *The Working Poor in Europe: Employment, Poverty and Globalization*. Cheltenham: Edward Elgar.

Bank of Italy (2013) *Il sistema industriale italiano tra globalizzazione e crisi*. Rome: Banca d'Italia.

Basso P (2011) Italia: el riesgo de frustrar las esperanzas. In M. Pajares and O. Jubany (eds), *Sindicatos e Inmigracion en Europa. 1990–2010* Barcelona: Icaria: 51–88.

Bengtsson E and Ryner M (2014) The (International) Political Economy of Falling Wage Shares: Situating Working-Class Agency. *New Political Economy*. Published online.

Buchanan J, Dymski G, Froud J, Johal S, Leaver A and Williams K (2013) Unsustainable Employment Portfolios. *Work Employment Society* 27(3): 396–413.

Callinicos A (2010) *Bonfire of Illusions: The Twin Crises of the Liberal World.* Cambridge: Polity.

Cambridge Econometrics (2011) *Study on the Competitiveness of European Industry in the Globalisation Era.* Cambridge: Cambridge Econometrics.

Caritas Migrantes (2012) *Immigrazione: Dossier statistico 2012.* Rome: Idos.

Castles S (2011) Migration, Crisis, and the Global Labour Market. *Globalizations* 8(3): 311–324.

Cillo R and Perocco F (2012) Trade unions and immigrant workers in the face of economic crisis. In O. Jubany and B. Güell (eds), Trade Unions, Economic Change and Active Inclusion of Migrant Workers. TEAM Research Report. Barcelona: Universitat de Barcelona, 177–196.

Cillo R, Perocco F and Scandolin P (2013) *Fieldwork Report Italy, CRAW Research Report.*

Esping-Andersen G (1990) *The Three Worlds of Welfare Capitalism.* Princeton: Princeton University Press.

EU Statistics on Income and Living Conditions – Statistical database. Available at: http://epp.eurostat.ec.europa.eu

Eurofound (2014) *Eurofound Yearbook 2013: Living and Working in Europe.* Luxembourg: Publications Office of the European Union.

European Central Bank (2008) *Labour Supply and Employment in the Euro Area Countries: Developments and Challenges.* Frankfurt/M: ECB.

European Commission (2012) *European Competitiveness Report 2012.* Luxembourg: European Union.

Fawcett Society (2013) *The Changing Labour Market: Delivering for Women, Delivering for Growth.* London: Fawcett Society.

Felipe J and Kumar U (2011) *Unit Labor Costs in the Eurozone.* Levy Economics Institute, Working Paper 651.

Ferreira HGF and Ravaillon M (2008) *Global Poverty and Inequality: A Review of the Evidence.* World Bank Policy Research, Working Paper 4623.

Ferrero M and Perocco F (eds) (2011) *Razzismo al lavoro.* Milan: FrancoAngeli.

Fine B (2014) *The Continuing Enigmas of Social Policy.* Geneva: UNRISD.

Fondazione Placido Rizzotto (ed) (2012) *Agromafie e caporalato. Primo rapporto.* Rome: FLAI-Cgil.

Foster JB, McChesney RW and Jonna RJ (2011) The Global Reserve Army of Labour and the New Imperialism. *Monthly Review* 63(6): 1–31.

Fraser N, Gutiérrez R and Peña-Casas R (eds) (2011) *Working Poverty in Europe: A Comparative Approach.* Basingstoke: Palgrave Macmillan.

Galieni S (2014) *La Cgil e i migranti dimenticati.* Corriere delle Migrazioni, June 17.

Gazier B (2008) Why Contemporary Capitalism Needs the Working Poor. *Prisme,* 14.

Geddes A, Craig G and Scott S (2013) *Forced Labour in the UK.* York: Joseph Rowntree Foundation.

Grimshaw D and Rafferty A (2011) Social Impact of the Crisis in the United Kingdom: Focus on Gender and Age Inequalities. In D. Vaughan-Whitehead (ed), *Work Inequalities in the Crisis.* Cheltenham: Edward Elgar, 525–570.

Gumbrell-McCormick R and Hyman R (2013) *Trade Unions in Western Europe: Hard Times, Hard Choices.* Oxford: Oxford UP.

Hermann C (2014) Structural Adjustment and Neoliberal Convergence in Labour Markets and Welfare: The Impact of the Crisis and Austerity Measures on European Economic and Social Models. *Competition and Change* 18(2): 111–130.

Kumarappan L, Jefferys S and Henry L (2013) *UK National Situation Report: Racism and Discrimination in Employment on Grounds of Ethnicity or National Origin (2003–2012)*. CRAW Research Report.

Kundnani A (2007) Integrationism: The Politics of Anti-Muslim Racism. *Race & Class* 48(4): 24–44.

Marx K (1976) *Capital: A Critique of Political Economy*. Vol. 1, Harmondsworth: Penguin.

OECD (2013) *International Migration Outlook 2013*. Paris: OECD.

Peña-Casas R and Latta M (2004) *The Working Poor in the European Union*. Dublin: European Foundation for the Improvement of Living and Working Conditions.

Powell M and Barrientos A (2011) An Audit of the Welfare Modelling Business. *Social Policy and Administration* 45(1): 69–84.

Pradella L (2010) *L'attualità del Capitale: Accumulazione e impoverimento nel capitalismo globale*. Padua: Il Poligrafo.

Pradella, L. (2014) New Developmentalism and the Origins of Methodological Nationalism. *Competition and Change* 18(2): 178–191.

Pradella L and Cillo R (2015) Immigrant Labour in Europe in Times of Crisis and Austerity: An International Political Economy Analysis. *Competition and Change* (forthcoming).

Roberts M (2014) UK Industry; Some Predictions for 2015 Onwards – and a Piketty Review. Available at: http://thenextrecession.wordpress.com

Schulten T (2013) *Wages and the Euro Crisis*, paper presented at the ILERA European Conference, Amsterdam.

UNAR (2013) *Immigrazione: Dossier statistico 2013*. Rome: Idos.

UNCTAD (2013) *World Investment Report 2013*. Geneva: UNCTAD Publications.

Vaughan-Whitehead D (ed) (2011) *Work Inequalities in the Crisis: Evidence from Europe*. Cheltenham: Edward Elgar.

Wimmer A and Glick-Schiller N (2002) Methodological Nationalism and Beyond: Nation-State Building, Migration and the Social Sciences. *Global Networks* 2(4): 301–334.

Wright K and Black R (2011) International Migration and the Downturn: Assessing the Impacts of the Global Financial Downturn on Migration, Poverty and Human Well-Being. *Journal of International Development* 23: 555–564.

Part II
Migrant Workers, Unfreedom and Forced Labour

4
Social Reproduction and Migrant Domestic Labour in Canada and the UK: Towards a Multi-Dimensional Concept of Subordination

Kendra Strauss

Introduction

Migrant labour is integral to both the contemporary global political economy and its key characteristic: uneven development. Uneven development, as often theorised, emphasises the economic and political institutions central to relations of production, rather than relations of reproduction. In this sense, frameworks for theorising uneven development, even where they draw attention to the role of social relations, tend implicitly to reproduce production/reproduction binaries. At the same time, the large and evolving literature on migration and care addresses commodification, privatisation and exploitation in the 'private' realm. Linking up the political economy of migrant labour and the political economy of social reproduction often remains an epistemological and methodological challenge.

In this chapter, I suggest that the concept of social reproduction can be utilised as a foundation on which to build a framework for making these linkages: in this sense, I am attempting further to develop some of the intersections between human geography, feminist political economy and feminist labour law in order to better conceptualise the processes that contribute to the exploitation of migrant workers. I do so by examining the political economy of migrant domestic work and social reproduction in Canada and the UK and focusing on the relationship between political economic and regulatory developments.

In highlighting both common and distinct features to the trajectories of these developments in Canada and the UK, I also suggest that the recalibration of norms of social reproduction occurring in both places may be related to changing relations of subordination. As labour law's traditional role in redressing subordination in the employment relation is increasingly under attack, so too is the idea that collective social welfare should redress the subordination of the social in capitalist market economies (see also Pradella and Cillo's chapter in this volume).

The political economy of migrant domestic labour

The efforts made by feminist political economists to link production and reproduction have, especially since the 1960s, focused on accounting (in literal and figurative senses) for the contribution of unpaid domestic work to the 'productive' economy (Hoskyns and Rai, 2007). Some have sought to develop and extend the notion of social reproduction referred to, but not fully mobilised, by Marx (1979) and especially Engels (2004). Thus feminists have highlighted the insufficiency of epistemologies that elide the contribution of unpaid and domestic labour, that create and sustain the idea of separate domains of 'economy' and 'society', and that allow theorists to argue (or assume) that non-wage and household labour are not productive or value-generating (Waylen, 1998). Heterodox political economists interested in richer understandings of labour markets also argued from the 1990s for theories that incorporated social reproduction as a key dimension of their social construction (Jonas, 1996; Peck, 1996).

How to theorise social reproduction – and in particular the range of activities, relations and sites it encompasses and seeks to explain – remains, however, an open question. In this chapter, I utilise a broad, multi-scalar definition of social reproduction that incorporates household and community dynamics over time, as well as the spatial, embodied dimensions which are themselves implicated in and shaped by the social construction of categories of difference like gender, race and ethnicity. At the same time, the specificity of capitalist relations of production and associated modes of value production and appropriation require recognition of the centrality of class dynamics (Braedley and Luxton, 2015), even as class itself remains open (like gender and race) to interrogation and contestation. Working-class women, especially Black and Minority Ethnic (BME) and migrant women, are doubly enrolled in reproductive work; not only does their household labour sustain the reproduction of labour power, but they are also disproportionately involved in providing commoditised domestic and care services.

Especially for female migrant domestic workers, then, gender, radical-isation and class dynamics interact not only in relation to their place in employment hierarchies in segmented labour markets but also in relation to their place in hierarchies of social reproduction. In both cases, their insertion into labour markets is often as unfree workers with precarious migrant status. This does not mean that all migrant domestic workers are all subject to 'modern slavery'. Rather, I refer here to the ways in which many immigration regimes require that 'unskilled' domestic workers and caregivers migrate as guest workers. Guest worker programmes often have conditional or – more often – non-existent paths to citizenship – they tie workers to a sponsoring employer – and require that they live-in as a condition of their visa. In this way, migrant domestic workers are clearly prevented from cir-culating as 'free' workers in the labour markets of destination countries. Although distinct from forced labour and domestic servitude, these con-ditions make migrant domestic workers (MDWs) extremely vulnerable to extreme labour exploitation. As theorised by Skrivankova (2010), free and unfree labour need to be understood as relations connected by a continuum of exploitation; MDWs' labour market position and precar-ious migrant status (Fudge, 2011; Goldring and Landolt, 2013) are not grounded in an ontological condition of unfreedom, but rather they are actively produced and negotiated by states, employers and workers themselves.

The exploration of the processes by which the unfreedom of some migrant workers is actively produced has emerged out of a longer tra-dition of work on migrant labour. Analyses of the role and importance of migration and migrant workers emerged in industrial sociology and political economy from the late 1970s, which followed the emergence of key debates about social reproduction a decade earlier. Michael Burawoy (1979), for example, pointed out that an important dimension of the political economy of migrant labour is that the social reproduction of families and communities takes place elsewhere and that specific legal and political forms of governance are put in place to regulate geo-graphical, spatial and occupational mobility of workers. These dynamics produce particular benefits for individual employers and capital more broadly (Arat-Koç, 2006). But they also highlight the role of the state in mediating the relationship between markets, workers and households in the context of socially determined norms of social reproduction.

In the late 1980s, research on immigration started to address the role and importance of women, mostly in the context of socio-cultural and economic integration (Pedraza, 1991); at the same time, analyses of legal mechanisms of control started to focus on the effects of characterisation on migrants with different statuses (Bosniak, 1988). Work that substantively addressed the specificity of migrant domestic workers as a distinct gendered and radicalised group also started to emerge in response to the growth of so-called guest worker programmes, such as the Live-in Caregiver Programme (LCP) in Canada (Arat-Koç, 1989; Fudge, 1997; Anderson, 2000; Parreñas, 2001; Stasiulis and Bakan, 2003). This literature contributed a range of insights on the political economy of migrant domestic labour and encompassed debates about the relative weight of different dimensions that contributed to the particular exploitation, and oppression, of migrant domestic workers. It also grappled more substantively with the role of the state in differentiating and institutionalising hierarchies of desirability as migrant status, including beyond non-Western contexts (Silvey, 2004; Wuo, 2010; Yeoh and Huang, 2010).

There are three dimensions of the specific character of *migrant* domestic labour that have been identified by feminists. First, the majority of domestic labour is performed by women, and even when performed for a wage, it continues to be done by women. There is therefore a relationship, mediated by processes of radicalisation and class formation, between women's status, the work they have traditionally performed and the way in which this work is valued. Second, the status attributed to domestic labour and the vulnerability of domestic workers are linked directly to *where* they labour: in private households. Feminist labour law scholars have highlighted the insufficiency of labour and employment law in regulating domestic labour because of their reliance on the separation of private and public spheres (Fudge, 2012). The role of labour law in addressing and redressing the subordinate status of labour in relation to capital in the employment relation is therefore limited by the traditional assumptions implied by the standard employment relation. The distinction between public and private spheres, in political economy and in law, thus contributes to the lack of visibility of domestics as *workers* and their exclusion from systems of labour rights and regulations.

Third, domestic work – how, and how much, domestic workers are paid – has a different (and variable) socially determined value than other kinds of labour, and it is affected by both dimensions described above. Where domestic workers are hired in dual-earner households, there is often what has been called a 'gendered loop': a domestic worker's wages relate, implicitly if not explicitly, to the woman's wage because the former is hired to replace the work that the latter would otherwise provide for 'free' (Pratt, 2004). In theorising the relationship between the political economy of migrant domestic work and social reproduction, however, it is also important to recognise the importance of status. In countries like the UK, domestic labour may *either* replace the work (usually done by women) in the home when they enter the labour market or be a determinant of status and class by substituting for familial labour in situations where women do not engage in waged work. Thus, although increasing female labour market participation and the continued (and increasing) reluctance of states to support collective institutions of social reproduction are important drivers of the increase in domestic service, class production and reproduction and the maintenance of status hierarchies continue to play a role – one that may be increasing due to changing distributions of income and wealth.

The final, and related, point to make is that more recent literatures have highlighted the ways in which the political economy of waged domestic labour is increasingly interrelated with the globalisation of markets (Elias, 2010; Beneria, Deere and Kabeer, 2012; Williams, 2012). Exporting workers has become a key means by which governments cope with unemployment and foreign debt, meaning remittances are increasingly crucial to the survival of households, communities and national economies (Sassen, 2002). Through the intersection of categories of social difference, such as race, class, gender, citizenship and sexuality, precarious migrant status is assigned to foreign domestic workers in ways that structure their unfreedom and privilege the social reproduction of some groups over others. This strategy, which values migrant domestic workers for their remittances or as a partial solution to crises of care in the minority world, allows the governments of both sending and receiving nations to ignore care drains and care deficits, respectively (Bakan and Stasiulis, 2003; Fudge, 2011).

(Re)producing precarity: The state, migration and regimes of social reproduction

The regulation of migrant domestic work reflects both general and specific tendencies within national polities in relation to the intersection of the political economy of social reproduction and migrant labour (Fudge and Strauss, 2014). The purpose of this section is to reflect briefly on differences between approaches to the regulation of guest worker programmes in Canada and the UK that have been specifically designed to place migrant workers in domestic employment and to link these approaches to broader trends in social re-structuring (especially in relation to public spending and the provision of public services).

The LCP in Canada is part of the Temporary Foreign Worker Programme (TFWP) which facilitates the migration of mostly women, predominantly from the Philippines, to work as domestic caregivers in Canadian households. The LCP requires that workers live-in, specifies the right to change employers (although this can in practice be difficult) and provides a route to settlement (through the ability to apply for landed immigrant status after three years, provided that the worker has been employed for at least 24 months providing full-time live-in care).[1] Extensive criticism from Philippine migrant workers, activists and academics (see, inter alia, Langevin and Belleau, 2000; Arat-Koç, 2001; Pratt, 2009) has over time produced some amendments to some conditions of the programme, including giving women the right to bring their dependent children with them when they migrate – although this too remains difficult in practice. However, the key conditions that construct caregivers' exploitability, especially the live-in requirement and high initial payments to placement agencies that result in de facto indentured labour (what Parreñas (2011) has called in other contexts 'indentured mobility'), have endured even as the number of them employed under the programme has risen. Research by Kelly et al. (2011), for example, documented 12,454 arrivals (including dependents) in 2009, up from just 3,303 in 2003. Citizenship and Immigration Canada (2014) reported a peak of 12,955 LCP entrants in 2007, followed by a gradual decline to around 6,000 in 2011–12. Although debate has often focused on the LCP as a privatised alternative to the public provision of childcare in Canada, an ageing population and the restructuring of care for the disabled mean that caregivers may increasingly be deployed in households in roles other than as nannies. Canada has a population of just over 35 million and has admitted 257,887 permanent residents in all classes in 2012, compared with 1,091,876 temporary residents, of whom nearly half were temporary foreign workers (Ibid.).

The Overseas Domestic Worker (ODW) visa in the UK, on the other hand, claims to be a more residual type of programme. It is designed to allow returning UK expatriates and foreign nationals approved to live or work in Britain to bring with them members of their domestic staff already employed by the household outside of the UK. Although one might assume that this applies to a relatively small high-income niche, the MDW NGO Kalayaan in UK[2] discovered through a Freedom of Information (FOI) request that from 2002 to 2012 up to 17,000 visas were issued annually (Roberts and Chaudry, 2013). The UK has a population of 63.7 million, just under twice that of Canada, and saw an estimated inflow of 532,000 immigrants in the year ending September 2013, of which 212,000 were classified as long-term migrants.[3] In other words, the ODW visa permits a proportionally larger inflow of migrant domestic workers relative to total migrant flows than does the LCP in Canada, although Kalayaan has pointed out that the majority of workers on the ODW visa leave because the visa does not provide a route to settlement. The ODW visa has, like the LCP programme, long drawn attention from campaigners due to the high reported incidence of exploitation. The ODW visa was introduced in 1998, replacing a system under which MDWs entered the UK on a 'concession' that tied them to their employers; the ODW visa granted them the right to change employers (though not to change sector) and enshrined their recognition as a 'worker' (its own status, different from that of employee) in the UK. Changes to the ODW visa in 2012, however, both removed the right to change employers *and* prevented the visa from being renewed after its reduced 6-month term has elapsed. Interestingly, these changes were justified by a government keen to cut non-EU migrants on the basis that they would *prevent* trafficking and labour exploitation (see Fudge and Strauss, 2014, for an analysis).

The different struggles and strategies of migrant workers and advocates *contra* state-imposed precarity and vulnerability and employer exploitation point to both common and particular relationships between the state, capital and the political economies of social reproduction and migrant labour. In Canada, a nation built on settler in-migration, perspectives against the LCP range from calls for its abolition to those advocating its fundamental reform (the latter often centring on the removal of the live-in condition, better enforcement of employment standards and landed status from the outset). For abolitionists, the point is in part that *because* Canada is a settler nation founded on a history of immigration – a history shaped by racist and white supremacist politics of citizenship – the country's need for workers should be reciprocated by an a priori right to permanent residence and a path to citizenship. In Britain, there are fewer voices calling for the abolition of the ODW visa,[4] perhaps out of fear that one of the only routes available to non-EU migrant domestic workers to enter the UK will be closed. Something more like the LCP would be, in this sense, an improvement on the situation in the UK.

In Britain, the current Conservative–Liberal Democrat coalition government has made reductions in immigrant numbers a key policy, leading to the closure of visa routes for non-EU workers. Because the UK is constrained, in relation to immigration policy, by its membership of the EU and common European market, the government has fixated instead on groups like foreign students and 'low-skilled' non-EU workers. Moreover, the pressure to retain such programmes from employers seeking to keep wages low is offset by strong anti-immigration sentiment among the Conservative base. Yet the UK government is clearly not yet willing to do away with a programme targeted at attracting wealthy individuals to the UK, instead proving its 'tough on immigration' credentials by reducing the employment protections embedded within the ODW visa. Moreover, because the ODW programme is not tied in any explicit way to the organisation of mainstream relations and institutions of care in the UK – it does not pretend to address a need for caregivers, unlike the LCP – the debate on the ODW programme is more peripheral to the UK's 'regime of social reproduction'.

What is clear is that the political economy of migrant domestic labour is related to, and supportive of, the polarising political economy of social reproduction in the UK and Canada. Although unique to each country (and varied within Canada's federal system), the political economy of both has been influenced by shifts (especially under conservative governments since 2006 in Canada and since 2010 in the UK) broadly characterised as neoliberal. These have included, in the UK and Canada, attacks on employment standards, labour law and unions under the rubrics of 'flexible labour markets' and 'cutting red tape'. In the UK, recent changes to the ODW visa have reduced protections for MDWs by removing their right to change employers. In Canada, reforms announced in June 2014 to the TFWP are framed in terms of protecting *Canadian* workers from labour market distortions wrought by the Conservative government's expansion of the Low Skill Pilot Programme, especially in the food services and hospitality sectors; the changes to the TFWP thus focus – like those to the ODW – on reducing the number of workers admitted under the programme, reducing the duration of work permits for low-wage workers and increasing fees associated with the programme. At the same time, both Canada and the UK have massively ramped up legislative and policy activity in the domains of trafficking for sexual exploitation and, to a lesser extent, forced labour and labour trafficking. Focusing on criminal law approaches to trafficking and forced labour, while simultaneously undermining labour law and employment standards, is producing the criminalisation of extreme labour exploitation and the normalisation of routine labour exploitation – with dubious benefits for migrant workers.

Both Canada and the UK have thus seen the deployment of the recent financial crisis, and related discourses of austerity, to affect socially conditioned norms of social reproduction. The refrain of inevitability in these discourses and policies is intended precisely to ratchet down expectations about what can be provided collectively and funded out of redistributive taxation. The recourse to migrant domestic labour – and in Canada's case temporary foreign labour more broadly – is part of this process. MDW programmes preserve and reinforce privilege (as poorly paid as MDWs often are, their services are far beyond the reach of many working families) in relation to privatised care, hold wages down for feminised and radicalised work, make collective organisation by workers difficult and block routes to settlement for migrant domestic workers who contribute to, but are unable to benefit from (and therefore make demands for), quality public services. These processes benefit capital, which is less beholden to contribute (through taxation and wages) to the costs of the social reproduction of labour power and which can also benefit directly from accumulation by dispossession (Harvey, 2004).

That the exploitation faced by MDWs has been met by general agreement on the need to tackle trafficking and modern slavery should not therefore be surprising. While anti-trafficking and anti-slavery efforts are diverse and include progressive and radical demands, state regulatory responses focus on the criminalisation of extreme exploitation and the promotion of human rights frameworks over sustained labour market reform grounded in a strong platform of workers' rights. This allows governments and fractions of capital to deplore trafficking and domestic servitude, while at the same time acting to undermine labour law and employment rights.

Conclusion: The subordination of the social

Governments in the UK and Canada aim to deter and punish extreme forms of exploitation perpetrated by traffickers, at the same time as they institutionalise 'routine' poor pay and conditions for the majority of migrant domestic and temporary workers. This highlights a significant tension in constructing the state, which institutionalises precarious migrant status, as the locus of regulation. The state also, however, remains a field for struggles over rights, including rights to socially defined levels of support for social reproduction in the spheres of community and household. The extent to which such rights are defined by market logics and the imperatives of accumulation can be understood as the *subordination of the social*; the nature and extent of social subordination are shaped by class struggle.

In labour law, the concept of subordination refers to the dependency of an employee in relation to an employer; labour law, as it has evolved in varied and context-specific ways, is intended to help achieve a balance of interests, rights and responsibilities between the parties involved in the employment relationship. If labour law itself has been challenged on multiple fronts, including by feminists who have highlighted the ways in which it has marginalised women's work and domestic labour (Fudge and Grabham, 2014), the concept of subordination is one that potentially has value and resonance beyond labour law's own conceptual 'jurisdiction'. Subordination in a more general sense refers to the condition, state or fact of being subordinate or subservient to a particular end, objective or need or the action of making subordinate in this way, and it is thus useful for analysing not only the balance of interests, rights and responsibilities between employer and employee (i.e. between capital and labour) but the balance of these dimensions more generally. Bourdieu, for example, can be read as theorising capital as a multi-dimensional relation that confers across different modalities the right to subordinate others (Bourdieu, 1984; on the social subordination of the family, see Fine, 1992).

What an analysis of the relationships between the political economy of migrant domestic labour and the political economy of social reproduction in the UK and Canada suggests, then, is the ongoing and intensifying subordination of the social in processes of state and labour market restructuring that privilege capital. This does not simply imply, however, that all processes and institutions that support social structures are somehow enrolled in, or dictated by, abstract market logics: 'the market' is itself a social construction, conjured into being by the activities of a variety of actors (including workers). Rather, it highlights the ways in which both regimes of social reproduction consolidated in post-war welfare states and those shaped by structural adjustment policies and new cash transfer programmes in 'developing' and 'emerging' economies are increasingly and explicitly hierarchical: equality and redistribution are made subordinate to norms of efficiency and cost-effectiveness that relate directly to surplus value extraction, accumulation and the maintenance of relations of power and status. In countries like the UK and Canada, this means the creation of labour markets segmented by migration status that are specifically designed to privilege the social reproduction of high-income citizens over lower-income groups, and finally migrant workers themselves. Uneven development, and the extensification of social reproduction produced by the mobility of workers, also becomes the justification for such hierarchies because workers can earn more in receiving countries than in sending countries. In this way, as the Philippine Women Centre in Canada puts it in relation to the LCP, migrant domestic workers 'mortgage themselves', enduring periods of unfreedom and sometimes of more extreme labour exploitation, in order to parlay their precarious migrant status into permanent residence – an option denied to workers on ODW visas in the UK.

Notes

1. Changes to the LCP proposed by the Canadian government in 2014 include the removal of the live-in requirement, but not the tie to a single employer, nor the condition of entry as a TFW (rather than an immigrant with permanent resident status).
2. www.kalayaan.org.uk
3. The methodologies for migration statistics in the UK and Canada are slightly different, given the context of common market for labour in the EU. Nevertheless, permanent resident numbers (Canada) can be compared with permanent immigrant numbers (UK) to give a sense of the size of immigration and migration flows. The key difference is that all those wanting to live *and work* in Canada need to apply through immigration channels, whereas citizens of the EU have the right to live and work in the UK.
4. Although at the time of writing, the ODW is the focus of a very energetic campaign in the context of the UK Modern Slavery Bill.

References

Anderson B (2000) *Doing the Dirty Work: The Global Politics of Domestic Labour.* London: Zed Books.

Arat-Koç S (1989) In the Privacy of Our Own Home: Foreign Domestic Workers as Solution to the Crisis of the Domestic Sphere in Canada. *Studies in Political Economy* 28(Spring): 33–58.

Arat-Koç S (2001) *Caregivers Break the Silence: A Participatory Action Research on the Abuse and Violence, Including the Impact of Family Separation, Experienced by Women in the Live-in Caregiver Program.* Toronto: Intercede.

Arat-Koç S (2006) Whose Social Reproduction? Transnational Motherhood and Challenges to Feminist Political Economy. In K. Bezanson and M. Luxton (eds), *Social Reproduction: Feminist Political Economy Challenges Neo-Liberalism.* Toronto: McGill-Queen's University Press, 75–92.

Bakan AB and Stasiulis D (2003) Introduction: Negotiating Citizenship. In AB. Bakan and D. Stasiulis (eds), *Negotiating Citizenship: Migrant Women in Canada and the Global System,* 1–10.

Beneria L, Deere CD and Kabeer N (2012) Gender and International Migration: Globalization, Development, and Governance. *Feminist Economics* 18(2): 1–33.

Bosniak LS (1988) Exclusion and Membership: The Dual Identity of the Undocumented Worker under United States Law. *Wisconsin Law Review* 6: 955–1042.

Bourdieu P (1984) *Distinctions. A Social Critique of the Judgment of Taste.* Cambridge, MA: Harvard University Press.

Braedley S and Luxton M (2015 forthcoming) Preface. In K. Meehan and K. Strauss (eds), *Precarious Worlds: Contested Geographies of Social Reproduction.* Athens, GA: University of Georgia Press, vi–xv.

Burawoy M (1979) The Functions and Reproduction of Migrant Labor: Comparative Material from Southern Africa and the United States. *American Journal of Sociology* 81(5): 1050–1087.

Citizenship and Immigration Canada (2012) *Facts and Figures 2012 – Immigration Overview: Permanent and Temporary Residents*. Available at: CIC http://www.cic.gc.ca/english/resources/statistics/facts2012/temporary/03 .asp (accessed 18 March 2014).

Elias J (2010) Gendered Political Economy and the Politics of Migrant Worker Rights: The View from South-East Asia. *Australian Journal of International Affairs* 64(1): 70–85.

Engels F (2004) *The Origin of the Family, Private Property and the State*. Chippendale, NSW: Resistance Books.

Fine B (1992) *Women's Employment and the Capitalist Family: Towards a Political Economy of Gender and Labour Markets*. London: Routledge.

Fudge J (1997) Little Victories and Big Defeats: The Rise and Fall of Collective Bargaining Rights for Domestic Workers in Ontario. In AD. Bakan and D. Stasiulis (eds), *Making the Match: Domestic Placement Agencies and the Racialization of Women's Household Work*. Toronto: University of Toronto Press, 119–145.

Fudge J (2011) The Precarious Migrant Status and Precarious Employment: The Paradox of International Rights for Migrant Workers. *Metropolis Working Paper Series*, No. 11–15. Vancouver: Metropolis.

Fudge J (2012) Blurring Legal Boundaries: Regulating for Decent Work. In J. Fudge, S. McCrystal and K. Sankaran (eds), *Challenging the Legal Boundaries of Work Regulation*. Oxford: Hart, 1–25.

Fudge J and Grabham E (2014) Introduction: Gendering Labour Law. *feminists@law* 4(1): 1–4.

Fudge J and Strauss K (2014 in press) Migrants, Unfree Labour, and the Legal Construction of Domestic Servitude: Migrant Domestic Workers in the UK. In C. Costello and M. Freedland (eds), *Migrants at Work: Immigration and Vulnerability in Labour Law*. Oxford: Oxford University Press, 9.

Goldring L and Landolt P (2013) *Producing and Negotiating Non-Citizenship: Precarious Legal Status in Canada*. Toronto: University of Toronto Press.

Harvey D (2004) The New Imperialism: Accumulation by Dispossession. *The Socialist Register* 40: 63–87.

Hoskyns C and Rai SM (2007) Recasting the Global Political Economy: Counting Women's Unpaid Work. *New Political Economy* 12(3): 297–213.

Jonas AEG (1996) Local Labour Control Regimes: Uneven Development and the Social Regulation of Production. *Regional Studies* 30(4): 323–338.

Kelly P, Park S, de Leon C and Priest J (2011) Profile of Live-In Caregiver Immigrants to Canada, 193–2009. *TEIDI Analytical Report*, 18.

Langevin L and Belleau M (2000) *Trafficking in Women in Canada: A Critical Analysis of the Legal Framework Governing Immigrant Live-in Caregivers and Mail-Order Brides*. Ottawa: Status of Women Canada.

Marx K (1979) *Capital: A Critique of Political Economy, Volume*. London: Penguin Books.

Parreñas RS (2001) *Servants of Globalization: Women, Migration and Domestic Work*. Redwood City, CA: Stanford University Press.

Parreñas RS (2011) *Illicit Flirtations: Labor, Migration, and Sex Trafficking in Tokyo*. Stanford, CA: Stanford University Press.

Peck J (1996) *Work-Place: The Social Construction of Labour Markets.* New York; London: Guilford Press.

Pedraza S (1991) Women and Migration: The Social Consequences of Gender. *Annual Review of Sociology* 17: 303–325.

Pratt G (2004) Valuing Childcare: Troubles in Suburbia. In K. Mitchell, SA. Marston and C. Katz (eds), *Life's Work: Geographies of Social Reproduction.* Malden, MA: Blackwell Publishing, 164–184.

Pratt G (2009) Circulating Sadness: Witnessing Filipino Mothers' Stories of Family Separation. *Gender, Place and Culture* 16(1): 3–22.

Roberts K and Chaudry S (2013) *Submission to the Joint Committee on Human Rights on the United Kingdom's Implementation of C.N. v. The United Kingdom (Application No. 4239/08).* London: Kalayaan and the AIRE Centre.

Sassen S (2002) Global Cities and Survival Circuits. In B. Ehrenreich and AR. Hochschild (eds), *Global Woman: Nannies, Maids and Sex Workers in the New Economy.* New York: Henry Holt, 254–274.

Silvey R (2004) Transnational Migration and the Gender Politics of Scale: Indonesian Domestic Workers in Saudi Arabia. *Singapore Journal of Tropical Geography* 25(2): 141–155.

Skrivankova K (2010) *Between Decent Work and Forced Labour: Examining the Continuum of Exploitation.* York: Joseph Rowntree Foundation.

Stasiulis D and Bakan A (2003) *Negotiating Citizenship: Migrant Women in Canada and the Global System.* London: Palgrave.

Waylen G (1998) Introduction. *New Political Economy* 3(2): 181–188.

Williams F (2012) Converging Variations in Migrant Care Work in Europe. *Journal of European Social Policy* 22(4): 363–376.

Wuo Y (2010) HOMEless: A case Study of Private/Public Inversion and the Temporal-Spatial Exclusion Faced by Migrant Domestic Workers. *Inter-Asia Cultural Studies* 11(3): 325–354.

Yeoh BSA and Huang S (2010) Foreign Domestic Workers and Home-Based Care for Elders in Singapore. *Journal of Aging & Social Policy* 22(1): 69–88.

5
Labour Exploitation of Non-EU Migrants in Slovakia: Patterns, Implications and Structural Violence

Matej Blazek

Introduction

Writing a few years after the countries of East and Central Europe joined the EU in 2004, Castles and Miller (2009: 116) named them 'future immigration lands'. Fuelled by the opening of new labour markets and dynamic economic growth, the number of migrants in Slovakia skyrocketed from 22,108 in 2004 to 73,783 in 2014 (ADP, 2014), although, as *with* its neighbours, Slovakia still retains one of the very smallest populations of migrants in the EU, in both absolute and relative numbers. Small numbers and their peripheral position in European migration flows are among the key reasons why the focus on migration in postsocialist European countries concentrates instead on the East–West flows of labour migrants (Burrell, 2009) and, to a lesser extent, on their return (White, 2014).

The chapter evaluates experiences of non-EU migrants in Slovakia with labour-related vulnerability, building on a pioneering national-scale study of the International Organization for Migration (IOM) conducted in 2012 (see Blazek et al., 2013; Blazek, 2014). Exploring migrants' experiences of exploitative labour in a country such as Slovakia adds to the existing understandings of migrant labour in two ways. First, rare empirical data from an East Central European region indicate patterns of migration, migration policy and migration politics that produce configurations of migrant workers' vulnerability similar to and simultaneously different from the known dynamics in Western Europe and elsewhere. While distinctive in many ways, Slovakia represents several traits of migration dynamics characteristic of the majority of post-socialist countries but not of Western Europe: small but increasing numbers of migrants, historical experience of ethnic homogeneity (Zubrzycki, 2001), lack of research on migrant communities (Blazek, 2014) and utilitarian migration policies driven by an antagonistic mixture of political populism and EU pressure (Vermeersch, 2005).

As the chapter builds on a wider research project concerned with various forms of violence, abuse and exploitation, it also looks at intersections of labour exploitation and other forms of marginalisation of some migrant groups, such as their exposure to violence in public spaces and to abuse at home. The socio-legal and institutional context of migration and the configurations of some migrant communities are shown to create conditions for a form of wider structural violence (Galtung, 1969) that embeds labour exploitation as one of its elements.

The chapter reviews patterns of migration, migration policy and politics in Slovakia, focusing on the importance of work in the lives of non-EU migrants, addressing especially migrants from Ukraine and East Asia as groups most exposed to labour exploitation. It outlines key data on migrants' experiences of labour exploitation and explains the underlying factors through a discussion of background policy and legal contexts. It reveals the intersections of migrants' experiences with other forms of violence and abuse, theorising the complexity of vulnerability as a structural condition.

All unreferenced primary data in the chapter come from the aforementioned IOM study (Blazek et al., 2013) drawing on information obtained from 690 questionnaires distributed across all non-EU migrant groups in Slovakia, followed by 83 interviews with individual migrants, as well as key stakeholders from organisations working with migrants.

Migration in Slovakia: Migrant workers, migration policy and politics

Migration to Slovakia

The structure of migration flows and the construction of migrants' positionalities as workers located in complex patterns of labour-related inequality and oppression are inter-related (McDowell, 2008). In contrast with most other countries where labour exploitation of migrants has been recorded and explored, especially in Europe, the intensity of migration to Slovakia has been relatively low and its patterns less complex, creating conditions for a distinctive character of migrant communities and migrants' labour.

Migration to Slovakia after 2004 has been shaped by three key trends: decreasing numbers of undocumented migrants, low numbers of refugees granted asylum and slow growth and changing structure of the overall migrant population. The number of recorded illegal border-crossings or stays decreased by 90 per cent between 2004 and 2013 (IOM, 2014), mainly as an effect of increased border security after its accession to the EU in May 2004 and the Schengen Area in December 2007. The number of asylum claims also decreased significantly, from 11,395 in 2004 to 441 in 2013 (APD, 2014), and Slovakia consistently records some of the lowest numbers of those granted asylum: less than 3 per cent of asylum seekers in 2013 were granted an actual refugee status, less than any other EU country, except for Malta and Greece (Eurostat, 2014).

As such, migrants who stay in Slovakia are predominantly documented, and their numbers have been constantly rising. However, the figures presented above are boosted particularly by EU citizens, whose proportion went up from 49 per cent of all migrants in 2004 to 63 per cent in 2013 (IOM, 2014). Thirty-eight per cent of all migrants come from only four post-socialist EU countries: the Czech Republic, Hungary, Romania and Poland (ADP, 2014). Ukraine maintains the highest and constantly growing numbers, increasing from 4,007 documented migrants outside the EU in 2004 to 7,137 in 2014. However, Ukrainians also represent the largest group of overstayers (Mrlianová et al., 2011), a significant feature of their likely marginalisation in the labour context, discussed in the following. The numbers of another key group of non-EU migrants from East and South East Asia (mainly Vietnam, China and South East Korea) rose dramatically between 2004 and 2009, but this growth decelerated since the recession in 2009.

King (2008) warns that a comparatively smaller size of migrant population does not necessarily result in homogeneous experiences and that letting countries with smaller numbers of migrants fly 'under the radar' might lead to overlooking substantial levels of vulnerability and marginalisation. As will be shown in the following, the size of migrant communities in Slovakia is a relevant factor in generating vulnerability, because it impacts power relations *within* migrant communities as well as *between* migrants and institutions.

Non-EU migrants and work

Although the number of legally working migrants has decreased over the last five years and just over 6,000 non-EU migrants had work permits in

2013, the proportion of adult non-EU migrants who declared any experience with work (documented or not) in the IOM research was 70 per cent. For migrants from the six most prominent non-EU countries of origin in Slovakia (Table 5.1), work is the primary motivation for migration for four – only migrants from Serbia and Russia named other factors as more important, mainly family or studies.

Whereas 46 per cent of all non-EU migrants indicated that work was their reason to come to the country, this number was 58 per cent for South Koreans, 69 per cent for Chinese, 70 per cent for Ukrainians and 75 per cent for Vietnamese. These groups also illustrate contrasting patterns of work in migrant communities in Slovakia. Korean migrants, for instance, almost exclusively work in middle and high managerial positions in Korean companies in Slovakia (especially the KIA factory in Žilina). The number of Korean migrants increased ten times between 2004 and 2010 because of investment after Slovakia joined the EU. Only men are usually economically active, but unlike other labour migrants from Asia, they often come with their families (27 per cent of Koreans were younger than 18 in 2010, considerably more than 17 per cent of migrants from China and 11 per cent from Vietnam), who are involved in social and cultural activities within their spatially and socially segregated communities. By contrast, migrants from China and Vietnam are mainly active in trade and restaurant businesses (see also Baláž and Williams, 2005) and most of them are in the productive age, joining established businesses of their relatives and acquaintances as a temporary or permanent workforce. While a smaller number of Vietnamese migrants came to Slovakia before 1989 as students and their ties with the Slovak population are relatively strong, the majority of Chinese and Vietnamese migrants live in compact and isolated communities, often sharing accommodation with other co-workers, who might or might not be family members. Younger adult migrants without families make up the majority of the workforce (Table 5.1).

Migrants from Ukraine are a distinct group and the only one of the four countries with constantly, albeit slowly, increasing numbers, even after the onset of the economic recession.[1] They form a relatively diverse group with respect to work experience. Some come to study, others with their families. Yet, most migrants from Ukraine come to Slovakia for work, utilising information from their relatives or (informal) work agents operating in Ukraine, and their stay in the country is largely opportunistic, depending on the availability of work. Unlike Asian migrants, most Ukrainians speak quite good Slovak and their physical appearance is not distinctive. Hence, they are more likely to engage without drawing attention. Relatively few Ukrainians run their

Table 5.1 Key groups of non-EU migrants in Slovakia according to the country of origin (Data as on 30 June 2014)

Rank	Country of origin	Number of migrants
1.	Ukraine	7,137
2.	Serbia	4,261
3.	Russia	2,748
4.	Vietnam	2,105
5.	China	1,957
6.	South Korea	1,556
7.	US	850
8.	Macedonia	678
9.	Turkey	389
10.	Israel	275

Source: Alien Police Department (2014).

own businesses and they usually work (documented or not) for Slovak employers in warehouses, in restaurants or at construction sites. However, the recruitment is usually organised collaboratively by powerful members of Ukrainian community and their Slovak partners, such as recruiters, gangmasters or lawyers. Similar to Chinese and Vietnamese migrants, Ukrainians often leave their families at home (25 per cent of Ukrainian men and 15 per cent of women stated they lived separately from their children) and share accommodation arranged by their labour providers. The percentage of Ukrainians who declared work experience in Slovakia was over 80 per cent, highlighting its significance in their lives.

Migration policy and politics

The current *Migration Policy of the Slovak Republic* (2011–2020) was adopted in 2011. For the first time, the country declared a commitment to 'active' migration management with a focus on high-skilled labour migration. While the government declared support to migrants in areas such as education, entrepreneurship, healthcare and legally, the focus on high-skilled migrants overlooked entirely the majority of migrants from the non-EU cohort. In addition, the policy declared a preference for 'culturally associated countries' of origin (meaning the white Western world), publicly interpreted by the Minister of Interior as a security measure and a step towards preventing segregation and tensions, citing the 'obvious failures of multiculturalism' as a rationale for the strategy (Chudžíková, 2011a). The second current relevant framework, the *Integration Policy of the Slovak Republic*, was adopted by the government in 2014, after previous integration policies were criticised heavily for their lack of accountability, implementation and monitoring mechanisms, and for the transfer of responsibility to non-state actors (Chudžíková, 2011b). The country scores particularly low in international comparative policy indicators such as Migrant Integration Policy Index (www.mipex.eu). While the framework itself was widely considered as an improvement on previous documents, it faced criticism during the public negotiation process because of the persistent lack of effective implementation.

Despite progress in the policy area, the predominant political discourse about migration is still dominated by narratives of security, control and assimilation (Chudžíková, 2011a; Blazek et al., 2013). Similar to other 'post-socialist' countries, the approach to migration management is based on an uneasy combination of political populism that frequently embraces xenophobic tendencies, alongside formal commitments to the EU calling for pro-migration policies (Vermeersch, 2005; Cerna, 2013). The majority of state funding is allocated to institutions regulating migration, with EU programmes being the predominant source of funding for activities supporting migrants (Blazek, 2014). For migrant workers from outside the EU, it means that individual local contacts (especially intimate partners) or the community of their compatriots are key sources of information and resilience, as the state fails to engage beyond its policing agenda; in fact, 36 per cent of non-EU migrants declared that they had never asked any formal institution for help.

Migrants in Slovakia and labour exploitation

Background to labour exploitation: Institutions, policies and law

Work is the key element in many non-EU migrants' lives in Slovakia, particularly those who come from Ukraine and Asia. Migrant workers with little awareness of their rights are dependent on informal contacts from their community to arrange not just their work but often also accommodation, food, transport or healthcare (cf. Scott et al., 2012). Apart from the lack of outreach mechanisms and engagement between migrant communities and the state, another factor is the importance of the Slovak language in communication with institutions for securing the necessary legal status and protection (Blazek, 2014).

There are differences between such arrangements in the Asian and Ukrainian communities. Much evidence exists about the deliberate and systematic exploitation of Ukrainian workers by their compatriots in collaboration with Slovak employers and agents. On the other hand, poor work conditions in Chinese or Vietnamese workplaces are often a result of the marginalisation of the employers themselves, as they lack the social and economic rights of Slovak citizens (see Wilkinson, 2014), and vulnerability is reproduced, rather than imposed.

No public institution in Slovakia currently actively addresses the labour exploitation of migrant workers or their rights. The focus of both immigration and regular police is on enforcing laws and policies rather than providing support, and there are indications of corrupt activities in the past. An illustration is the practice explained by a research participant from Ukraine who had overstayed and worked illegally in Slovakia for more than ten years. He used to carry a 50-euro banknote in his passport in case he is stopped by the police, calling it his 'business card'. The work of labour inspection is focused on the detection of undocumented labour, with an emphasis on prosecuting the employers and especially the workers, rather than providing support to victims. Migrant entrepreneurs, especially petty traders from East and Southeast Asian communities, declared their perception of systematic harassment by the Inspectorate. No trade unions or similar organisations are active in supporting migrants in Slovakia, unlike some partners in Western Europe (Krings, 2009).

However, it is the legislation and in particular its implementation that fundamentally limits opportunities to tackle exploitative and forced labour. First, immigration law is in practice given priority over labour law, so a victim of labour exploitation without valid work permit is seen first as an illegal immigrant rather than a victim of crime. This is illustrated by the case of a restaurant owner, confidentially reported by a research participant. The owner was recruiting workers from India but never arranged necessary work documents for them. He stopped paying their salary soon after they arrived, and when their discontent was too difficult to handle, he would report them to the police himself, after getting rid of any tangible evidence that they had worked for him, repeating this tactic several times. While victims of human trafficking or 'extremely exploitative labour' can be offered 'tolerated stay', a temporary form of permit and itself a transposition of the EU legislation (Directive, 2009/52/EC), this is in practice very rare for victims of human trafficking and has not happened for victims of exploitative labour yet.

Secondly, the condition for recognising the worker's status and rights is possession of a legally valid work contract written in the Slovak language (see Dwyer et al., 2011). Thirty-three per cent of non-EU migrants declared to the IOM that their understanding of the language was limited or non-existing, and only 29 per cent declared that their comprehension of Slovak was very good. A common practice in some sectors was then to provide only verbal contracts, or differing versions of contracts in different languages – neither is a valid document, but migrants are usually unaware of this. The last option is particularly sophisticated, because the employer retains a valid contract document in Slovak and does not employ the worker illegally. An example of this was a case of Thai masseuses with little knowledge of English and no knowledge of Slovak, who signed eight-hour contracts in both languages. The employer interpreted this to them as eight paid hours of actual massaging, whereas they spent well over ten hours per day at work.

Slovakia lacks a number of mechanisms identified in other countries that help to tackle exploitative and forced labour. Although sectors and industries with a high risk of the presence of exploitation (see Scott et al., 2012, for a UK example) have been identified, and these findings have been integrated into the new *Integration Policy*, no regulation or monitoring framework has been implemented. While the most vulnerable groups of migrants are known, outreach activities receive no funding and even the work of non-state agencies will probably be reduced after the European Integration Fund was dissolved in 2015. A multi-agency approach (Anderson and Rogaly, 2005) to address exploitative labour of migrants is underdeveloped, partly because of the lack of active engagement by some key institutions (such as trade unions, non-active in the area of migrant rights) and partly because of the lack of positive relations between migrant communities and the state. The law recognises human trafficking as defined in the Palermo Protocols, but unlike some other West European countries (Skrivankova, 2010), it does not acknowledge the vulnerability of migrants or define forced labour as a separate offence (FLMG, 2014). Finally, the migration status legislation has been criticised lately and suggestions have been made to liberalise the right to stay, particularly for the most vulnerable migrants (Blazek et al., 2013); yet the political view on migration continues to be among the most restrictive within the EU.

Extent of labour exploitation

In terms of the overall numbers, the IOM estimated that 11 per cent of all working adult non-EU migrants in Slovakia have some experience of forced labour and a further 18 per cent might be at high risk (see Blazek, 2014; the numbers are calculated from ILO [2009] and Skrivankova's [2010] methodology). The most at-risk group of migrants are Ukrainians, particularly men, who experience forced labour 2–3 times more frequently than other migrants. Despite good general levels of education, these migrants find themselves marginalised, a process fostered by a combination of pressure from those who organise such work (including, especially, confinement, debt bondage or direct threats, see Blazek, 2014), strong motivation to earn money and often subsidise the family in Ukraine, and their intensely suspicious attitude towards formal institutions (the research documented cases of migrants who did not see their children for more than five years, because of travel costs, despite the relative proximity of Slovakia and Ukraine).

However, further indicators of labour exploitation (Scott et al., 2012) show even more signs of labour exploitation – 22 per cent conduct activities beyond their contract, and more than 41 per cent work more than 48 hours average per week (the maximum legally allowed time), including regular work and overtime – and of vulnerability: 25 per cent of all working adult non-EU migrants do not understand their Slovak contract. As noted, vulnerability rather than deliberate exploitation is more prominent in Vietnamese and Chinese communities. In petty trade, such long hours are worked by both workers and employers, and while the workers have little leeway to circumvent this, they usually see it as a normal economic practice rather than exploitation. However, many Vietnamese migrants also work for transnational industrial firms and they most often referred to forced overtime work (under the threat of losing the job) and unpaid salaries among their experiences of exploitation, indicating forced labour practices. As their right to stay depends on their work permit and because of the lack of wider institutional support, they have even fewer opportunities to address this pressure than their Slovak co-workers.

To summarise, work is the key motivation and factor of livelihood for a considerable segment of non-EU migrants in Slovakia. Some groups, particularly migrants from Ukraine and East Asia, are particularly exposed to labour exploitation and forced labour, and their vulnerability is fuelled by two factors – socio-legal and institutional migration contexts in Slovakia, where the state pursues restrictive policies rather than offering support to vulnerable groups – and the importance of ties within migrant communities that privilege certain informal actors, some of whom abuse this position to organise and perpetuate exploitative practices, often together with Slovak partners.

Intersections of violence, abuse and exploitation: Migrants and structural violence

The term 'structural violence' has been used in the literature on migration in various contexts, describing phenomena ranging from the implications of institutional exclusion (Larchanché, 2012) to structural exposure to the violence of criminal gangs (Slack and Whiteford, 2011). Two elements are important for understanding the term. First, structural violence is not the same as oppression, as it refers to dynamics which expose victims to actual violence or risk of violence, not just disadvantage, marginalisation or exclusion (Alvarado and Massey, 2010). Secondly, as Galtung (1969) explains, structural violence is not equal to institutional violence as it entails wider sets of relations associated with one's positionality that encompass more than one institution.

We conducted a chi-square test of the relationships between migrants' experiences with forced labour and other forms of violence: (1) hate crime attack in public (verbal or physical); (2) repeated physical attack in public; (3) repeated experience of control by a household member (e.g. of movement, contact, access to money, documents, communication technologies, food, sleep or healthcare); (4) repeated experience of psychological violence (threats or humiliation) by a household member; and (5) repeated experience of physical violence (including sexual and against property) by a household member. The relationship was in all five cases statistically significant at the 0.01 level, indicating that victims of forced labour are likely also to experience other forms of violence.

Two conclusions from these statistics based on the qualitative findings are important. First, the experience of forced (and exploitative) labour and other forms of violence might be coincidental, but often they are related, and secondly, other forms of violence serve as additional methods of control in forced labour situations. For instance, Ukrainian research participants cited a system of accommodation where male migrants working in shifts took turns to sleep in a room with a capacity much smaller than was appropriate for the number of people, who were subjected to strict discipline. The violence and control from household members do not refer to intimate partners here but rather refer to the providers of accommodation associated with the employers (see Blazek, 2014), but also to other co-workers, as conflicts and violence are not uncommon in confined spaces (cf. McGrath, 2013). However, we also recorded a situation where a female migrant from Southeast Asia presented her relationship with the employer as intimate, while simultaneously declaring experiences with both forced labour and domestic abuse.

On the other hand, even if these experiences are not necessarily related, they indicate that most vulnerable migrant workers are simultaneously exposed to other forms of abuse and have limited capacities to tackle them. Hate-motivated attacks are experienced not only by migrants from Asian or African countries but also by Ukrainians whose physical appearance is identical to Slovaks, but where differences can be identified by language or accent. Yet with any forms of violence, including incidents not related to migrants' specific position, for example robberies, there is still the additional factor of marginalisation, because most migrants do not trust the police, many do not have the necessary knowledge about their rights and the existing supportive mechanisms, and many are afraid to engage with formal institutions because of threats from their employers or other community members.

These findings suggest that migrant workers in Slovakia are not just vulnerable to exploitative labour but many are also victims of structural violence. Structural violence is ultimately embodied and manifested in acts of interpersonal violence (Barak, 2003), but it is at the same time systematic, personal and indirect, in the sense that it does not necessarily come from a single source, instead being a product of complex socio-economic dynamics, and it targets any member of a certain social group rather than specific individuals (Farmer, 2004). Even those victims of incidents unrelated to their migrant identity might suffer from what Quesada et al. (2011) termed 'structural vulnerability', a lack of means to cope with the difficulties caused by their positionality as migrants.

Conclusions

The findings from Slovakia suggest an urgent need to focus on experiences of migrants in countries that are normally not seen as 'immigration lands', as even relatively small migrant cohorts might experience profound abuse and exploitation. The case of Slovakia illustrates how emerging migration flows in a country with little history of immigration gave rise to a specific socio-legal and institutional context which nurtured labour exploitation of vulnerable migrants through a lack of institutional engagement and the marginalisation of whole communities.

In addition, the findings show that labour exploitation is often experienced along with other forms of violence, whether in parallel or as their direct component. I discuss this phenomenon through the concepts of structural violence and vulnerability, a system of conditions exposing individuals from certain groups to acts of violence in various spheres of their lives with little capacity to tackle this. Lewis et al. (2014) have suggested a need to rethink the relations between 'precarious work' and 'precarious lives' due to the degree in which precarity exceeds the realm of work. While drawing on a different conceptual tool, I suggest that the problem of migrants' labour exploitation is an issue not just of work but rather of the broader configurations of migrants' lives from the arena of intimate privacy to their positionality in wider state structures.

Acknowledgements

The IOM research informing this chapter was funded by the European Integration Fund (Grant nr. SK 2011 EIF P2/1 IP). Sona Andrášová and Nina Paulenová equally contributed to the completion of the project, but the paper does not necessarily present IOM's views and the IOM takes no responsibility for its content.

Note

1. It is conceivable that the recent war on the eastern periphery of Ukraine may drive higher numbers to migrate.

References

ADP (2014) *Statistical Overview of Legal and Illegal Migration in the Slovak Republic.* Bratislava: Alien Department Police.
Alvarado SE and Massey DS (2010) In Search of Peace. Structural Adjustment, Violence, and International Migration in Mexico and Central America 1979–2002. *The Annals of the American Academy of Political and Social Science* 630(1): 137–161.
Anderson B and Rogaly B (2005) *Forced Labour and Migration to the UK.* London: Trades Union Congress.
Baláž B and Williams AM (2005) Winning, then Losing, the Battle with Globalization: Vietnamese Petty Traders in Slovakia. *International Journal of Urban and Regional Research* 29(3): 533–549.
Barak G (2003) *Violence and Nonviolence: Pathways to Understanding.* London: Sage.
Blazek M, Andrášová S and Paulenová N (2013) *Skúsenosti Migrantov a Migrantiek na Slovensku s Násilím [Experiences of Migrants in Slovakia with Violence].* Bratislava: International Organization for Migration.
Blazek M (2014) Migration, Vulnerability and the Complexity of Violence: Experiences of Documented Non-EU Migrants in Slovakia. *Geoforum* 56: 101–112.
Burrell K (eds) (2009) *Polish Migration to the UK in the 'New' European Union after 2004.* Aldershot: Ashgate.

Castles S and Miller M (2009) *The Age of Migration. International Population Movements in the Modern World*. Basingstoke: Palgrave.

Cerna L (2013) Understanding the Diversity of EU Migration Policy in Practice: The Implementation of the Blue Card Initiative. *Policy Studies* 34(2): 180–200.

Chudžíková A (2011a) Migration Strategy: An Attempt to Homogenize Society by 2020? *Minority Politics* 3/2011: 11–12.

Chudžíková A (2011b) Strategy of Integration of Foreigners in the Slovak Republic: Unclear Goals, Unclear Results. *Minority Politics* 1/2011: 6–7.

Dwyer P, Lewis H, Scullion L and Waite L (2011) *Forced Labour and UK Immigration Policy. Status Matters?* York: Joseph Rowntree Foundation.

Eurostat (2014) *Asylum Applicants and First Instance Decisions on Asylum Applications: 2013*. Available at: http://ec.europa.eu/eurostat/en/web/products-data-in -focus/-/KS-QA-14-003 (accessed 8 October 2014).

Farmer P (2004) An Anthropology of Structural Violence. *Current Anthropology* 45(3): 305–325.

FLMG (2014) *Forced Labour: What Next?* Durham: Forced Labour Monitoring Group.

Galtung J (1969) Violence, Peace and Peace Research. *Journal of Peace Research* 6: 167–191.

ILO (2009) *The Cost of Coercion*. Geneva: International Labour Organization.

IOM (2014) *Migration in Slovakia*, Available at: http://www.iom.sk/en/about-migration/migration-in-slovakia (accessed 8 October 2014).

King R (2008) Across the Sea and over the Mountains. Documenting Albanian Migration. *Scottish Geographical Journal* 119(3): 283–309.

Krings T (2009) A Race to the Bottom? Trade Unions, EU Enlargement and the Free Movement of Labour. *European Journal of Industrial Relations* 15(1): 49–69.

Larchanché S (2012) Intangible Obstacles: Health Implications of Stigmatization, Structural Violence, and Fear among Undocumented Immigrants in France. *Social Science & Medicine* 74(6): 858–863.

Lewis H, Dwyer P, Hodkinson S and Waite L (2014) Hyper-Precarious Lives: Migrants, Work and Forced Labour in the Global North. *Progress in Human Geography*, early view.

McDowell L (2008) Thinking through Work: Complex Inequalities, Constructions of Difference and Trans-National Migrants. *Progress in Human Geography* 32(4): 491–507.

McGrath L (2013) Many Chains to Break. The Multi-Dimensional Concept of Slave Labour in Brazil. *Antipode* 45(4): 1005–1028.

Mrlianová A, Ulrichová N and Zollerová M (2011) *Praktické opatrenia v boji proti nelegálnej migrácii v Slovenskej Republike* [*Practical measures to combat illegal migration in the Slovak Republic*]. Bratislava: IOM and EMN.

Quesada J, Hart LOK and Bourgois P (2011) Structural Vulnerability and Health: Latino Migrant Laborers in the United States. *Medical Anthropology: Cross-Cultural Studies in Health and Illness* 30(4): 339–362.

Scott S, Craig G and Geddes A (2012) *Experiences of Forced Labour in the UK Food Industry*. York: Joseph Rowntree Foundation.

Skrivankova K (2010) *Between Decent Work and Forced Labour: Examining the Continuum Exploitation*. York: Joseph Rowntree Foundation.

Slack J and Whiteford S (2011) Violence and Migration on the Arizona-Sorona Border. *Human Organization* 70(1): 11–21.

Vermeersch J (2005) EU Enlargement and Immigration Policy in Poland and Slovakia. *Communist and Post-Communist Studies* 38(1): 71–88.

White A (2014) Polish Return and Double Return Migration. *Europe-Asia Studies* 66(1): 25–49.

Wilkinson M (2014) Demonising 'the other': British Government Complicity in the Exploitation, Social Exclusion and Vilification of New Migrant Workers. *Citizenship Studies* 18(5): 499–515.

Zubrzycki G (2001) 'We, the Polish Nation': Ethnic and Civic Visions of Nationhood in Post-Communist Constitutional Debates. *Theory and Society* 309(5): 629–668.

6
Understanding and Evaluating UK Efforts to Tackle Forced Labour

Alex Balch

Introduction

Forced labour[1] is recognised as a worldwide problem, directly affecting millions of people, generating some US$150 billion annual profits (ILO, 2014a). Since 2000, the issue has been entangled in the developing international regime to tackle human trafficking[2] and is often subsumed within broader definitions of 'modern slavery'.[3] This chapter evaluates the UK's response to forced labour, locating this within the international context. It argues that the main problems can be traced to policy framing and implementation, in turn relating to national preferences over economic governance and the regulation of workplace rights. It draws on a study of the problems of regulation and enforcement to tackle forced labour in the UK (Balch, 2012), forming part of a four-year research programme into forced labour funded by the Joseph Rowntree Foundation (JRF).

Forced labour in the UK: What we know

In November 2014, the British government published a scoping study exploring the extent of 'modern slavery'. It estimated that between 10,000 and 13,000 individuals were experiencing slavery-like conditions in the UK, nearly five times more than previous estimates (HO, 2014). It is notable that the report, confirming the fears of many of those conducting research into the topic since the early 2000s, generated little shock or surprise.

Knowledge about dangerous levels of exploitation was heightened by the tragic death of 23 Chinese migrant workers in Morecambe Bay in February 2004. A year later a study by COMPAS (University of Oxford's

'Centre on Migration, Policy and Society') and the TUC (Trades Union Congress) reported forced labour, where 'the immigration status of workers was used to coerce them into work or services' (Anderson and Rogaly, 2005: 59). The TUC went on to create a Commission on Vulnerable Employment (COVE), which reported that 'employment practices attacked as exploitative in the nineteenth century are still common today' (TUC, 2007: 7). Importantly, while these reports highlighted migrants as a group likely to be affected, they all pointed out that forced labour also appeared to affect non-migrants: immigration status (see Waite et al. Chapter 10, this volume) was only one of several factors increasing vulnerability.

This evidence resonated with related research exploring the influence of neoliberal ideas in economic policymaking. Many have argued that the preference for a flexible workforce equates to a strategy of 'disposability' (Kundani, 2007) producing exploitable labour through 'precarity', ranging from 'illegalised, seasonal and temporary employment to homework, flex- and temp-work to subcontractors, freelancers or so-called self-employed persons' (Neilson and Rossiter, 2005).

A second wave of research provided more detail, in particular the 2010–14 forced labour programme funded by the JRF (see Skrivankova 2014b). We now have more information about the scope of forced labour, the different economic sectors most affected (Geddes et al., 2013), the role of immigration rules (Burnett and Whyte, 2010; Dwyer et al., 2011) and the asylum system (Lewis et al., 2014) in creating vulnerability, gaps in enforcement and regulation (Balch, 2012), and the role of business (Lalani and Metcalf, 2012) and changing business models (Allain et al., 2013).

This growing body of independent research on forced labour in the UK is now supported by government reports and statistics. The creation of a National Referral Mechanism (NRM) in 2009, as part of the UK's anti-trafficking efforts, provides quarterly figures, sub-divided into those trafficked for sexual exploitation, forced labour and domestic servitude (with the important caveat that this does not include non-trafficked individuals in situations of forced labour). A small, but growing, number of prosecutions provide case studies and enforcement data from regulators also provide anecdotal evidence.

UK policy and practice to tackle forced labour

How can we characterise the UK response to forced labour? Until the rise of anti-trafficking campaigns in the early 2000s, there was no formal policy. It was assumed that such crimes not only contravened basic human rights but would also likely involve the breaking of other laws, and so could be dealt with by the police and the courts. The UK is indeed a signatory to International Labour Organization (ILO) conventions and human rights treaties which outlaw the practice, but forced labour was historically considered to be a foreign policy or development issue – a problem for poor countries and authoritarian states (Geddes et al., 2013). Evidence of forced labour within the UK has exposed the baselessness of these assumptions. Gradually, a new approach has developed, albeit in a piecemeal and incremental fashion.

An offence of trafficking for forced labour was included with the introduction of new legislation on human trafficking, brought in following agreement reached on the issue in Palermo in 2000 through the UN Office on Drugs and Crime (UNODC). However, in the UK case this was incorporated within immigration legislation and did not cover forced labour if a trafficking element was not involved. Pressure to provide more legal clarity eventually led to an offence of forced labour being included in the 2009 Coroners and Justice Act. While this move was widely praised for finally creating a standalone offence (Liberty and ASI, 2009), it was not accompanied by a comprehensive renovation of existing policy. Also, in terms of outcomes, the new law has not led to a large number of prosecutions, perhaps due to low awareness or understanding among law enforcement agencies (ATMG, 2013: 33). Legislation was also passed to create a new agency dealing with worker exploitation – the Gangmasters Licensing Authority (GLA). This was established following the Morecambe Bay tragedy to licence and regulate labour providers in agricultural, shellfish and food production sectors.

Despite the ratification and implementation of the Council of Europe (CoE) Convention, and incremental legislative adjustments, commentators remained critical of the UK response to severe forms of exploitation. A scathing report from a think-tank closely linked to the Conservative Party (CSJ, 2013) formed the context within which the Coalition government announced a new 'Modern Slavery Bill' in the summer of 2013. It was claimed that the Bill would make the UK a 'global leader' in the fight against human trafficking and modern slavery. Before considering this in greater detail, the next section summarises the main criticisms and weaknesses in the UK's response to forced labour, focusing on the framing and the implementation of policy.

Policy framing

The way in which forced labour is 'framed' as a policy issue is crucial to both explaining the phenomenon and also for deciding upon appropriate responses. Public policy analysis has shown that in areas of political complexity, battles over ideas and causal assumptions result in competing policy 'frames' (Schoen and Rein, 1994). These are important because they can influence the kinds of policy instruments which are selected and the ways they are applied or implemented (Hall, 1993). In the case of forced labour, competing frames can be associated with several different international frameworks 'authored' by different institutions that have developed distinct pathways and policy agendas. While they have subsequently converged and overlapped to a certain extent, they still differ on emphasis and priority (see Table 6.1).

The international dimension is highly relevant because discussions over human trafficking and forced labour (or modern slavery) have often been held at the international level. As in other areas of 'global concern' such as climate change (Haas, 2004), the role of international networks of expertise and advocacy coalitions has traditionally been important to anti-slavery movements. Table 6.1 demonstrates the contrasts between different international programmes, each with its own emphasis: the criminal justice focus of the UNODC and anti-trafficking, the enhanced 'human rights' dimension injected by the CoE Convention, the 'soft-law' approach of the UN on business and human rights, and the 'workplace rights' approach of the ILO.

Prior to the Coroners and Justice Act, law and policy on forced labour in the UK fell almost entirely within the developing anti-human trafficking regime, framed in the UK as a question of transnational organised

Table 6.1 Competing or complementary? A comparison of international frameworks for tackling forced labour

Author	Frame	Policy
UNODC	Transnational organised crime (TOC), immigration	The 3-Ps' agenda – protection, prevention and prosecution (which became 4 with the addition of 'partnership')
CoE	TOC, immigration but with enhanced human rights provisions	As above, but with more defined responsibilities for states with respect to victims
UN SC	CSR (Corporate Social Responsibility)	Three-pillar framework: 'Protect, Respect, and Remedy' (Ruggie 2011)
ILO	Workplace rights	'Prevention, protection, remedies, enforcement, and international cooperation' (ILO 2014b; ILO 2014c)

crime, immigration and border control. This was demonstrated by the way discussions progressed over the CoE Convention and the fact that responsibility for implementation was delegated to the UK Border Agency (Balch and Geddes, 2011). This policy framework now encompasses a range of activities, including public awareness-raising campaigns; training of frontline workers; tackling the environment for exploitation; implementing processes of identification ((NRM) – see below); funding for accommodation/support of victims; working with other countries; coordinating policing efforts; and improving help for victims (Chenti et al., 2012).

While the CoE Convention featured enhanced protection of human rights when compared with the Palermo Protocol, the emphasis remained on criminal justice and forced labour as a type of human trafficking. A problem with this framing is that some incidences of forced labour might be overlooked by enforcement agencies because of the emphasis within anti-trafficking policies on sexual exploitation and immigration. There is now overwhelming evidence that cases of forced labour can occur without a trafficking or immigration element (see Geddes et al., 2013).

The particular framing adopted by the UK can be traced to an aversion towards understanding forced labour as either an issue for businesses to address (i.e. through the UN GP) or a question of more rigorous enforcement of workplace rights (as per ILO recommendations). This could be partially attributed to timing and the fact that those interested in these kinds of approaches were initially slow to grasp the opportunity provided by the anti-trafficking regime (Chuang, 2013). In addition, path-dependencies mean the 'immigration frame' has persisted, despite this being a central focus of most critical analyses (ATMG, 2010; CSJ, 2013).

The UN Guiding Principles on Business and Human Rights and ILO frames position forced labour as a product of endogenous factors, rather than exogenous, where partnership is needed to protect human rights. From these perspectives, forced labour results from a combination of economic structures, the organisation of labour markets and the ways in which businesses operate and are regulated. These frames implicitly or explicitly identify problematic business practices; however, the UK has shown an inability or reluctance either to enforce rules or act to protect the rights of workers (Balch, 2012). This is unfortunate because much research on forced labour establishes links between the phenomenon and increasing levels of informality in labour markets, the lengthening of (product and/or labour) supply chains, the increase in outsourcing of company functions (see Smith, this volume), and shifting recruitment and subcontracting practices, which include the use of intermediaries and temporary labour agencies (see Ewart-James et al., this volume).

Implementation

Criticisms of the UK's efforts to tackle human trafficking and forced labour are not just about framing. They also relate to problems with the implementation of that system put in place by the government (ATMG, 2013) and pre-existing gaps in labour market regulation (Balch, 2012). Definitional issues also translate into implementation problems. As not all forced labour involves human trafficking, individuals can fall outside of the protection offered to victims under anti-trafficking policies. However, even protection of victims identified and supported through the NRM can be undermined by other government targets, such as on removals of foreign nationals, or restrictions on access to benefits for immigrants. There are also wider questions over the appropriateness of anti-trafficking campaigns (Andrijasevic and Anderson, 2009). In the case of forced labour, as a crime fundamentally economically driven, anti-trafficking campaigns focusing on global crime syndicates and sexual exploitation are ineffective – instead the response needs to be tailored to its economic context (CSJ, 2013: 36).

This connects with deeper problems of a fragmented infrastructure in place in the UK to deal with labour exploitation (Balch, 2012). Government-commissioned research by the Migration Advisory Committee (MAC) on migration in low-skilled occupations identified a structural vulnerability to exploitation in the UK economy. The report found that UK employers are only likely to be inspected once every 250 years on average. The authors expressed serious concerns that enforcement is 'under-resourced' and the penalties for non-compliance 'too weak' (MAC, 2014: 4).

Those agencies established to regulate or inspect the workplace have different goals, levels of capacity and sectoral jurisdiction. While they potentially help in combating forced labour, there is no unified labour inspectorate, assuming responsibility for policy and implementation (unlike most other EU countries). Instead, the main economy-wide inspectorate is the Health and Safety Executive, which has 'a declining inspectorial presence' (Whyte and Tombs, 2013). Inspection is generally limited to occupation safety and health, where only around 6 per cent of reported accidents are investigated (ILO, 2006). Outside the police, the GLA would appear to be the regulatory agency best suited to investigating forced labour. Many commentators have recommended an extension to the remit and resources of the GLA, the only pro-active regulator seeking to identify and prevent forced labour (ECHR, 2010; Geddes et al., 2013; Robinson, 2014). These have included widespread demands for more sectors to be subject to the GLA's licensing system for labour providers, to a request from the recruitment industry for the GLA to have powers to investigate forced labour (REC, 2014: 7–8). However, it currently remains tied to a narrow slice of the labour market and faces constant pressure to do less, rather than more – reducing 'burdens' on compliant business and making inspections more risk-based and targeted.[4]

A key feature of UK policy on workplace rights is that protection is theoretically achieved by individuals knowing their rights and taking it upon themselves to act in order to remedy their situation (Balch, 2012). However, as noted above with reference to government anti-trafficking efforts, other policies appear to be in tension with this. The 2014 Immigration Act, for example, increased restrictions on access to benefits, legal aid and the right of appeal, making it significantly more difficult for migrants experiencing exploitation to seek redress. Policy on employment relations has sought to move away from resolution through collective action and towards the use of individual claims via employment tribunals. However, this has been undermined by the introduction of tribunal fees (in July 2013), which led to a drop of over 50 per cent in claims made by individuals in the following month (Burns, 2013), reducing the possibility of redress for workers, particularly those in precarious economic situations.

The Modern Slavery Bill: Leading 'the global fight'?

The announcement of a new Modern Slavery Bill by Home Secretary Theresa May in 2013 came as a surprise to some (Skrivankova, 2014a), but it follows a well-established pattern, where politicians, billionaire entrepreneurs and even religious leaders line up to claim the mantle of the original abolitionists. How cynically should we interpret the Coalition government's claim that the Bill was driven by a desire to 'lead the global fight' against 'modern slavery'? To what extent does it represent a re-framing of the UK approach to forced labour?

The rhetorical and symbolic power of the word 'slavery' (Quirk, 2011) provides an attractive cause for those seeking to further their careers or prestige on the national or international stage. We saw this in 2007 when the then-Home Secretary John Reid seized upon a symbolic opportunity by signing the CoE Convention on a desk used by William Wilberforce. The political calculations behind the new legislation included the hope that it would be positive news for the government in the final legislative session before the 2015 general election. It also served a number of political functions: as a rebuttal to opposition (Labour Party) arguments regarding immigration and exploitation (e.g. Cooper, 2013); as a career opportunity for ambitious parliamentary players (the Home Secretary is a potential candidate to succeed David Cameron as leader of the Conservative Party); and as a topic with the potential to gain cross-party support, it could help detract from the Conservatives' 'nasty party' tag (Balch, 2013).

It is worth noting that the record of the Coalition government on these issues up until the announcement of a new Bill had been quite mixed, with a noted aversion to new legislation. On human trafficking, it was (initially) reluctant to sign up to the EU's 2011 Directive on trafficking, claiming that the legislation would make little difference to the UK's anti-trafficking efforts.[5] Anti-Slavery International (ASI, 2011) (with the campaigning organisation '38 Degrees' and the *Independent on Sunday*) organised a petition and claimed the subsequent reversal of the government position over the EU directive as a campaign victory. A new Bill somewhat contradicts the government's own internal review completed in 2012 which concluded that there should be no radical revision of existing law, nor any new 'bespoke' law on human trafficking (IDMG, 2012).

On domestic servitude the record is no better. The UK government opted not to sign the (June 2011) ILO convention on domestic workers, which aimed to tackle the 'historical and continued exclusion of domestic workers, mainly women and girls, from labour protection' (ILO, 2011: 1). The government raised concerns that 'requiring a licensing system would provide difficulties' and health and safety measures would be problematic because 'national occupational health and safety regulations do not apply to domestic workers' (Ibid.: 51). The UK's Confederation of British Industry (CBI) was one of the few organisations to vote against the ILO Convention (it passed with a majority of 83 per cent), the UK government itself abstaining.

How then should we assess the shift to 'modern slavery' that the UK appears to have adopted? While the legislation was still being debated within Parliament, policy changes had already started. The anti-trafficking unit within the Home Office has been re-named as the Modern Slavery Unit and the government has made a number of statements regarding the direction and priorities of the new approach (Bradley and May, 2014).

In legal terms, the law consolidates and so appears to be no radical departure, but if passed it will represent the third change in forced labour law in a decade. Aside from the confusion this might create for the criminal justice system, there are also a number of dangers in seeking to extract political capital from anti-slavery initiatives. The new Bill defines modern slavery as encompassing 'slavery, human trafficking, forced labour and domestic servitude' (Bradley, 2014).[6] This risks 'exploitation creep' (Chuang, 2013), where different forms of severe exploitation are re-defined as slavery, and a criminal justice approach dominates over labour market interventions or additional responsibilities for business. The UK government's pledge to 'work with business' on modern slavery seems to confirm this (May, 2014), and the content of the draft Bill is more suggestive of a 're-branding' of anti-trafficking policy than a recognition that forced labour requires a tailored response.

Behind the questions of personality, prestige and party politics driving the Modern Slavery Bill, there are deeper political divisions influencing the direction the UK has taken towards forced labour. These result from the connection between the politics of business regulation, cheap labour and immigration. These are areas more likely to be subject to neoliberal ideas due to the influence of 'private sector' interests in public policymaking (Crouch, 2011). This has led to the dominance of certain economic sectors (such as finance) alongside a decline in collective bargaining and practices historically serving to protect the interests of workers (Peters, 2011).

Conclusions: Addicted to cheap labour?

The reluctance to adopt a workplace rights frame can be linked to wider economic policies. There is a strong desire on the part of governments to appear 'business-friendly'. This has arguably led to moves increasing the risk of forced labour in the UK, for example, with removal of regulations around employment rights through the 'red-tape challenge'.[7] Ironically, an enhancement of workplace rights through a nationwide inspectorate could reduce 'burdens' because it would simplify the byzantine system of inspectorates and agencies. The current system is complex and inefficient. The prioritisation of job creation and labour market flexibility has led to very uneven protection across sectors (Balch and Scott, 2011) and is far from providing the 'level playing field' that businesses claim to prefer.

Forced labour is a crime where those responsible are likely to be employers or businesses, but the prioritisation of 'business crime' in the UK has always been much lower than 'conventional crime' (Tombs,

2002). The offence of corporate manslaughter, for example, led to only two convictions between 1965 and 2000, and 20,000 deaths following its introduction (Slapper, 2000). While it would be misleading to claim that there is no regulation or inspection of business in the UK, the system is certainly weak, complex and unwieldy, and almost no inspections look for problems in employment regulations (Balch, 2012). The government's MAC (2014), as noted, expressed serious concerns at its weakness. The 'business-friendly' approach adopted by successive governments explains why NGO demands for a more robust approach to regulation of business (McQuade, 2014) are likely to be ignored in favour of alternative arguments to develop good practice and non-binding codes of conduct (Robertson, 2014). However, it is difficult not to see this as an opportunity missed, particularly when some of the business responses to the question of supply chains in the Bill were against the government position, and for further legislation (ETI, 2014).

The problems with the current policy frame are exacerbated by populist pressures, which mean workers at the bottom of the labour market suffer the dual effects of exploitation and welfare chauvinism. The politics of austerity and government responses to the financial crisis have led to an acceleration of welfare reforms already begun under Labour, including the representation of immigrants as 'undeserving' in a sometimes populist debate on the role of the welfare state (Hamnett, 2014).

Even if government policies facilitating the supply of cheap labour are a defensive measure against the risk of businesses seeking even more informal/illegal sources (King and Rueda, 2008), evidence of forced labour is symptomatic of an imbalance between the democratic system and economic governance. The UK's preferences over business regulation, cheap labour and immigration certainly contribute to creating a more risky environment, influencing both the framing and implementation of policies to address forced labour.

Notes

1. This chapter uses the definition of forced labour provided by Article 2 of the ILO's Forced Labour Convention No. 29 (1930) as 'all work or service that is exacted from any person under the menace of any penalty and for which the said person has not offered himself voluntarily'.
2. The definition of human trafficking in the Palermo Protocol (2000) included forced labour in the list of possible types of exploitation: 'the exploitation of the prostitution of others or other forms of sexual exploitation, forced labor or services, slavery or practices similar to slavery, servitude or the removal of organs'.
3. 'Modern slavery' is an umbrella term often used to incorporate multiple types of contemporary 'slavery-like' practices. These have included (inter

alia) bonded labour, forced labour, domestic servitude, human trafficking and forced marriage.
4. At the time of writing, the UK government has committed to a review of the GLA's role.
5. European Scrutiny Committee, 9 March 2011 – Hansard: http://www .publications.parliament.uk/pa/cm201011/cmselect/cmeuleg/428-xxii/42805 .htm
6. The UK government launched a 'modern slavery' website as part of an information campaign on 31 July 2014: https://modernslavery.co.uk
7. http://www.redtapechallenge.cabinetoffice.gov.uk/home/index/

References

Allain J, Crane A, LeBaron G and Behbahani L (2013) *Forced Labour's Business Models and Supply Chains*. York: Joseph Rowntree Foundation.
Anderson B and Rogaly B (2005) *Forced Labour and Migration to the UK*. TUC: London.
Andrijasevic R and Anderson B (2009) Anti-Trafficking Campaigns: Decent? Honest? Truthful? *Feminist Review* 92(1): 151–156.
ASI (2011) *Anti-Slavery Campaign Victory as the Government Signs Up to the EU Trafficking Directive*. London: Anti-Slavery International.
ATMG (2010) *Wrong Kind of Victim? One Year On: An Analysis of UK Measures to Protect Trafficked Persons*. London: Anti-Trafficking Monitoring Group.
ATMG (2013) *In the Dock: Examining the UK's Criminal Justice Response to Trafficking*. London: Anti-Trafficking Monitoring Group.
Balch A (2012) *Regulation and Enforcement to Tackle Forced Labour in the UK: A Systematic Response?* York: Joseph Rowntree Foundation.
Balch A (2013) Slavery Bill No Use Without Shift in Attitudes towards Migrants and Work. In The Conversation, Available at: https://theconversation.com/ slavery-bill-no-use-without-shift-in-attitudes-towards-migrants-and-work -21621 (accessed 20 February 2015).
Balch A and Geddes A (2011) Opportunity from Crisis? Organisational Responses to Human Trafficking in the UK. *British Journal of Politics and International Relations* 13(1), 26–41.
Balch A and Scott S (2011) Labour Market Flexibility and Worker Security in an 'Age of Migration'. In M. Bommes and G. Sciortino (eds), *Foggy Social Structures: Irregular Migration, European Labour Markets and the Welfare State*. Amsterdam: Amsterdam University Press, 143–169.
Burnett J and Whyte D (2010) *Wages of Fear: Risk, Safety and Undocumented Work*, PAFRAS (Positive Action for Refugees and Asylum Seekers), Liverpool: University of Liverpool.
Burns E (2013) *Employee Claims against Employers Tumble Immediately following Introduction of Tribunal Fees*. hughjames.com, Hugh James Associates (Firm News).
Chenti M, Pennington J and Galos E (2012) *The UK's Response to Human Trafficking: Fit for Purpose?* London: IPPR – Institute for Public Policy Research.
Chuang J (2014) Exploitation Creep and the Unmaking of Human Trafficking Law. *American Journal of International Law* 108(4): 609–655.

Cooper Y (2013) *Speech on Immigration Institute for Public Policy Research*. London: Institute for Public Policy Research.

Crouch C (2011) *The Strange Non-Death of Neo-Liberalism*. Malden, MA: Polity.

CSJ (2013) *It Happens Here: Equipping the United Kingdom to Fight Modern Slavery. Slavery Working Group*. London: Centre for Social Justice.

Dwyer P, Lewis H, Scullion L and Waite L (2011) *Forced Labour and UK Immigration Policy: Status Matters?* York: Joseph Rowntree Foundation.

ECHR (2010) *Inquiry into the Meat and Poultry Processing Sectors*. London: Equality and Human Rights Commission.

ETI (2014) *Position Statement on Modern Slavery Bill*. London: Ethical Trading Initiative.

Geddes A, Craig G and Scott S (2013) *Forced Labour in the UK*. York: Joseph Rowntree Foundation.

Haas P (2004) When Does Power Listen to Truth? A Constructivist Approach to the Policy Process. *Journal of European Public Policy* 11: 569–592.

Hall P (1993) Policy Paradigms, Social Learning and the State: The Case of Economic Policymaking in Britain. *Comparative Politics* 25: 275–296.

Hamnett C (2014) Shrinking the Welfare State: The Structure, Geography and Impact of British Government Benefit Cuts. *Transactions of the Institute of British Geographers* 39(4): 490–503.

HO (2014) *Modern Slavery: An Application of Multiple Systems Estimation*. London: Home Office.

IDMG (2012) *First Report, Inter-Departmental Ministerial Group on Human Trafficking*. London: UK Home Office.

ILO (2006) *General Survey on Labour Inspection. International Labour Conference, 95th Session, Report III (Part 1B)*. Geneva: International Labour Organization.

ILO (2011) *Decent Work for Domestic Workers, Report IV (2A)*. Geneva: International Labour Organization.

ILO (2014a) *Profits and Poverty: The Economics of Forced Labour. Special Action Programme to Combat Forced Labour (SAP-FL); Fundamental Principles and Rights at Work Branch (FPRW)*. Geneva: International Labour Organization.

ILO (2014b) *Text of the Protocol to the Forced Labour Convention, 1930. International Labour Conference, 103rd Session*. Geneva: International Labour Organization.

ILO (2014c) *Text of the Recommendation on Supplementary Measures for the Effective Suppression of Forced Labour. International Labour Conference, 103rd Session*. Geneva: International Labour Organization.

King D and Rueda D (2008) Cheap Labor: The New Politics of 'Bread and Roses' in Industrial Democracies. *Perspectives on Politics* (2): 279–297.

Kundani A (2007) *The End of Tolerance: Racism in 21st Century Britain*. London: Pluto Press.

Lalani M and Metcalf H (2012) *Forced Labour in the UK: The Business Angle*. York: Joseph Rowntree Foundation.

Lewis H, Dwyer P, Hodkinson S and Waite L (2014) *Precarious Lives: Forced Labour, Exploitation and Asylum*. Bristol: The Policy Press.

Liberty and ASI (2009) *Joint Briefing on the Coroners and Justice Bill for the Committee Stage of the House of Lords*. London: Liberty and Anti-Slavery International.

MAC (2014) *Migrants in Low-Skilled Work: The Growth of EU and Non-EU Labour in Low-Skilled Jobs and Its Impact on the UK*. London: Migration Advisory Committee.

May, Theresa and Lord Taylor of Holbeach (2014) 'Modern Slavery: How the UK Is Leading the Fight' Written ministerial statement, laid in the House of Commons by Theresa May (Home Secretary) and in the House of Lords by Lord Taylor of Holbeach, UK Home Office: London.

McQuade A (2014) *Voluntary Guidance on Slavery Is Pointless – Only Radical Action Will Help. Supply Chain Hub*. London: Guardian Sustainable Business.

May T (2014) *Modern Slavery: How the UK Is Leading the Fight. Written Ministerial Statement to Parliament*. London: UK Parliament.

Neilson B and Rossiter N (2005) From Precarity to Precariousness and Back Again: Labour, Life and Unstable Networks. *Fibreculture* 5.

Peters J (2011) The Rise of Finance and the Decline of Organised Labour in the Advanced Capitalist Countries. *New Political Economy* 16(1): 73–99.

Quirk J (2011) *The Anti-Slavery Project: From the Slave Trade to Human Trafficking*. Philadelphia: University of Pennsylvania Press.

REC (2014) *Labour Policy Review: Exploitation Law – Fit for Purpose. Submission to Consultation on Employment Policy*. London: Recruitment and Employment Federation.

Robertson M (2014) *Good Business Practice, as Well as New Laws, Are Needed to Stop Forced Labour. Supply Chain Hub*. London: Guardian Sustainable Business.

Robinson C (2014) *Preventing Trafficking for Labour Exploitation*. Working Paper No. 1. London: Focus on Labour Exploitation (FLEX).

Ruggie J (2011) Report of the Special Representative of the Secretary-General on the Issue of Human Rights and Transnational Corporations and Other Business Enterprises. A/HRC/17/31, Seventeenth session, agenda item 3, Human Rights Council.

Schoen D and Rein M (1994) *Frame Reflection: Toward the Resolution of Intractable Policy Controversies*. New York: Basic Books.

Skrivankova K (2014a) The Word Slavery Has Come to Occupy the Political Arena. In Migration Pulse (Migrants Rights Network), Available at: http://www.migrantsrights.org.uk/migration-pulse/2014/word-slavery-has-come-occupy-political-arena (accessed 20 February 2015).

Skrivankova K (2014b) *Forced Labour in the United Kingdom*. York: Joseph Rowntree Foundation.

Slapper G (2000) *Blood in the Bank. Social and Legal Aspects of Death at Work*. Aldershot: Ashgate.

Tombs S (2002) Understanding Regulation? *Social and Legal Studies* 11(113): 219–243.

TUC (2007) *Hard Work, Hidden Lives*. Report of the Commission on Vulnerable Employment, TUC.

Whyte D and Tombs S (2013) *Triennial Review of the Health and Safety Executive: Submission to the Department for Work and Pensions*. Liverpool: Institute for Employment Rights.

Part III
The Vulnerability of Asylum Seekers

7
The Contribution of UK Asylum Policy 1999–2010 to Conditions for the Exploitation of Migrant Labour

Tom Vickers

Introduction

This chapter argues that our understanding of UK asylum policies can be deepened through a political economy analysis. The chapter focuses on the period 1999–2010, drawing on research conducted in Newcastle upon Tyne between 2007 and 2010 (also see Vickers, 2012, 2014a, 2014b).[1] Policy changes directed at asylum seekers[2] during this period included forced dispersal from 1999, prohibition of paid work from 2002 and a significant increase in immigration detention. These policies, alongside the detained fast track system and reductions in access to appeals and legal aid, amount to an increasingly punitive system that has been widely criticised by bodies such as the Independent Asylum Commission (IAC, 2008b) and that has provoked widespread resistance from those within the system and their supporters (Gill et al., 2012; Anti-Raids Network, 2014; Vickers, 2014a), yet the overall policy direction has continued. This suggests there may be even more powerful pressures pushing for a continuation of the current direction.

Explanations of the hostile policy climate that focus exclusively on the influence of the media, or voter attitudes, do not explain why these policies have been enacted at this particular time. Indeed, Philo et al. (2013) argue that British governments have actively used the media to cultivate public hostility towards refugees. An explanation is also needed for the consistency in policy direction across different political parties in power, including the Labour Party between 1997 and 2010 and the Conservative and Liberal Democrat parties in coalition since 2010, and for the focus on asylum seekers, out of all proportion to their numbers relative to other forms of migration (Cohen, 2006: 5–6; Crawley, 2006: 22–24). If we consider the distinctive characteristic of asylum to be the claim to citizenship based solely on the needs of a group or individual, then a political economy approach directs attention to some powerful reasons for Britain's capitalist class to restrict asylum during this period:

- The increasing push since the 1970s to further commodify labour power as part of a neoliberal[3] policy approach (Lavalette and Pratt, 2006), requiring the elimination of claims based on human needs rather than market forces.
- The destruction of the socialist bloc at the end of the 1980s, which both removed the political value of granting asylum to 'dissidents' in order to embarrass their socialist countries of origin (Schuster, 2003) and made available a large pool of highly skilled labour in nearby Eastern Europe, who were under economic pressures to migrate.

(Hardy, 2008)

In the context of a policy approach of 'managed migration', with rights to move to Britain increasingly tailored to the labour needs of capital, asylum represented an exception, with claims based on universal human rights. Even where refugees' labour is needed within Britain, the fact that refugees move regardless of whether their labour is needed or not represents a threat to the dominance of neoliberal criteria. Restrictions on access to asylum between 1999 and 2010 helped counter this threat. Table 7.1 shows the general decline in numbers of applications between 1999 and 2010, while refusal rates have remained high, exceeding 80 per cent for three consecutive years and exceeding 70 per cent in nine out of twelve years.

In October 2013, *The Observer* reported statements by a Home Office spokesperson that officials dealing with asylum cases were expected to secure a rejection in at least 60 per cent of cases (Taylor, 2013), and in January 2014 *The Guardian* cited written Home Office guidelines offering rewards to officials meeting a 70 per cent rejection target (Taylor and Mason, 2014). These restrictions on access to asylum contributed to conditions for more intense exploitation of other migrants' labour, by making it more difficult in practice to assert economic, political and social rights. The creation of a separate welfare and housing system for asylum seekers in 1999, the prohibition of paid work in 2002 and the increasing use of immigration detention, all served to make it harder for refugees to build links with non-refugees. This both made it more

Table 7.1 UK asylum applications and refusal rates
1999–2010

Year	Asylum applications*	Refusal rates**
1999	71,160	52%
2000	80,315	74%
2001	71,025	72%
2002	84,130	63%
2003	49,405	83%
2004	33,960	88%
2005	25,710	83%
2006	23,610	78%
2007	23,430	73%
2008	25,930	69%
2009	24,485	72%
2010	17,790	75%

Note: *Includes applications made at the port of entry and
after arrival in the UK.
**Final decisions made that year, including applications
which may have been made in a previous year.
Source: Figures from UK Home Office Immigration Statistics
(https://www.gov.uk/government/statistics).

difficult for refugees to resist the injustices of the asylum system and countered the potential for refugees from oppressed countries to form alliances with British working-class people, by removing opportunities for day-to-day contact and struggle – over shared conditions of housing and work, for example – which could threaten international divisions of labour.

The remainder of this chapter sketches some key features of the political economy approach that informs this analysis, before discussing the role of migrant labour in the British economy and the implications of specific asylum policies.

British capitalism and the international reserve army of labour

This chapter employs an analysis of contemporary capitalism that draws on Lenin's ([1916] 1975) theory of imperialism. Imperialism is understood here as a phase of capitalism characterised by the merger of banking and manufacturing capital into monopoly finance capital and the division of the world into countries with a high concentration of capital ownership and consequently financial, political and military power and countries with low levels of capital ownership, whose people and resources are exploited for the benefit of the owners of capital. Based on their relative positions within the international capitalist system, the former countries are characterised as imperialist countries, and the latter as oppressed countries, while recognising that there is a dynamic continuum between the two categories, with continuous struggles for imperialist countries to maintain and extend their dominance relative to their rivals, for less powerful capitalist countries to aspire to imperialist status, and for oppressed countries to mitigate or overturn their oppression. Struggles of oppression and resistance exist within oppressed and imperialist countries, as well as between them, and these are shaped by, and shape, the position of these countries within the imperialist system. The chapter employs an analysis of the state, drawing on Lenin ([1917] 1972), as a set of interlocking institutions ultimately serving the interests of the British capitalist class (outlined in more detail in Vickers, 2014b).

Countries' position within capitalism has emerged historically, driven by the internal dynamic of the capital accumulation process. Accumulation of capital produces a tendency for the rate of profit to fall (Marx, [1894] 2006); eventually an over-accumulation of capital results in insufficient opportunities for investment relative to the mass of accumulated capital, and the accumulation process fails (Grossman, [1929] 1992). One of the consequences of this process is that as capital accumulates in the main capitalist centres – the imperialist countries – there is a drive to export capital abroad, to countries with lower concentrations of capital and where conditions can be created for a higher rate of profit, maintaining the average rate of profit as an incentive for continued investment. An international division of labour is an integral part of the division of countries into imperialist and oppressed categories (see also Smith Chapter 2, this volume). Profitable conditions in oppressed countries often include lower health and safety and environmental standards, lower pay and a lower 'social wage' in the form of state services and financial support. In 2011, Britain earned a rate of return on investments in Asia and the rest of the world, excluding the EU and the US, of 3.3 per cent and 3.0 per cent, respectively, compared to 2.5 per cent return on other countries' investments in the UK (ONS, 2013a: 17), a significant difference considering the sums involved. At the end of 2012, Britain's total external assets stood at £10,222.9 billion (ONS, 2013b: 6), more than 6.5 times UK GDP. For Foreign Direct Investment, which accounts for around 10 per cent of the UK's total overseas assets, the UK received rates of return of 19 per cent and 16 per cent, respectively, for investments in Africa and Asia, compared to a rate of return of 4 per cent on direct investments into the UK (ONS, 2013c): this represents a parasitic relationship and conditions of super-exploitation in oppressed countries. Material underdevelopment of countries oppressed within imperialism has historically prevented these countries' domestic production from fulfilling their own populations' needs, thus simultaneously generating markets for imperialist exports, and maintaining a reserve army of labour for imperialist countries (Castells, [1975] 2002; Miles, 1987; Chinweizu and Jameson, 2008).

As Castells ([1975] 2002: 85) argues, the relationship between capital, labour and mobility is not simply economic but mediated by political systems and relationships that arise from the economic base and impact back upon it. Control over one's mobility is rooted in a person's relationship to capital, both in terms of where their country of citizenship stands within imperialism and their class position within that country. As Foster et al. (2011: 6) point out, the production of super-profits in oppressed countries through conditions that can be characterised as super-exploitation depends on the immobility of labour. While capital is free to move across borders, the movement of workers from oppressed countries is therefore heavily regulated (Barber and Lem, 2008: 4).

The 'New Migration' from Eastern and Central Europe

The year 2004 saw a significant development in freedom of movement and employment for citizens designated 'migrant workers' from the 'Accession 8' (A8) countries in Eastern and Central Europe, with the further addition of the 'A2' countries, Romania and Bulgaria, in 2007. Datta et al. (2007: 49) suggest that A8 workers may have been a preferred source of labour compared to migrants from outside the EU, both for their 'whiteness' and on the understanding that they would be more likely to return to their country of origin than people who have travelled greater distances. By 2007, there were an estimated 1.4 million registered migrant workers in the UK, around half of whom had arrived from the A8 and A2 countries since 2004, and somewhere between 300,000 and 800,000 unregistered migrant workers (Craig et al., 2007: 22). Even for those who were registered, many worked in conditions so exploitative as to meet the international definition of 'forced labour' (Ahmad, 2008: 857; Geddes et al., 2013). The Workers Registration Scheme (WRS) was established, in the words of the Home Office, to provide 'transitional measures to regulate A8 nationals' access to the labour market...and to restrict access to benefits'. Access to the labour market was regulated by the requirement to register for the WRS, but this did not apply to those classified as 'self-employed'. Those designating themselves self-employed were thereby denied many employment rights, even where they were dependent on a single employer for work (Dwyer et al., 2011). While on the WRS, migrants had severely restricted access to unemployment, child and housing benefits. In the first quarter of 2010, 71 per cent of requests by A8 workers for tax-funded, income-related benefits were refused (Home Office, 2010: 23–24). This gave these workers a distinct relationship to capital, to the benefit of the capitalist class. It further explains their preference for Eastern European workers over refugees, who, once they were granted refugee status, had far greater rights to remain in Britain and access state support (Chinweizu, 2006), although these rights have been reduced by the shift from indefinite leave to remain to an initial five years. Under the WRS, A8 migrants only had access to out-of-work benefits once they had completed 12 months in continuous employment. The WRS ended in 2011 and the restrictions on A2 migrants ended in 2014, but they were replaced by regulations restricting access to benefits for all EU migrant workers, extending the exploitative conditions previously affecting A8 and A2 migrants to also include the growing numbers of migrants fleeing the results of crisis and austerity in Southern Europe.

Refugees in Britain and the management of migration

Refugees occupy an ambiguous position in the international division of labour, seeking refuge on the basis of universal human rights yet also available to be called on for their labour, depending on the needs of capital (Kay and Miles, 1992: 4–7). To the extent that refugees 'put down roots' in Britain and gain access to resources and networks of support, they are in a stronger position to resist the demands of capital and assert greater control over their mobility, based on their own needs and priorities. Refugees have faced significant barriers to integration for a long time (Bloch, 2002) and continue to do so (Carnet et al., 2014). The ability to put down roots and rebuild their lives in Britain was increasingly obstructed from 1999 by key policy interventions targeted at refugees without status, designated 'asylum seekers'. While the increased use of detention (Silverman, 2011) also has significance within these processes of social control (Gill, 2009), this chapter will focus on dispersal and the prohibition on paid work, due to their role in isolating refugees within community settings, where it might be expected that there would be more opportunities for integration compared to detention. The qualitative research drawn on here included multiple in-depth qualitative interviews and focus groups with 18 refugees, some with status and some without, supplemented by interviews with the staff of four voluntary and community sector organisations.

Under the dispersal system, Temple et al. found asylum seekers' attempts to reconstitute communities were restricted by allocations of resources, which tended to exclude refugees without status from integration initiatives; hostile environments in dispersal areas, which in some cases kept people confined to their homes; and prohibition of paid work (Temple et al., 2005: 23–26). These factors were also identified in my research, framed and given added force by the asylum decision-making process itself. Overall, the refugees I interviewed presented experiences of the UK asylum process as unreasonable, unclear and unjust. One way of interpreting this is that a fog of complexity and bureaucracy covers up for the fact that a formally 'fair' process is in practice set up to fail all but a few (Tyler, 2010), regardless of their need (BID, 2009). Access to a fair consideration of cases has been undermined by reductions to legal aid and the right of appeal (IAC, 2008b) and an approach to refugees' claims that the Independent Asylum Commission termed a 'culture of disbelief' (IAC, 2008a), echoing the findings of the earlier Glidewell Panel in 1996. The political economy approach outlined above suggests this may be a functional arrangement for capitalism, fulfilling two related but contradictory needs of imperialism. On the one hand, the absolute priority accorded to capital's demand for labour as the basis for migrants to live in Britain is reinforced by the likelihood of being refused asylum, necessary for the continuation of the imperialist division of labour. On the other hand, the British state's image as an upholder of universal human rights and liberty is maintained by the formal fairness of the system, which is necessary for the claims to moral authority so often used to justify Britain's imperialist interference and domination in other countries.

Dispersal

Since 1999 'dispersal' – the forced resettlement of refugees without status to towns and cities across the UK – has been a key element in the British state's attempts to manage refugees. The Immigration and Asylum Act 1999 transferred coordination of housing from local authorities to the National Asylum Support Service (NASS), operating under the direction of the Immigration and Nationality Directorate (IND).

In selecting areas for dispersal, little consideration was given to social and economic infrastructure or existing community networks or resources (Griffiths et al., 2005: 41–42), and the main priority in selecting areas was the availability of cheap housing. In many cases refugees were dispersed to largely white areas with high levels of deprivation, which were given no preparation for the new arrivals (Hewitt, 2002; Hynes, 2011). Racism played a central role in isolating refugees' experiences from the consciousness of British workers (Temple and Moran, 2005). Refugees' lack of control over where they are dispersed contributed to particular problems of isolation for some refugees, such as women refugees experiencing domestic violence (Chantler, 2010: 96–97). Refugees dispersed to Newcastle from 1999 encountered considerable hostility, as well as solidarity. An article, titled 'Police hunt four illegal immigrants: Asylum seekers go on the run', in the local *Evening Chronicle* is symptomatic of the hostile reception, referring to four men who had come from Holland in the back of a lorry and then run away from the driver (Hickman, 2002). While dispersal disrupted existing networks and was carried out in a way that generated hostility from some in the areas where asylum seekers were dispersed, it also led to new forms of resistance (Webber, 2012), including alliances between refugees and non-refugees (Vickers, 2014a).

A political economy approach can help us to understand the dispersal system as part of a system for managing oppression, in the context of refugees' particular class position in the international capitalist system. Capital has little interest in most refugees remaining in Britain, because they are driven by imperatives that override demand for their labour, and consequently the state has little interest in providing any but the most basic means of survival. The existence of coherent and self-conscious diasporas with a sense of shared identity between immigrants in imperialist countries and their oppressed countries of origin, rather than with the national ruling classes of their new home, poses a threat to national borders on both an ideological and practical level (Gilroy, 2001: 124). Major dispersal areas included cities with little history of migration from refugees' countries of origin. The dispersal process thus played a significant political role in breaking up diasporic networks, removing their potential as a basis for resistance, or even a degree of independence from the state. The state has even less interest in helping refugees integrate with other working-class people. Such integration could both offer solidarity for refugees' attempts to remain in Britain and advance their rights, and fundamentally threaten the divisions among workers of different countries, which imperialism relies on to undermine resistance to the super-exploitation of oppressed countries. By disrupting connections with other refugees, support networks and other sections of workers, the dispersal system undermined the potential for collective resistance and increased pressure for refugees to accept the positions assigned to them in international divisions of labour, concentrated disproportionately in low-paid sectors of the economy, often in far lower-skilled roles than those for which they are qualified (Bloch, 2007; Cebulla et al., 2010; Fletcher, 2011).

The prohibition on paid work

While some categories of migrant workers continued to receive encouragement to come to Britain, most refugees without status were prohibited by law in 2002 from seeking paid work[4] or even accessing work-based training, cutting them off from legal areas of the British labour market (Phillimore and Goodson, 2006: 1721). Even prior to this, the 'right to work' had already been restricted to refugees with status and to the 'primary claimant' on each asylum application, and even then only once the person had been in Britain for at least six months (Dumper, 2002: v). This excluded many women from paid work as 'secondary claimants' on family members' applications, and legally enforced their role of unpaid domestic labour in the work of social reproduction in the family.

In a capitalist society, where survival and self-worth for the majority are tied to the sale of one's labour power, refugees interviewed in Newcastle spoke about the negative impact on their self-esteem and mental health as a result of forced inactivity due to being denied the right to undertake paid work. The experience of being a refugee, particularly one who has not been granted some form of 'leave to remain', was strongly characterised by insecurity and dependency on the state, enforced by the prohibition on paid work:

> [T]he asylum seeker is limited, he's not allowed to work ... his income is very low, and he doesn't know the outcome of his decision, so any time he can be deported or can be accepted, so he is in limbo.
>
> (Refugee without status, arrived 2002)

This insecurity, and the legal restrictions on many kinds of action which might have improved their situation, contributed to an intense sense of dependency:

> I've always been independent ... but now it's as if I'm in prison ... there's nothing that proves that I'm an adult, I am just at home, just wait[ing] for somebody to give [things to me].
>
> (Refugee without status from Cameroon, arrived 2008)

By coming to Britain under imperatives other than those of the labour market, refugees have broken discipline with the reserve army of labour and have contradicted the neoliberal terms for international mobility. In response, asylum policies combine to disempower refugees and enforce their dependency on the British state and with it their responsiveness to be re-disciplined into the reserve army (see also Waite et al. Chapter 10, this volume). This both keeps them in an oppressed position and manages this situation by enforcing compliance with the terms of their oppression. It also serves as an example of what happens to those who break neoliberalism's imperatives. Such an observation is not meant to imply the impossibility of resistance; indeed, the development of the structures of control described here has been influenced by the interplay between oppression and resistance, as the British state and those seeking to resist its oppression of refugees have each had to shift their tactics in response to the other (Vickers, 2014a, 2014b).

Conclusions

Refugees occupy an indeterminate class position, particularly acute while their cases are under consideration. They are part of the international reserve army of labour, but a 'part out of place', with a potential to disrupt the normal functioning of the division of labour on a political as well as an economic level. Refuge from persecution represents a powerful form of needs-based claim, the severity of which makes it harder to dismiss compared to more 'ordinary' claims such as access to food and shelter.[5] Refugees' trajectory is in most cases from countries oppressed on a national basis, with which they may maintain connections in identity, communication and transfer of resources. Regardless of their class position in their country of origin, their present position within Britain is most often among the poorest sections of the working class, in conditions that hold the potential to forge alliances across racialised divisions (for an example, see Vickers, 2014a). From 1999, government policy specifically mitigated against this, by breaking up existing networks based on refugees' countries of origin, through dispersal, and impeding the formation of new ones based on common elements of class position within Britain, through a prohibition on paid work. With the exception of individuals who 'escape' the collective position of the majority, for example through paid employment in the refugee sector, the trajectory of most refugees after arrival in Britain is challenging. If they secure leave to remain, they may gain inclusion into a more regularised but still exploited section of the working class. If they are refused asylum, destitution and highly exploitative conditions of employment are likely to follow (British Red Cross 2010, and see following chapters in this part), amounting in some cases to forced labour (Lewis et al., 2014), and/or individuals may be subject to deportation. By undermining rights to remain in Britain and access resources based on human need, rather than labour market demand, this also creates conditions for more intense exploitation of other migrants' labour.

Notes

1. The implications of the global economic crisis of 2007 onwards are beyond the scope of this chapter, although it is important to note that while levels of labour migration dropped, the crisis did not remove Britain's structural dependency on migrants' labour (Sporton, 2013).
2. A constructed category of refugees whose claims have not been accepted by the British state.
3. A policy approach characterised by aggressive privatisation and deregulation.
4. From 2005 asylum seekers could apply for permission to work if they had been waiting for 12 months for a decision on their asylum claim, although this could be granted or refused at the discretion of the Home Office. In 2010, further restrictions were introduced to limit the occupations those granted permission to work could undertake to a 'shortage list'.
5. Although the severity of refugee claims also has the potential to produce a form of exceptionalism, with individual claims to asylum acknowledged while other needs-based claims continue to be ignored.

References

Ahmad AN (2008) The Labour Market Consequences of Human Smuggling: 'Illegal' Employment in London's Migrant Economy. *Journal of Ethnic and Migration Studies* 34(6): 853–874.

Anti-Raids Network (2014) Notes for a Brief History of Resistance in UK Detention Centres. Available at: https://network23.org/antiraids/2014/05/08/notes-for-a-brief-history-of-resistance-in-uk-detention-centres/ (accessed 29 August 2014).

Barber PG and Lem W (2008) Introduction: Migrants, Mobility, and Mobilization. *Focaal: European Journal of Anthropology* 51: 3–12.

BID (2009) *Out of Sight, Out of Mind: Experiences of Immigration Detention in the UK.* London: Bail for Immigration Detainees.

Bloch A (2002) *Refugees' Opportunities and Barriers in Employment and Training.* London: Department for Work and Pensions.

Bloch A (2007) Refugees in the UK Labour Market: The Conflict between Economic Integration and Policy-Led Labour Market Restriction. *Journal of Social Policy* 37(1): 21–36.

Carnet P, Blanchard C and Apollonio F (2014) *The Move On Period: An Ordeal for New Refugees.* London: British Red Cross.

Castells M ([1975] 2002) Immigrant Workers and Class Struggles in Advanced Capitalism: The Western European Experience. *The Castells Reader on Cities and Social Theory.* I. Susser (ed). Malden, MA: Blackwell.

Cebulla A, Daniel M and Zurawan A (2010) *Spotlight on Refugee Integration: Findings from the Survey of New Refugees in the United Kingdom.* London: Home Office.

Chantler K (2010) Women Seeking Asylum in the UK: Contesting Conventions. In I. Palmary, E. Burman, K. Chantler and P. Kiguwa (eds), *Gender and Migration: Feminist Interventions.* London: Zed Books, 86–103.

Chinweizu C (2006) Asylum and Immigration: Maximising Britain's Economy. *Fight Racism! Fight Imperialism!* (190 June/July).

Chinweizu C and Jameson N (2008) Immigration and the Reserve Army of Labour in Britain. *Fight Racism! Fight Imperialism!* (201 February/March).

Cohen R (2006) *Migration and Its Enemies: Global Capital, Migrant Labour and the Nation-State.* Aldershot: Ashgate.

Craig G, Gaus A, Wilkinson M, Skrivankova K and McQuade A (2007) *Contemporary Slavery in the UK.* York: Joseph Rowntree Foundation.

Crawley H (2006) Forced Migration and the Politics of Asylum: The Missing Pieces of the International Migration Puzzle? *International Migration* 44(1): 21–26.

Datta K, McIlwaine C, Wills J, Evans Y, Herbert J and May J (2007) The New Development Finance or Exploiting Migrant Labour? Remittance Sending among Low-Paid Migrant Workers in London. *International Development Planning Review* 29(1): 43–67.

Dumper H (2002) *Missed Opportunities: A Skills Audit of Refugee Women in the Teaching, Nursing and Medical Professions.* London: Greater London Authority.

Dwyer P, Lewis H, Scullion L and Waite L (2011) *Forced Labour and UK Immigration Policy: Status Matters?* York: Joseph Rowntree Foundation.

Fletcher G (2011) *Finding Routes for Refugees to Use Their Skills and Experience and Contribute to the North East Region's Economic Future.* Gateshead: Regional Refugee Forum North East.

Foster JB, McChesney RW and Jonna RJ (2011) The Global Reserve Army of Labor and the New Imperialism. *Monthly Review* 11(1): 1–31.

Geddes A, Craig G and Scott S with Ackers L, Robinson O and Scullion D (2013) *Forced Labour in the UK.* York: Joseph Rowntree Foundation.

Gill N (2009) Governmental Mobility: The Power Effects of the Movement of Detained Seekers around Britain's Detention Estate. *Political Geography* 28(3): 186–196.

Gill N, Conlon D, Oeppen C and Tyler I (2012) *Networks of Asylum Support in the UK and USA: A Handbook of Ideas, Strategies and Best Practice for Asylum Support Groups in a Challenging Social and Economic Climate.* Available at: http://www.esrc.ac.uk/my-esrc/grants/RES-000-22 -3928-A/outputs/Download/116f00b0-3bc0-484c-afa4-60476a64b8a7 (accessed 5 September 2012).

Gilroy P (2001) *Against Race: Imagining Political Culture Beyond the Color Line.* Cambridge: The Belknap Press of Harvard University Press.

Griffiths D, Sigona N and Zetter R (2005) *Refugee Community Organisations and Dispersal: Networks, Resources and Social Capital.* Bristol: The Policy Press.

Grossmann H ([1929] 1992) *The Law of Accumulation and Breakdown of the Capitalist System.* London: Pluto Press.

Hardy J (2008) Polish-UK Migration: Institutions, Capital and the Response of Organised Labour. *EAEPE Conference 'Labour, Institutions and Growth in a Global Knowledge Economy'*. Rome.

Hewitt RL (2002) *Asylum-Seeker Dispersal and Community Relations – An Analysis of Developmental Strategies*. London: Centre for Urban and Community Research Goldsmiths College.

Hickman B (2002) Police Hunt Four Illegal Immigrants: Asylum Seekers go on the Run. *Evening Chronicle*. Newcastle.

Home Office (2010) *Control of Immigration: Quarterly Statistical Summary*. London: United Kingdom January–March 2010.

Hynes P (2011) *The Dispersal and Social Exclusion of Asylum Seekers: Between Liminality and Belonging*. Bristol: Policy Press.

IAC (2008a) *Fit for Purpose Yet? The Independent Asylum Commission's Interim Findings*. London: Independent Asylum Commission.

IAC (2008b) *Deserving Dignity: How to Improve the Way We Treat People Seeking Sanctuary*. London: Independent Asylum Commission.

Kay D and Miles R (1992) *Refugees or Migrant Workers? European Volunteer Workers in Britain 1946–1951*. London: Routledge.

Lavalette M and Pratt A (2006) *Social Policy: Theories, Concepts and Issues*. London: Sage.

Lenin VI ([1916] 1975) *Imperialism, the Highest Stage of Capitalism*. Moscow: Progress Publishers.

Lenin VI ([1917] 1972) *The State and Revolution*. Moscow: Progress Publishers.

Lewis H, Dwyer P, Hodkinson S and Waite L (2014) *Precarious Lives: Forced Labour, Exploitation and Asylum*. Bristol: The Policy Press.

Marx K ([1894] 2006) *Capital, Volume 3*. London: Penguin.

Miles R (1987) *Capitalism and Unfree Labour: Anomaly or Necessity?* London: Tavistock Publications.

ONS (2013a) *The Pink Book 2013, Part 3: Geographical Breakdown*. London: Office for National Statistics.

ONS (2013b) *The Pink Book 2013, Part 1: Current Account*. London: ONS.

ONS (2013c) *Foreign Direct Investment Involving UK Companies, 2012*. London: ONS.

Phillimore J and Goodson L (2006) Problem or Opportunity? Asylum Seekers, Refugees, Employment and Social Exclusion in Deprived Urban Areas. *Urban Studies* 43(10): 1715–1736.

Philo G, Briant E and Donald P (2013) *Bad News for Refugees*. London: Pluto.

Schuster L (2003) *The Use and Abuse of Political Asylum*. London: Frank Cass Publishers.

Silverman SJ (2011) *Immigration Detention in the UK*. Oxford: The Migration Observatory.

Sporton D (2013) 'They Control My Life': The Role of Local Recruitment Agencies in East European Migration to the UK. *Population, Space and Place* 19(5): 443–458.

Taylor D (2013) Home Office Accused of 'Fixing' Asylum Figures. *The Observer* 27 October.

Taylor D and Mason R (2014) Home Office Staff Rewarded with Gift Vouchers for Fighting Off Asylum Cases. *The Guardian* 14 January.

Temple B and Moran R, with Fayas N, Haboninana S, McCabe F, Mohamed Z, Noori A and Rahman N (2005) *Learning to Live Together: Developing Communities with Dispersed Refugee People Seeking Asylum*. York: Joseph Rowntree.

Tyler I (2010) Designed to Fail: A Biopolitics of British Citizenship. *Citizenship Studies* 14(1): 61–74.

Vickers T (2012) *Refugees, Capitalism and the British State: Implications for Social Workers, Volunteers and Activists*. London: Ashgate.

Vickers T (2014a) Developing an Independent Anti-Racist Model for Asylum Rights Organising in England. *Ethnic and Racial Studies* 37(8): 1427–1447.

Vickers T (2014b) Opportunities and Limitations for Collective Resistance Arising from Volunteering by Asylum Seekers and Refugees in Northern England. *Critical Sociology*, DOI: 10.1177/0896920514526623

Webber F (2012) *Borderline Justice: The Fight for Refugee and Migrant Rights*. London: Pluto.

8
Precarity at Work: Asylum Rights and Paradoxes of Labour in Sweden

Maja Sager

Introduction

The fields of migration politics and labour market politics are closely linked in many ways. Some of these links are explicit and obvious, but nevertheless they need to be closely examined. It is crucial to examine legislative or discursive links to labour market dynamics, particularly in relation to refugee migration, as these links risk damaging basic human rights principles. People's urge for mobility is channelled into processes of precarisation and labour market segmentation through the categorisation of rights and status intrinsic to migration controls, through racist discrimination, and through racialisation of work and the production of deportability (see, e.g., Balibar and Wallerstein, 2002; de Genova, 2005). This chapter examines some connections and overlapping issues between labour and refugee migration regulations to highlight and problematise these processes.

The chapter focuses on the subjective experiences at the intersections between migration and asylum processes in Sweden on the one hand and conditions in the labour market and discursive conflations between labour market protectionism and nationalism/nativism on the other. The analysis centres on the case of Mira, who will be presented below, but the material stems from a larger body of ethnographic material consisting of in-depth interviews, field notes, debate and information material from asylum rights organisations as well as from authorities and politicians. The material has been gathered through interviews with ten refused asylum seekers and nine asylum rights activists,[1] and my own participation and activism in migration rights movements from 2005 up to the present. The interviews that are analysed for this piece were conducted between 2006 and 2009. The analysis is also framed by news stories and legislation from the same time period that contextualise and highlight subjective experiences.

The concept of precarity is used to examine interviewee experiences with migration and labour. Participant experiences highlight the double character of labour as exploitative while offering the possibility of enhanced security. The material was gathered during a period characterised by a shift in the political landscape from a left-wing to a right-wing government and by an opening up for employer-driven labour immigration. The analysis relates to the way the policy changes came to create links between asylum and labour migration policies in the subjective experiences of these shifts. In the final section I contextualise the analysis of subjective experiences in the tensions between protectionist approaches to labour immigration on the one hand and neoliberal labour market approaches on the other.

Asylum rights and paradoxes of labour: Mira's story

Mira is a middle-aged woman from Kosovo. She is member of an ethnic minority group and after years of harassment she left Kosovo to apply for asylum in Western Europe. She migrated to Sweden in 2004. After two years her asylum application and a series of appeals had been refused and all of her chances to request asylum were exhausted. Mira could not face the prospect of deportation and remained in the country irregularly, partly supported by a local asylum rights organisation and partly by irregular work.

I met Mira for a series of interviews between 2006 and 2009. She was worried about being deported back to Kosovo, but she also could not see any other possibility to receive leave to remain in Sweden. She described her life as very constrained. She spoke limited Swedish and she mostly just stayed in an apartment that she shared with an activist in a local migration rights group, scared of getting lost if she left. At one point I asked her to take photos of her everyday life, and the next time we met she returned the camera with only three pictures taken and said that there was nothing happening in her life that she could photograph. However, she did have a job. In the next section we will consider the concept of precarity as a lens to explore Mira's experiences in the informal labour market, and how these experiences became linked to her struggle to gain either asylum or a residence permit in Sweden.

Precarity at work

The concept of precarity has been applied in several, slightly differing, modes (Butler, 2004; Standing, 2011). I use the concept as an analytical tool with the potential to describe an understanding of the labour market's subject positions as influenced by a range of social and political arenas. The interplay of these different arenas creates precarity in work as well as in housing, everyday mobility and time management, hence producing a lack of security and stability across all aspects of everyday life. Work insecurity thus produces subject positions that link to other areas of policy and life:

> [T]he exploitation of workforce happens beyond the boundaries of work, it is distributed across the whole time and space of life. Precarity means exploiting the continuum of everyday life, not simply the workforce.
>
> (Neilson and Rossiter, 2005, cited in Tsianos and Papadopoulos, 2006)

Secondly, the concept of precarity carries the analytical capacity to link and highlight different positions in the neoliberal labour market, such as irregular and regulated work or workers, and migrant workers and citizens (Las Precarias a la Deriva, 2004; Tsianos and Papadopoulos, 2006; Anderson, 2007; Papadopoulos et al., 2008: 222ff; Waite, 2009). The concept of precarity has the potential to consider issues beyond boundaries of citizenship and legal status, de-centring the labour market to understand marginal positions in the labour market as *central*. By connecting processes of gendered and racialised segmentation of the labour market to irregular work, the concept of precarity helps us to challenge the hegemonic representations of irregular work conditions or undocumented workers as exceptions and deviations in an otherwise 'healthy' labour market.

Mira's work experiences, and the production of these experiences through her irregular position, illustrate how precarity expands into other aspects of life. She summarises her conditions as an irregular worker at a pizzeria:

> There are no contracts or anything like that, no verbal agreement either, and [...] the owner, or the responsible one, can just, today, decide that now you have to leave. It has been very unstable. [...]

the boss seems to change his mind every time his mood swings, so one doesn't know from one day to another if there will be any work.

Mira describes here a lack of both basic labour rights and even logic through which she can understand or build expectations of work. She has to comply with her employer's shifting needs and mood swings. Precarisation is a general process in a gendered, radicalised and flexibilised labour market affecting workers with all forms of legal status, but the fear of deportation, along with other aspects of irregularity, reinforces the precarity experienced by irregular workers further. First, there is the urgent need to work to gain some sense of security in her insecure, irregular position. Secondly, the insecurity and fear produced by the threat of deportation prevent the worker from demanding better work conditions or in some cases from demanding to get paid (Sager, 2011; Bloch, 2014; Lewis et al., 2014: see also Waite et al. Chapter 10, this volume). The threat of deportation also constantly creates stress in other aspects of the working day. Mira gave several accounts of stressful and scary situations throughout our conversations.

> When I'm working I'm very worried that I will be taken by the police, because I'm a hidden refugee, but also because I work 'on the black'. So every time I'm out in the streets I'm worried and I'm also worried in my workplace.

> When I was on the way back from work one day a colleague gave me a lift, went over the speed limit and got us stopped by the police ... it went on for about half an hour, they wanted to see his papers and all that [...] When I got home ... I couldn't sleep that night [...] the man who was driving said to us afterwards 'god, my legs are shaking!' He was afraid of losing his driver's license, but I felt that my whole heart was shaking!

As we can see in these quotes, insecurity is connected not only to the actions of an employer but also to the risk of being exposed to police or government officials either at the workplace or during travel to or from work. Finally, other studies have shown that the irregular conditions produce vulnerability in other situations. For example, irregular migrants may be more vulnerable to crime because they cannot reach out to authorities for assistance (Khosravi, 2006). This general vulnerability is a part of the continuum of life that is exploited in the case of irregular migrants. This takes us to the next section, the role of work and the workplace as somehow reducing precarity at the same time as exploiting it.

Work as a strategy against precarity

In accounts of labour exploitation there is a risk of making agency invisible. At the same time that a worker may be critical towards her working condition, or understand that she is being exploited, the work process can also entail opposing elements of positive feelings regarding the work and/or the workplace. I argue for a two-fold perspective on the role of work in irregularity. Although work such as Mira's is characterised by exploitation and precarity, it can paradoxically also provide a source of increased security in certain ways.

> Maja: Can you tell me something about your daily routines?
>
> Mira: Yes, ok, I wake up and go to work. And whilst everyone else feels like going back home as soon as possible, I feel on the contrary that I want to stay . . . the day passes faster if I have something to do, as I don't have anything special to do right now and I don't see my future, I have no clear idea about what will happen. So that is why I prefer being at work, it makes the hours pass by.
>
> Maja: You say you don't meet any people, but don't you see anyone at work?
>
> Mira: Yes, the people at the pizzeria, and they all speak the same language.
>
> Maja: Ok, does anyone there know about your situation?
>
> Mira: No one knows I am staying irregularly, they only know I am applying for asylum, but not that I am irregular.

Mira returned several times during the interviews to the feeling of emptiness and 'nothingness' that permeated her everyday life. In that situation, despite the awareness of being exploited and fear about being easily exchanged, she appreciated the potential of the job site to provide her with an everyday routine and a community of colleagues who became valuable to her. With the understanding of precarity as an experience that is built up across the 'continuum of everyday life', every element that reduces the harshness of irregularity can be understood as a stake in the struggles over the boundaries of irregularity and the limits of precarisation. Mira also mentions that she enjoys speaking in her first language to her colleagues and that no one reflects much on her status. They think that she still is in the asylum process and therefore entitled to work. They do not know that she is actually hiding from the authorities.[2] Despite her precarious situation, she spends her days in an environment where she is 'regular' and she fits into the world because she can 'pass' as an asylum seeker with the right to be in the country during her asylum process – she is not seen as 'deportable' and hence not viewed as being vulnerable.

The quotes above suggest that Mira's everyday presence at the workplace reduces some of the tension in her situation and in that way allows her to take a temporary 'pause' from the full experience of irregularity. Another important aspect of having a job is the significance of a (relatively) regular wage in this situation that otherwise is characterised by a lack of social rights and/or welfare support. Even a precarious job can in some ways reduce the insecurity related to income, accommodation and health. An income makes it a bit easier to *stay*, to avoid deportation and to continue to explore ways of acquiring a residence permit. So, although the workplace is characterised by exploitation, it also carries a possibility of enhanced security – and it is in the ambiguous meeting between the two that precarity is constructed.

Institutionalised precarity

This section explores the way in which Mira's experiences were framed by a specific political shift in Sweden. In 2006, the new right-wing government[3] initiated a labour immigration reform. Previously, the former Social Democratic government had developed a commission to investigate ways of opening up their borders to increased labour immigration (SOU, 2006: 87). However, the new government's proposal converted a restrictive labour immigration policy that was regulated, together with the trade unions, to an employer-driven system in which assessments of demand were left to the individual employers. This reform, implemented in 2008, included a possibility clause for asylum seekers who had a job to apply for a temporary work permit within two weeks after a refused asylum application. The two-week limitation of this mechanism was not fully detailed when the proposal first was presented in 2006, but it was rather loosely referred to as a possibility to 'shift queues' from being an asylum seeker to being a labour migrant. The main purpose of the reform was related to labour immigration politics. However, due to the side-effect of the possibility of 'queue-shifting' from asylum seeker to migrant worker for asylum applicants, the reform came to play an important role in the debate on (and subjective experiences of) refugee migration. There was now an actual possibility for some asylum seekers to get a 'second chance' as labour migrants (a shift in status which suited employers – see Vickers Chapter 7, this volume). The queue-shifting exercise offered hope to many people who were already living in a situation as irregular migrants after their asylum application had been refused. Although the law, as finally implemented in 2008, only allowed this 'queue-shifting' within two weeks after the refusal, it was the phrase 'shifting queues' that started to spread along the grapevine in 2006, hence influencing people's strategies and approaches to their irregular situation. When the reform proposal was presented in 2006, it was done in the aftermath of an intense period of campaigning and claim-making around asylum and migration rights. In this context, the reform was repeatedly used as a response to critiques of restrictive asylum assessments and harsh living conditions for refused asylum seekers. Representatives from the new government regularly referred to the opening up of labour migration and the concept of 'queue-shifting' when they were confronted with critical questions about asylum seekers' and especially refused asylum seekers' situations (Sager, 2011: 145–146). In a hearing, organised in November 2006 by an advocacy group for refused asylum seekers living irregularly, the representative from one of the government parties explicitly responded to critiques:

> We will also present a proposal about the possibility for an asylum seeker to work or take an internship from the first day of their arrival in Sweden, and that will later on enable a 'shift of queue', that is that one can go from being asylum seeker to be... to apply for a residence permit as a labour immigrant [...] When it comes to the grounds required to get a residence permit *as* an asylum seeker they will of course stay constant, so it will still be possible to stay if one meets the asylum requirements. By making it possible for those who can get a job to apply for a residence permit on other grounds, it will make it easier for those who apply for asylum.
>
> (Representative from the Moderate Party,
> parliament hearing 15/11/2006, field notes)

So although the reform, as it finally was phrased in the legislation, is a labour market issue, with the small window for 'queue-shifting', the way it was mobilised in the debate gave it a larger role also in the field of refugee migration.

I met Mira for interviews regularly between 2006 and 2009, hence the debate and eventually the implementation of the law were constantly framing this period in Mira's life. At the time when the first suggestions about a change in legislation appeared in the debate, our conversations often considered her chances to receive a work and residence permit through this reform. She wanted to know what I thought about her chances, whether she would be able to find formalised employment or not, and so on. Mira's employer had mentioned in passing that they might be able to formalise her employment, but the actual conditions at her workplace did not give her much hope that there had been any substance behind that offer. Her actual work situation stood in stark contrast to the requirements of the new legislation.

> Mira: It is difficult with the work. I work informally in the pizzeria so it is very insecure. And the boss changes workers as often as you change your socks. So, as far as I can tell right now, this workplace will not be much help.

A short period after this conversation, the pizzeria where Mira worked suddenly closed and the owner cut all contact with Mira without paying her last month's wages. Mira not only lost the money but also lost the possibility of a validated employment situation that she hoped to use to earn a residence permit within the new legislation. If Mira had already had issues claiming rights in relation to her employer, this connection between a possible residence permit and the individual employer further increased the precarity entailed in the relationship.

These links, and the institutionalisation of precarious irregular work, become more clearly discernible if they are looked at in the context of two factors. First, the characteristics of the labour migration reform meant that some of the features that drive workers into precarity would still be attached to the position of the temporary regular worker (Bonfanti, 2014). The temporary work permits are tied to a specific employer during the first two years and thereafter to a specific work sector for another two years. This part of the legislation carries implications. A worker who is afraid of deportation will remain in a precarious and vulnerable position in relation to an employer because their work and residence permit is dependent upon that position, but also the racialised and gendered segmentation of the labour market is reinforced when migrants become 'locked into' certain work sectors. Critiques at the time, and studies that have followed up the reform, point out the risk for a continuous precarity in such a situation. In a critical evaluation of the reform, Bonfanti (2014: 378) writes: '[T]he overlapping between the category of labour migrants and that of asylum seekers risks to subordinate the recognition of the asylum right to the educational and professional background of the individual, namely to his/her level of desirability for the Swedish labour market.' The link between refugee migration and labour migration regulation becomes reinforced when the latter is used as a political tool to avoid taking responsibility for restrictive asylum assessments and human rights violations inside and along the borders of the Schengen area.

Many other European countries, among them Denmark and Norway, have linked asylum legislation to labour market legislation through demands on participation in integration programmes as another condition for gaining a permanent residence permit. An example of this in Danish legislation is that migrants, including refugees, who do not participate in the integration programmes will not be granted permanent resident permits (Emilsson, 2008: 39ff; The Danish Immigration Service, 2015). In Sweden, the boundary between the two areas has been more clearly demarcated. The right to the full protection that a permanent residence permit can offer has not been conditioned by demands for labour market participation (although the integration programmes entail demands on active participation on the labour market as conditions for receiving any welfare support), but in practice the boundary between the two policy areas has not always remained clear.

Precarity between neoliberalism and protectionism

Social anthropologist Nicholas de Genova has analysed how the US migration regulation has been managed. US policies have historically shaped migrating individuals into a cheap and flexible workforce. Guest worker programmes, the design of work visas and the management of irregular migrants' rights/lack of rights, together with the threat of deportation, come together to produce precarious labour conditions and 'flexible' cheap labour (de Genova, 2005). In the Swedish context, there is a tradition of a well-regulated labour market combined with strong trade unions that have contained the growth of informal labour markets. Although the strength of labour rights and unions has been declining in recent decades, this tradition is still understood as relatively strong. This means that there is scepticism towards understanding the production of an informal market and precarious labour conditions as an *actual part of* the Swedish labour market. Rather, these processes are seen as deviations from the 'normally' well-regulated labour market. However, the production of these precarious forms of labour can be seen as an organising principle of the general labour market.

The movement towards a more restrictive refugee policy in Sweden accelerated in the early 1990s after years of a relatively open refugee policy. The debate about asylum rights and refugee policy has often been related to protectionist and 'nativist' ideas (de Genova, 2005; Schierup et al., 2006) about the national labour market. Ever since the period of increased immigration to Sweden commenced during the latter half of the twentieth century, migration policy and the debates surrounding migration have in part been shaped within the frames of labour market policies. For instance, the major national organisations representing workers and employers were central actors in drawing up regulations and quotas for, as well as the 1972 cessation of, labour immigration (Schierup et al., 2006: 199).

The framing of migration policies within labour market policies created an opening for inclusive policies that aimed to prevent immigration from becoming 'a vehicle for wage and welfare dumping' through inclusive approaches to migrants' civil and social rights (Ålund and Schierup, 1991; Schierup et al., 2006: 218). Further, the restrictions of labour immigration policies after 1972 did not have a direct effect on refugee policies at the time – on the contrary, the 1970s and 1980s saw the most inclusive era of refugee reception. Nevertheless, given the shift in the 1990s from a refugee policy based on principles of solidarity to a more restrictive path (Schierup et al., 2006: 220), it seems that the historical link between regulation of migration and the 'needs' of the national labour market as a central reference in the political approach to immigration eventually also influenced debates on refugee migration.

Zolberg (1999) divides the attitudes towards migration between material and cultural dynamics. The material dynamics are framed by the capitalist economy. The interests involved in migration are, the employers' interest to increase their labour pool to keep wages down and the trade unions' interest to control immigration to counter 'wage dumping' and decreased labour rights. Cultural dynamics relate to identity and the conflict in this dimension is between extreme right or conservative groups that consider immigration a threat to an imagined 'national identity' or 'national life style' and those who either do not believe in these kind of culturist entities or believe that immigration would 'improve' national culture and identity (Zolberg, 1999: 83ff).

Zolberg's categorisation seems pertinent for an understanding of what is at stake in the Swedish debates on labour and migration. However, I would argue that the dimensions are not separated from each other but rather have an effect on each other. While the economic dimension might have been the foundation for a more restrictive stance to migration, the restrictiveness may itself have *constructed* a cultural dimension. Although the periods of restrictive labour migration and restrictive refugee migration are not entirely synchronous, it seems that the protectionist position of the social democratic regime eventually spilled over from labour migration to refugee migration. Knocke discusses how discourses surrounding labour immigration during the 1960s and 1970s produced ideas about migrants as deviants and carriers of problematic cultures (Knocke, 2006. See also: Molina, 1997; Tesfahuney, 1998; SOU, 2005: 56). The discourses surrounding both restrictions on labour migration and on refugee migration often perpetuate notions of 'our' and 'their' culture. Even the materially-based discussion about 'wage dumping' and decomposition of labour rights sometimes includes references to cultural traditions in 'other' national labour markets.

However, whilst the protectionist approach of the social democracy and the labour movement seems to eventually have become linked also to the field of refugee migration, the discussion about labour immigration reform displayed how the right-wing parties' politics also created connections between labour market policies, migration policies and asylum rights. The way migration policies link to labour market policies – and how Zolberg's cultural and material dimensions tend to coalesce – can be further explored through an understanding of racialised patterns of labour market segmentation.[4] The processes that cause the development of informal and precarious labour conditions can be correlated to two aspects of the global restructuring of labour markets in late capitalism: neo-liberal deregulation and segmentation of labour markets, and the racialised and gendered segregation of the work force (Wallerstein, 2002; Mulinari and Neergaard, 2004: 38ff). These mechanisms are inherent to the capitalist labour market (Wallerstein, 2002), but in the context of the Swedish (and European) welfare state(s) these processes become ever more pronounced and stark in relation to the increasing presence of irregular workers.

Informal and precarious work is not only confined to undocumented workers and should not be understood as a marginal phenomenon, but rather as central to the organisation of the labour market in the global neo-liberal order. The informal economy and the flexibilisation and deregulation of the labour market are expanding in relation to many work sectors and different categories of workers. These processes reinforce and deepen the racialised and gendered segmentation of labour markets (Mulinari and Neergaard, 2004: 38ff).

In an analysis of the development of migration policies and programmes in the European Union (EU), Hansen identifies 'the *most fundamental contradiction in the EU's migration policy'* as 'the EU's *double* and increasing *need* for migration and migrants' (2008: 203, original emphasis, my translation) as both labour force and population reserve *and* as a political tool to conceal conflicts of interest by the scapegoating of migrants for various social problems. The political shift at stake here is a further turn away from refugee immigration and the opening up for expansion of provisional labour immigration. When access to a temporary residence permit (and thereby the access to civil rights) is conditioned by one's position in the labour market, the individual is reduced to a cog in the labour force and consequently deprived of many of the rights attached to citizenship or permanent residence permit. In this sense the informal/irregular labour market does not limit its consequences to the precarious working conditions of the irregular migrants workers who are exploited by it, but it links deeper into the processes of segmentation and racialisation of the labour market.

Conclusion

The analysis in this chapter has traced some links and overlaps between labour and refugee migration regulations focusing on the case of Mira. I have also discussed how these links were reinforced and institutionalised through the particular characteristics of the employer-driven labour migration that was introduced in Sweden in 2008, and through the role the 'queue-jumping' reform was given in government discourses on asylum rights.

The chapter analyses the processes of precarisation in Sweden in the subjective experiences of work and in the institutionalisation of precarity. This linking between migration, asylum rights and labour in everyday life through the effects of these policies should be carefully analysed as a way to develop a critical understanding not just of how migration policies affect migrants' lives, but also to reveal how migration policies regulate labour market interests and mobilise migration as a tool for managing public opinions and democratic deficit.

Notes

This chapter is based on parts of the analysis in my PhD thesis *Everyday Clandestinity: Experiences on the Margins of Citizenship and Migration Policies* (2011). Another version of the analysis is published in Swedish in *Arbete. Intersektionella perspektiv* edited by Mulinari and Selberg (2011).

1. Of course these categories do not exclude each other – most of the asylum seeking interviewees could also be described as activists, and some of the activists had experiences of seeking asylum.

2. Asylum seekers in Sweden can apply for a work permit if the asylum assessment is estimated to take longer than four months and if they meet the following criteria: 'You provide proper identity papers or in some other way help to prove your identity; your application is to be considered in Sweden; there are solid reasons for your application for asylum. You will not be granted a permit if you have been issued a refusal of entry with immediate effect.' (Migrationsverket, 2014).
3. In the national election 2006, the former Social Democratic minority government (supported by the socialist LeftParty and the centre-left Green party) lost and instead a right-wing alliance between four right-center parties formed a coalition government that stayed in power two electoral periods until September 2014.
4. Labour market segmentation means that the labour market is divided into an *internal* and an *external* labour market. The internal labour market is regulated by labour rights and offers relatively safe work conditions – in this market one finds the 'core labour force'. The external labour market works as a reserve labour market with precarious work conditions and demands of high levels of flexibility. Conscious or unconscious racist attitudes can lead to racialised groups being referred to the external labour market. But these attitudes are mainly an effect of the way that institutionalised racist practices among employers, state institutions or the labour unions result in 'the labour force [being] sorted, categorised and finally allocated' (Mulinari and Neergaard, 2004: 39–41, my translation).

References

Ålund A and Schierup C (1991) *Paradoxes of Multiculturalism: Essays on Swedish Society*. Aldershot: Avebury.

Anderson B (2007) *Battles in Time: The Relation Between Global and Labour Mobilities*. University of Oxford, Centre on Migration, Policy and Society, Working Paper No. 55.

Balibar E and Wallerstein I (2002) *Ras, nation, klass*. Göteborg: Daidalos.

Bloch A (2014) Living in Fear: Rejected Asylum Seekers Living as Irregular Migrants in England. *Journal of Ethnic and Migration Studies* 40(10): 1507–1525.

Butler J (2004) *Precarious Life: The Powers of Mourning and Violence*. London: Verso.

Bonfanti S (2014) 'New Rules for Labour Immigration': Delving into the 2008 Swedish Reform of Labour Migration and Its Effects on Migrants' Well-Being. *The Journal of International Migration and Integration* 15: 371–386.

Danish Immigration Service (2015) *New to Denmark: Permanent Residence Permit*. Available at: http://www.nyidanmark.dk/en-us/coming_to_dk/permanent-residence-permit/permanent-residence-permit.htm (accessed 24 January 2015).

De Genova N (2005) *Working the Boundaries*. Durham and London: Duke University Press.

Emilsson H (2008) *Introduktion och integration av nyanlända invandrare och flyktingar. Utredningar, granskningar, resultat och bristområden*. NTG-asyl & integration.

Hansen P (2008) *EU:s migrationspolitik under 50 år. Ett integrerat perspektiv på en motsägelsefull utveckling*. Lund: Studentlitteratur.

Khosravi, S (2006) Territorialiserad mänsklighet: irreguljära immigranter och det nakna livet. In SOU 2006:37 *Om välfärdens gränser och det villkorade medborgarskapet rapport*. Stockholm: Fritze.

Knocke W (2006) Fyrverkeri och forskning. In: Apitzschm U, Mulinari D and Räthzel N (eds), *Bortom etnicitet: festskrift till Aleksandra Ålund*. Umeå: Boréa.

Las Precarias a la Deriva (2004) *A la deriva por los circuitos de la precariedad femenina*. Madrid: Traficantes de Sueños.

Lewis H, Dwyer P, Hodkinson S and Waite L (2014) *Precarious Lives: Forced Labour, Exploitation and Asylum*. Bristol: The Policy Press.

Migrationsverket (2014) *Working While Seeking Asylum*. Available at: http://www.migrationsverket.se/English/Private-individuals/Protection-and-asylum-in-Sweden/Adults-seeking-asylum/Work.html (accessed 20 May 2015).

Molina I (1997) *Stadens rasifiering: etnisk boendesegregation i folkhemmet*. Diss. Uppsala: Univ.

Mulinari D and Neergaard A (2004) *Den nya svenska arbetarklassen: rasifierade arbetares kamp inom facket*. Umeå: Boréa.

Papadopoulos D, Stephenson N and Tsianos V (2008) *Escape Routes: Control and Subversion in the Twenty-First Century*. London: Pluto.

Sager M (2011) *Everyday Clandestinity: Experiences on the Margins of Citizenship and Migration Policies*. Diss. Lund: Lunds universitet.

Schierup C, Hansen P and Castles S (2006) *Migration, Citizenship, and the European Welfare State: A European Dilemma*. Oxford: Oxford University Press.

SOU 2005:56. Utredningen om strukturell diskriminering på grund av etnisk eller religiös tillhörighet, 2005. *Det blågula glashuset: strukturell diskriminering i Sverige: betänkande*. Stockholm: Fritzes.

Standing G (2011) *The Precariat: The New Dangerous Class*. London: Bloomsbury Academic.

Tesfahuney M (1998) *Imag(in)ing the Other(s): Migration, Racism, and the Discursive Constructions of Migrants*. Diss. Uppsala: Univ.

Tsianos V and Papadopoulos D (2006) *Precarity: A Savage Journey to the Heart of Embodied Capitalism*. Available at: http://transform.eipcp.net/transversal/1106/tsianospapadopoulos/en (accessed 12 December 2010).

Waite L (2009) A Place and Space for a Critical Geography of Precarity?. *Geography Compass* 3(1): 412–433.

Wallerstein I (2002) Kapitalismens ideologiska spänningar: Universalism kontra rasism och sexism/ Bourgeoisien som begrepp och verklighet. In E. Balibar and I. Wallerstein (eds), *Ras, nation, klass*. Göteborg: Daidalos.

Zolberg A (1999) Matters of State: Theorizing Immigration Policy. In C. Hirschman, P. Kazinitz and J. Dewind (eds), *The Handbook of International Migration. The American Experience*. New York: Russell Sage Foundation, 71–93.

9
Bangladeshi Fruit Vendors in the Streets of Paris: Vulnerable Asylum Seekers or Self-Imposed Victims of Exploitation?

Donghyuk Park

Introduction

Beginning in early 2008, unprecedented numbers of Bangladeshi asylum seekers entered France in search of humanitarian protection and improved economic prospects. Over subsequent years, Bangladesh has become one of the most important sending countries of asylum seekers to France (OFPRA, 2012). Bangladeshi asylum migration to France remains under-researched and the lack of historical and cultural ties between the two countries offer few clues as to the causes of migration, making it difficult to understand the experiences of asylum seekers. More investigation is needed on migration trajectories, the specific strategies used to enter France and how these strategies have affected migrants' legal and economic integration.

In the context of economic crisis and growing populism on the European continent, migrant populations have faced multiple constraints. First, the economic crisis starting from 2008 destabilised the legal and economic conditions of migrant populations in European countries and pushed them into irregular situations (Frontex, 2009). Irregular migrants struggle to maintain their lives in the country of migration, and even in times of crisis, which expose their marginal status, they struggle not to return to the country of origin. Migrant populations instead seek ways to diversify their mobility and residential strategies, so as to extend their stay. Secondly, the political understanding of migration has often been unclear, misleading, politicised and associated with illegal border crossing (Collyer et al., 2012; Düvell, 2012;

Hess, 2012). While European governments make a clear distinction between legal and irregular migration, a growing number of them favour formally criminalising the latter (Dauvergne, 2008; Schuster, 2011). In this context of hardening external borders and softening internal ones, irregular migrants within the EU sometimes find themselves in the ironic situation of benefitting from these more extreme border policies, as they are balanced by internal freedom of movement. Unlike those crossing EU external borders, they are no longer subject to stringent identity controls.

The social exclusion and marginalisation of migrant populations contribute to the changing perceptions of migrants by their host societies. Migrants are forced to adapt to the structures of increasingly unfavourable working conditions and are subject to deteriorating legal and economic conditions. As a result, migrants are largely perceived as working solely in low-skill, low-wage employment sectors, including food services, hospitality and cleaning, where they become commodified (Bernardot, 2012), temporary workers (Jounin, 2009; Chauvin, 2010), ethnicised (Bertheleu, 2007), irregular and unwelcome (Fassin et al., 1997).

While conducting my research on Bangladeshi working asylum seekers in Paris, I observed growing numbers of impoverished asylum seekers being driven into the informal work of street fruit vending. Amid a persistent economic crisis and an increasingly hostile political atmosphere towards migrant populations in France, I observed that Bangladeshi asylum seekers are also caught in legal and economic limbo. In this chapter, I use the term 'working asylum seeker' and define it as those who benefit from the temporary protection of a host country where they not only have claimed asylum but also have constrained legal rights to work, and who are nevertheless engaged in jobs in the formal or informal sector. Working asylum seekers share their legal vulnerability with those such as 'undocumented', 'irregular migrants' or *sans-papiers*, who are all vulnerable to precarious legal-social conditions. In this research, I suggest that these working asylum seekers, operating on the street, represent the contemporary figure of precarious, temporary, unauthorised and deportable aliens.

Being an asylum seeker in France: Constrained access to legal rights to work

The current refugee laws dictate that upon arrival respondents are prohibited from entering the formal labour market for at least one year if their refugee status is pending. However, if an application for asylum has not received a response within one year from the French refugee authority (L'Office français de protection des réfugiés et apatrides, OFPRA), or the asylum application receipt or *récépissé* has been renewed, normally with a validity of three months, a temporary work permit can be requested from the applicant's local prefecture. Although French policy stipulates that asylum seekers are able to obtain temporary work permits after one year, the process is plagued with problems. First, the applicant must submit numerous documents, such as a work contract or a strong supporting letter from a potential employer (stating his or her desire to hire the applicant). When successful, an applicant obtains a temporary work permit; however, the duration is limited to less than three months, corresponding to the validity of asylum receipt.

Moreover, due to the limited duration of the work permits, and uncertainty about their legal validity, potential employers are reluctant to hire asylum seekers and instead prefer to pay them under the table, *au noir*, opening them up to exploitation (see also Sager and Waite et al., this volume). The work permit is renewable every three months and it is the key document allowing them to work both in the formal and informal sectors of the economy, including fruit vending. If they can no longer renew the document, there is more chance to be excluded from both formal and informal job markets, including the fruit vending job.

Working asylum seekers whose claims have already been rejected face even worse conditions, as they must live without financial and legal support from the state. In effect, the temporary residence permit issued to asylum seekers leads many of them to feel that they are in legal limbo, because it enables them to avoid deportation while nonetheless making it difficult for them to legally to earn a *living*.

In this chapter, I focus on the case of street vendors as an illustration of the legal and economic constraints faced by many Bangladeshis as it is understood and interpreted. Using empirical research on Bangladeshi working asylum seekers in France, it shows how French refugee policy, which is thought to protect the rights of asylum seekers, in fact imposes constraints that increase their legal and economic vulnerability. I argue that in the absence of a right to work during the initial application period, working in the 'ethnicised' economy appears to augment income levels in the short term but paradoxically leaves subjects vulnerable to coercive state powers of control and punishment (Foucault, 1975). I explain it by illustrating how seeking a job in the formal sector of the economy produces legal constraints. Although asylum seekers can work legally under certain circumstances, current policy has in practice limited the programme's potential to provide regular employment to most asylum seekers.

The methodology of the research

This chapter is based on my doctoral research concerning Bangladeshi asylum seekers in Paris. For this chapter, 16 representative interviews with male working asylum seekers were selected from among the 40 interviews conducted for the doctoral project. All interviewees were aged below 40 years, with an average age of 32 years. All participants were informed about the nature of my research and gave verbal consent. Many of the vendors whom I had never encountered before had already heard of me and were willing to share their individual experiences confidentially. Owing to their irregular status, and out of concern for ethical issues in research (Düvell et al., 2010), I have anonymised their names in this chapter.

Participant observation was used as the basis for the project, to survey personal demographic data and individual migratory and work experiences. Along with in-depth interviews, this was carried out at first with three key fruit vendors on a regular basis from 2009, modelled on existing ethnographic research with street book vendors (Duneier, 1999). Later, I conducted interviews with 13 individuals, asking prepared questions to obtain general data on age, education level, work experiences, migration trajectories, income level and difficulties encountered as street vendors. Each interview took around 15–30 minutes. The interviews were conducted mostly in Bengali with some English. As I have only a working competence in Bengali, a Bengali fruit vendor assisted me with interpretation.

It should be noted that while the research method used here generates knowledge about the conditions of certain working asylum seekers, it should not be assumed that these vendors represent Bangladeshi migrants or asylum seekers as a whole. Nevertheless, it illustrates a selected group of migrants in the informal sector that has become significantly visible within the influx of asylum seekers to France since 2009.

Bangladeshi in France: Increasing asylum migration

Bangladeshi communities in the UK have been well-scrutinised from historical and anthropological perspectives (Gardner, 1995; Gardner and Osella, 2004; Peach, 2006; Lewis, 2011), with respect to community development (Neveu, 1993; Eade and Garbin, 2002; Garbin, 2002; Eade, 2010; Maxwell, 2012), and in relation to diaspora networks and their roles (Garbin, 2002; Smith and Garbin, 2008). Bangladeshi migration phenomena have also been studied in other European countries, especially in Italy (Knights, 1996; King and Black, 1997; Knights, 1997), in Spain (Zeitlyn, 2006) and more recently in Portugal (Mapril, 2011), focusing on migration experiences and trajectories.

In France, while some existing research focuses on other South Asian populations (Dassaradanayadou, 2007; Dequirez, 2007; Goreau-Ponceaud, 2008), detailed accounts of Bangladeshi migration to France are rare (Moliner, 2009). Although Bangladeshi asylum seekers to France have existed for decades, they have only recently attracted extensive political attention, culminating in a special French delegation being sent in 2010 to Bangladesh to investigate the origins of asylum claims (OFPRA, 2010). The number of Bangladeshi asylum seekers has increased since 2006, doubling now to 3,140 per year. The year 2011 was marked by a slight increase in numbers to 3,462. However, the number of applications for refugee status dropped to 999 in 2012, after Bangladesh was listed in 2011 as one of the 'safe countries' by the French refugee authority in December 2011.[1] The demographic data show that around 95 per cent of Bangladeshi asylum seekers in France are males aged under 50 years, and over 96 per cent live in Paris or its suburban areas (OFPRA, 2012). Bangladeshi asylum seekers have low education, language and skills levels, which contribute to high unemployment.

The Bangladeshi migration trajectories include rural–urban migration, direct rural–international migration, transit migration and secondary movement among EU countries. There is no reliable official data indicating migration trajectories of Bangladeshis in France; however, all respondents from my fieldwork had passed through at least one other country before reaching France. Among the 16 interviewees, 12 responded that they first arrived in Italy and travelled to France and 3 responded that they first entered the UK. One interviewee responded that he arrived in Sweden, then decided to come to France to claim asylum. All the interviewees answered that they entered France between 2009 and 2011, a period of increased Bangladeshi asylum claims in France. The geographical origin of respondents varied, ranging from Dhaka, the capital of Bangladesh, and its sub-districts to other regional districts such as Sylhet, Noakali. My fieldwork findings suggest that many Sylhetis living in other EU countries have migrated to France, from countries like the UK and Italy, to find protection and job opportunities.

Although, more than 90% of asylum claims were based on political motivations (OFPRA, 2012), many applicants had been informed of favourable economic conditions in France prior to migration, usually by their families or friends who already lived in the country. The respondents had worked as street vendors during the initial period of stay, for an average of 16 months. The longest period of street work was 36 months and the shortest was 2 months. Only two had some university education; five had only attended primary school; and the remainder had completed some high school. Prior to coming to France, they were self-employed, farmers, students or unemployed.

The lack of regular and durable labour opportunities along with material/financial shortages creates precarious conditions for migrants (Goldring et al., 2009; see other chapters in this volume). Financial need forced them to find jobs urgently. Migration is an expensive livelihood investment project (Siddiqui, 2003) and migration costs to Europe are known to be around 7,000–15,000 euros. After arrival, living expenses demand substantial financial resources, well beyond the 11.35 euros/day *allocation temporaire d'attente* (ATA) allocated to applicants in 2014. All qualified asylum seekers receive the ATA from the government and it can be combined with other income from work for up to 12 months if an asylum seeker is working.

Migrants frequently share living quarters (Damaris Rose and Ray, 2001) and pool to buy food in bulk in order to reduce the cost of living. As other financial resources are depleted, ironically some migrants depend on counter-remittances from their families, reversing the intended flow of money. Being marginalised and lacking alternatives, asylum seekers turn to marginalised sectors or temporary work without contracts, leaving them legally and economically precarious.

Street fruit vending as constrained livelihood strategies

A typical day for a Bangladeshi fruit vendor begins with hauling his fruit pushcart loaded with various seasonal fruits to assigned spots, usually near subway station entrances. Each individual sets up a temporary fruit stand constructed of wooden boards and disassembled produce boxes. The pushcarts, containing remaining stock, are moved away from the stands to suggest that there is no further inventory than what is displayed, which is a simple strategy to reduce the potential for police controls and confiscation. The fruit boxes stacked nearby suggest hours of outdoor work by bodies unprotected from the cold and the heat, which is not obvious to the public who are unaware of this larger, unseen inventory. This account of street fruit vendors is consistent with the experience of migrant street vendors in Paris generally, including sellers of flowers, grilled corn and chestnuts, copied DVDs and cheap accessories just like other migrants in irregular situations. Nevertheless, working in the informal economy is considered an effective economic coping strategy by many asylum seekers whose financial conditions and legal rights often deteriorate over time. Asked why they were working as a street vendor, respondents often mentioned that it was a livelihood strategy since they lack the legal right to work during the often-lengthy claims process.[2]

Working in the service sector, self-employment or using co-ethnic networks appears to be the last resort when finding better employment is not always guaranteed. In the case of fruit vendors, prospective employees are only selected from within their ethnic network, as the following statement illustrates:

> He worked here before with me. It's always like that. If you don't know anyone, if you don't have friends, you have no work. He came to France and because he knows me, I got this work for him.
>
> (S, fruit vendor)

Much of the literature on migrant niche economies shows the positive effects of ethnic concentration. An ethnic niche economy is defined as a sector that has a high concentration of co-ethnic population (Waldinger and Bozorgmehr, 1996) and where entry barriers are determined by common ethnicity. Ethnic economies provide products that were previously unavailable to consumers within a specific geographical area. The predominance of a particular population within ethnic entrepreneurship is understood to be associated with shared cultural heritage or way of living (Bonacich and Modell, 1980). Employment opportunities for refugees in host countries are very competitive (Bloch and Levy, 1999; Colic-Peisker and Tilbury, 2006) and they often compete with other irregular migrants for informal work. In addition, social and legal constraints experienced by ethnic migrants drive these employable but excluded populations into ethnic economies. Successful integration in the ethnic economy requires the augmentation of the self-reliance of individuals, to increase income and networks effectively. Evidence shows that interpersonal relationships and self-employment networks are crucial employment strategies and have led to declining unemployment rates among Bangladeshi migrants in the UK (Maxwell, 2012).

Bangladeshi street fruit vendors in France share these characteristics and this emphasises the importance of co-ethnic networking. Fruit vending is developed and upheld by actors themselves in order to increase individual income levels as a short-term livelihood strategy (Crawley et al., 2011). Although fruit selling on the street is one of the least desired jobs, it is also a viable survival strategy for the most vulnerable asylum seekers. Moreover, unlike other asylum seekers in the initial period who endure prolonged unemployment, fruit vendors are able to achieve some stability, through their earnings, for the first phase of adaptation to a new country.

Fruit vending work and organisation

Since 2008, street fruit vending has become an important income-generating strategy, with the number of vendors increasing progressively. In the single administrative area (*arrondissement*) of Paris where this research was conducted, the number of vending stands increased from 7 to 19, representing employment of more than 30 regular and temporary vendors between 2009 and 2013. Similarly, there are many other fruit stands in other areas of Paris and its suburbs. These fruits stands operate independently within geographically divided areas managed by different owners. Based on my observation, I estimated that there are more than 200 fruit stands operated across Paris and its suburbs.

The hierarchical system assigns roles and responsibilities to various participants and divides types of work, working hours and income. There are three groups of actors in the street vending market: the owners of fruit stands; collectors (or intermediaries); and the vendors. Owners hire low-wage labourers who are willing to bear with long hours of labour-intensive work; the 2008 migration surge provided abundant low-cost labour to these fruit vending networks. Pre-established networks, individual legal status and experience within the sector are determining factors in fruit stand ownership. The informal character of the business increases the value of established networks. Prior to 2008, Bangladeshi migrants were just one of many ethnic groups engaged in street fruit vending. The subsequent influx of Bangladeshi asylum seekers provided abundant accessible labour and allowed these existing vendors to ascend the hierarchy and control the fruit vending market. These owners have improved legal status, allowing them to stay legally in France.

Like us, they [owners] were asylum-seekers or someone who already had documents. You know, they arrived before us. They came at least 4 or 5 years ago. If I had arrived here a year earlier, maybe I would have been the boss. But I am selling fruit and my boss is even younger than I am.

(T, fruit vendor)

The collectors/intermediaries rely heavily on relationships based on mutual trust. With their superior knowledge of business operations, they manage sales and distribution and collect revenues from vendors. Because of the nature of their work, owners and intermediaries are relatively protected from public visibility unlike the final group, the vendors themselves, who endure the most precarious conditions.

The average working week is six nine-hour days, often with no breaks. Some vendors are willing to work a seventh day to earn increased income. Wages are roughly proportionate to the revenue a vendor has generated and often amount to 20–30 euros per day. Usually, the overall income made by vendors is less than 1000 euros per month.

I work every day and I receive more or less 1000 euros per month. There are days that I don't work. With this money, it's ok for the moment. I can live with that. But I need a more secure job like in a restaurant where I can work indoors.

(N, fruit vendor)

There are no significant wage differences among vendors. Nevertheless, owner–employee relationships determine how the best-performing locations are assigned, thus affecting potential income levels. If a vendor sells more, he can expect income to increase by about 5 euros per 20–30 euros in extra sales.

I know my boss and manager, they are my friends. So they put me on the good sales point where I could make more money than the others. Everyone gets paid proportionally so it is better to work the same amount of time to make more money. If I worked at another spot, I would make less money.

(R, fruit vendor)

Increasing market size beginning from 2008 has modified the structure of the fruit vending network and has entrenched hierarchies, as 'owners' and 'employees' have become distinctive roles. When accessing this fruit vending network, one's existing personal network is a key determinant. Though several vendors, those in higher-trust relationships with owners, were able to increase their income level, most other vendors remained precarious, with lower income levels and difficult working conditions.

Contested presence of fruit vendors in public space

Police controls result in short-term incarceration at a police station, being released after a short period of time, usually less than a day. Almost all of the respondents replied that they have been arrested at least once and have been put into the police station. It is a traumatic experience as they fear deportation and it is costly for vendors as random police controls result in significantly reduced income. Frequently, merchandise is confiscated, a fine of 100–150 euros is levied and the remainder of the day's wages is lost. Owners are aware of the risks and they normally do not ask vendors to pay for the lost merchandise, but vendors are responsible for lost wages and paying fines. The vendors are only fined for illegal sales on public space but their legal status of asylum seeker has protected them from being deported.

Also, new legislation[3] criminalising all types of unauthorised sales on public property has made it difficult to operate in this sector of the informal economy. With this legislation, what was previously 'informal' activity has become 'criminal' by law and the vendors can be punished accordingly. It has targeted burgeoning informal street vendor networks mainly run by migrant populations in Paris, with fruit vending having been specifically investigated. Several arrests have been made.[4] While owners faced further investigation, fruit vendors were freed, as they were considered 'victims' of criminal networks.[5]

Moreover, the situation for fruit vendors is becoming more complicated as the entrance of new migrants from a different region of Bangladesh – Sylhet – has given rise to conflict. Sylhetis have been replacing other vendors. Many vendors complained about the new arrivals, accusing them of unethical and discriminatory practices, as follows:

> They are shameless to take such a disgraceful job, very greedy, non-cooperative and ultimately very regionalist. Unlike other 'Bengalis' or 'Bangladeshis' who are expected to be morally respectful to communities and up-holders of tradition, Sylhetis only think about their own destiny and safety.
>
> (T, vendor)

Other vendors have complained that the recently arrived Sylheti vendors are exacerbating their precarious situation by dominating the business and excluding other Bangladeshi regional groups. As entry-level job opportunities are rare, this inter-ethnic competition within the ethnic economy creates increased precariousness among existing unemployed Bangladeshi asylum seekers.

Conclusion

The institutionalised processes of refugee policy, bureaucracy and limited access to legal rights increases the vulnerable conditions of working asylum seekers in France. While enduring challenging working conditions and limited legal rights, working asylum seekers are highly visible, leading to police controls and possible incarceration. Applying for asylum is perceived as an alternative to obtaining a temporary residence permit, but it remains the least desirable strategy for many economically desperate asylum seekers as it prohibits them from legally accessing the local labour market.

Nevertheless, working in the informal ethnic niche economy of fruit vending is a nearly unavoidable step for many unauthorised asylum seekers, who may then find themselves 'criminalised' due to their illegal activity. Overall, street vending provides a short-term financial cushion as well as the opportunity to learn about other job opportunities, potentially allowing them to find higher-paying jobs with better legal protections. But it is a risky strategy, as they become victims of a system that they themselves have participated in creating and which they work to maintain. This research suggests that the current French refugee policy should extend asylum seekers' right to access the formal labour market.

Notes

This research was presented at the conference session entitled *Vulnerable Workers, Forced Labour, Migration and Ethical Trading*, organised on the 14th of December 2012 at the University of Leeds. I deeply appreciate the valuable comments received from editors for my drafts. The chapter stems from the author's doctoral research on Bangladeshi asylum seekers in France.

1. An applicant from the listed countries could not benefit from the temporary residence permit and their application is treated with special procedures, thus leaving less chance for an applicant to stay in France.
2. The refugee determination process takes more than 18 months, on average.
3. The French government has prohibited all non-permit holders from selling in public spaces, making the action a *délit*, a criminal offence punishable by

up to 6 months in prison as well as fines, rather than a *contravention*, a lesser, ticketable, offence. See *la Loi 2011–267 du 14 mars 2011 art. 51.*
4. Arrests included some fruit wholesalers who sold substandard low-quality fruits to groups of 'South Asian' origin migrant fruit vending networks.
5. LeParisien 7 December 2011, *Les dessous d'un juteux trafic de fruits*, http://www.leparisien.fr/rungis-94150/les-dessous-d-un-juteux-trafic-de-fruits-07-12-2011-1756098.php

References

Bernardot M (2012) *Captures.* Bellecombe-en-Bauges: Éd. du Croquant.
Bertheleu H (2007) Sens et usages de 'l'ethnicisation'. Le regard majoritaire sur les rapports sociauxethniques. *Revue européenne des migrations internationales* 23: 7–28.
Bloch A and Levy C (1999) *Refugees, Citizenship, and Social Policy in Europe.* Houndmills, Basingstoke, Hampshire New York: Macmillan Press; St. Martin's Press.
Bonacich E and Modell J (1980) *The Economic Basis of Ethnic Solidarity: Small Business in the Japanese American Community.* Berkeley: University of California Press.
Chauvin S (2010) *Les agences de la précarité journaliers à Chicago.* Paris: Seuil.
Colic-Peisker V and Tilbury F (2006) Employment Niches for Recent Refugees: Segmented Labour Market of the 21st Century Australia. *Journal of Refugee Studies* 19: 203–229.
Collyer M, Düvell F and De Haas H (2012) Critical Approaches to Transit Migration. *Population, Space and Place* 18: 407–414.
Crawley H, Hemmings J and Price N (2011) Coping with Destitution Survival and Livelihood Strategies of Refused Asylum Seekers Living in the UK. *Oxfam GB Research Report.* Oxfam.
Damaris R and Ray B (2001) Le logement des réfugiés à montréal trois ans après leur arrivée: le cas des demandeurs d'asile ayant obtenu la résidence permanente. *JIMI/RIMI* 2: 455–492.
Dassaradanayadou SL (2007) Tamouls indiens – de Pondichéry à la France: Diasporas indiennes dans la ville. *hommes & migrations* 1268–1269.
Dauvergne C (2008) *Making People Illegal: What Globalization Means for Migration and Law.* Cambridge; New York: Cambridge University Press.
Dequirez GL (2007) Tamouls sri lankais le little Jaffna. *hommes & migrations* 1268–1269.
Duneier M (1999) *Sidewalk.* New York: Farrar, Straus and Giroux.
Düvell F (2012) Transit Migration: A Blurred and Politicised Concept. *Population, Space and Place* 18: 415–427.
Düvell F, Triandafyllidou A and Vollmer B (2010) Ethical Issues in Irregular Migration Research in Europe. *Population, Space and Place* 16: 227–239.
Eade J. (2010) Representing British Bangladeshis in the Global City: Authenticity, Text and Performance. *Institute for Culture and Society Occasional Paper Series* 1: 1–21.
Eade J and Garbin D (2002) Changing Narratives of Violence, Struggle and Resistance: Bangladeshis and the Competition for Resources in the Global City. *Oxford Development Studies* 30: 137–149.

Fassin D, Morice A and Quiminal C (1997) *Les lois de l'inhospitalité les politiques de l'immigration à l'épreuve des sans-papiers.* Paris: Éd. la Découverte.

Foucault M. (1975) *Surveiller et punir: naissance de la prison,* Paris: Gallimard.

Frontex. (2009) The Impact of the economic crisis on illegal migration to EU. Warsaw. Frontex Risk Analysis Unit. Available at: http://www.europarl.europa. eu/meetdocs/2009_2014/documents/libe/dv/frontex_/frontex_en.pdf.

Garbin D (2002) Bidesh Taka: Argent, Migration et Politiques Transnationales entre Banglatown(Londre) et Sylhet(Bangladesh). *Journal des Anthropologues* 5: 55–77.

Gardner K (1995) *Global Migrants, Local Lives: Travel and Transformation in Rural Bangladesh.* Oxford, England, New York: Clarendon Press; Oxford University Press.

Gardner K and Osella F (2004) *Migration, Modernity, and Social Transformation in South Asia.* New Delhi; Thousand Oaks, CA: Sage.

Goldring L, Berinstein C and Bernhard J (2009) Institutionalizing Precarious Immigration Status in Canada. *Citizenship Studies* 13: 239–265.

Goreau-Ponceaud A (2008) *La diaspora tamoule: trajectoires spatio-temporelles et inscriptions territoriales en Île-de-France.* Bordeaux: Université de Bordeaux III.

Hess S (2012) Denaturalising Transit Migration. Theory and Methods of an Ethnographic Regime Analysis. *Population, Space and Place* 18: 428–440.

Jounin N (2009) *Chantier interdit au public enquête parmi les travailleurs du bâtiment.* Paris: la Découverte.

King R and Black R (1997) *Southern Europe and the New Immigrations.* Brighton; Portland, OR: Sussex Academic Press.

Knights M (1996) Bangladeshi Immigrants in Italy: From Geopolitics to Micropolitics. *Transactions of the Institute of British Geographers, New Series* 21: 105–123.

Knights M (1997) Migrants as Networkers; The Economics of Bangladeshi Migration to Rome. In R. King and R. Black (eds), *Southern Europe and the New immigrants.* Brigton: Sussex Academic Press, 113–137.

Lewis D (2011) *Bangladesh: Politics, Economics, and Civil Society.* Cambridge; New York: Cambridge University Press.

Mapril JMF (2011) The Patron and the Madman: Migration, Success and the (In)visibility of Failure among Bangladeshis in Portugal. *Social Anthropology* 19: 288–296.

Maxwell R (2012) *Ethnic Minority Migrants in Britain and France: Integration Trade-Offs.* New York: Cambridge University Press.

Moliner C (2009) Invisible et modèle? première approche de l'immigration sud-asiatique en France. *Rapport d'étude pour la Direction de l'Accueil, de l'Intégration et de la Citoyenneté.* Paris: Ministère de l'Immigration, de l'Intégration, de l'Identité nationale et du Développement solidaire.

Neveu C (1993) *Communauté, nationalité et citoyenneté de l'autre côté du miroir, les Bangladeshis de Londres préf. de Jean Copans.* Paris: Éd. Karthala.

OFPRA (2010) OFPRA Rapport d'activité 2010.

OFPRA (2012) OFPRA Rapport d'activité 2012.

Peach C (2006) South Asian Migration and Settlement in Great Britain, 1951–2001. *Contemporary South Asia* 15: 133–146.

Schuster L (2011) Turning Refugees into 'Illegal Migrants': Afghan Asylum Seekers in Europe. *Ethnic and Racial Studies* 34: 1392–1407.

Siddiqui T (2003) Migration as a Strategy of the Poor: The Bangladesh Case. *Regional Conference on Migration, Development and Pro-poor Policy Choices in Asia.* Dhaka.

Smith MP and Garbin D (2008) A Diasporic Sense of Place: Dynamics of Spatialization and Transnational Political Fields among Bangladeshi Muslims in Britain. *Transnational Ties: Cities, Identities, and Migrations.* New Brunswick, London: Transaction Publishers.

Waldinger RD and Bozorgmehr M (1996) *Ethnic Los Angeles.* New York: Russell Sage Foundation.

Zeitlyn B (2006) *Migration from Bangladesh to Italy and Spain.* Refugee and Migratory Movements Research Unit.

10
Refused Asylum Seekers as the Hyper-Exploited

Louise Waite, Hannah Lewis, Stuart Hodkinson and Peter Dwyer

Introduction

This chapter delves into the worlds of refused asylum seekers – worlds too often characterised by conditions of destitution. This destitution does not simply 'occur'; rather it is *produced* and *enforced* through immigration policies and the structural erosion of welfare support. Successive UK governments have systematically tiered entitlement for migrant groups and undermined the basic rights of asylum seekers who from 1999 onwards have had diminishing financial support and accommodation. In 2002, permission to work for asylum seekers who had not received an initial decision on their claim within six months was removed as employment was considered a 'pull factor' encouraging unfounded asylum claims (Bloch and Schuster, 2002). In 2003, a cashless voucher system (known as Section 4 support) was introduced for refused asylum seekers temporarily unable to leave the UK. Both were deliberately punitive to deter continuing residence in the UK. While there is a lack of evidence substantiating any effect of assumed 'pull factors' for seeking asylum in the UK, the government insists that denying work rights is central to deterrence of people claiming asylum. It is now widely recognised that refused asylum seekers routinely experience enforced destitution due to the intentional restriction of their rights (Crawley et al., 2011; Bloch, 2013, see also Vickers in this volume).

The government expects all refused asylum seekers to either voluntarily return or be deported. However, there is a significant 'deportation gap' (Sigona and Hughes, 2012) between those eligible for deportation and numbers actually removed. Many refused asylum seekers continue to be monitored through requirements to report to a local immigration or police office. Others stop reporting and live outside the system fearing the threat of being returned to their country of origin. The Home Office is also unable to return certain refused asylum seekers to their country of origin if foreign governments refuse to provide appropriate travel papers or cooperate with removals (McIntyre and Mogire, 2012). A case resolution exercise involving 500,500 'legacy' claims made before 2007 but still unresolved led to 172,000 grants (36 per cent) and 37,500 (8 per cent) removals, and 98,000 asylum cases assigned to a 'controlled archive', meaning these individuals were untraceable and may or may not still be in the UK (Vine, 2012). No accurate estimate is possible of the numbers since 2007, but due in part to the legacy process, the overall population of refused asylum seekers in the UK is likely to have dropped from an estimated 450,000 or more in 2007 to around 50,000–150,000 at the end of 2013. However, this population is being continually swollen by current high asylum refusal rates. In the last quarter of 2013, the Home Office refused 64 per cent of initial asylum decisions (of 3,070 cases) and dismissed 69 per cent of appeals (of 1,811 cases).[1]

In this chapter, we draw on research data from an Economic and Social Research Council project carried out between 2010 and 2012. Fieldwork was conducted in the Yorkshire and Humber region of the UK. We interviewed 30 asylum-seeking and refugee participants comprising 12 women and 18 men, aged between 21 and 58 years, who came from 17 countries in Africa, the Middle East, Central Europe and South and Central Asia. Interviews typically lasted between 2 and 3 hours and involved biographical accounts of migrating to the UK, entering the asylum system and experiences of work guided by semi-structured prompts. The material for this chapter derives from a sub-set of 17 individuals who told us of their experiences of working while living as 'refused asylum seekers'. Throughout the chapter interviewees are referred to using a pseudonym of their choice.

Over the last few years a number of studies have emerged describing the lives of refused asylum seekers (Dwyer and Brown, 2005; Lewis, 2007; Lewis, 2009; Blitz and Otero-Iglesias, 2011). There has been less research, however, into this group's working experiences and even less documenting their experiences of exploitation at a time of growing evidence of migrant labour exploitation in general (Anderson and Rogaly, 2005; Craig et al., 2007; van den Anker, 2009). Our focus in this chapter is on how refused asylum seekers negotiate survival within destitution. A large part of these survival strategies revolves around work – both for-cash labouring in low-paid sectors and also as labour that is transactionally exchanged. The first section explores refused asylum seekers' informal support structures, the next broaches the reasons individuals access paid work, the third describes how individuals are able to access work and their experiences within 'illegal' work and the final section documents the albeit limited cases of resisting the exploitation that is too frequently encountered. We conclude that the exploitation of vulnerable refused asylum seekers is sometimes so chronic that it amounts to 'hyper-exploitation'.

Destitution and survival

As noted above, the removal of support payments and housing when an asylum case is refused triggers destitution in most cases. The feelings described here by Frank are illustrative of the desperation that frequently ensues:

> But when I became destitute, no roof over my head, no income to support me, nothing. So I'm just like someone who is thrown into a desert, so at that moment, I felt the pinch and I started thinking, what can I do next?

Alternative survival strategies must be swiftly found; often, this initially involves informal support from friends, family and acquaintances, as well as from community organisations, faith groups or charities: 'I survived, because there was an organisation, when you go there, they give you I think, a kilo of rice with some nuts and noodles' (Pascual). Voluntary sector support is becoming evermore insecure due to the UK public expenditure cuts, eroding services provided by agencies offering temporary shelter and basic necessities for destitute migrants. As with other research, we found refused asylum seekers are increasingly reliant upon support from networks that are ethno-cultural or faith-based (Gupta, 2007).

For destitute refused asylum seekers, such support is vital. Rose, who had experienced life on the streets following refusal, was enormously grateful when taken in by a couple she met through a local church and she was happy to provide exchange services:

> Anything that needed doing in the house, housework, they had a child, sometimes to take the child to school ... they were feeding me, they were housing me, so I was doing what I could ... they were just Christians helping a fellow Christian.

While destitute, Gojo stayed in two different households, where she did domestic chores and childcare, but similar to Rose she felt the relationship with her hosts was largely positive and cordial. For refused asylum seekers, residing in others' homes has the advantage of keeping them less visible and thus less liable to detection by authorities. Maintaining a basic livelihood in private spheres such as the household reduces engagement in paid-economy activities that are deemed riskier. However, despite these perceived protection advantages, there are perils too. For many situations we encountered, unpicking where 'exchange' ends and 'compulsion' begins is complex and highly contingent (Crawley et al., 2011). Support offered to destitute asylum seekers by others who themselves may be only marginally better off can be interpreted as altruistic, mutually supportive or resource pooling (Cross, 2013), but there is a fine line between house guest and servant (Lewis, 2007). Transactional relationships can be more voluntary, as described above, or may become servile and disempowering, as in the case of Jay, whose romantic relationship descended into an abusive, coercive care arrangement. Jay was expected to take on a role as carer, cleaner and cook and be on call for sex in return for food and accommodation. When he tried to negotiate an improvement in his conditions, he was coerced to work without money through the threat of denunciation:

> [S]he used to tell me sometimes – oh you fucking African if you do anything I will call the immigration office and they will send you back to your country.

Although some interviewees accessed support through tight co-ethnic or co-faith groups, others feared exposure of their status within such networks (Sigona, 2012). Fear of denunciation to authorities and deportation generates mistrust that erodes social relationships: 'you fear to disclose your illegality to even some of the people that you know because you not sure of them' (John). Some were kept alive through chance acquaintances. Nanda, for example, moved in with someone she met at an English class, but quickly she began to fear the precarious nature of this support: 'And how many days is she gonna give me food, how many days?'

Informal support is demonstrably often variable, both between individuals and also across *time* for any one individual, underlining that destitution is a *process* not an event. However, it is not uncommon for informal support to be experienced as double-edged – vital to keep starvation and homelessness at bay, but also laced with relations of dependency that can develop into feelings of restricted choice or entrapment. If and when such informal support networks become exhausted, many refused asylum seekers find themselves entering undocumented working, the subject of the next section.

Pushed into the labour market

Experiences of refused asylum seekers entering the labour market vary. It may take place before or even alongside accessing informal support. Some refused asylum seekers enter undocumented work as an absolute last resort, a survival-related decision contingent on declining choices in a 'tunnel of entrapment' (Morgan and Olsen, 2009) that ends in destitution:

> It was after that [refusal] that I felt myself very desperate to survive. [...] I had to work to stay alive... and I didn't have an alternative choice.
>
> (Parviz)

Others in our research took up work not necessarily because they were 'at the end of the road' with regard to survival but due to the competing pressures to make urgent remittances to families back home, to fund legal representation, to avoid exhausting limited resources and to contribute to 'hosting' struggling families. In this latter regard, some refused asylum seekers felt ashamed of the burden they placed on friends. John had repeatedly not been paid for a cleaning job and was overjoyed when his first payment enabled him to contribute to his host's household:

> I do the shopping and I'll put the money on the table there, so people could see you are, you are also feeling the pains they are going through, because I was a little bit of a burden there.

Assanne similarly described the pressure to contribute to the family helping him, but compounding this was his need to pay the legal costs of a fresh asylum claim, which led him to find an informal manual job in a clothes recycling factory. The particular push for Gojo was to send money for her daughter; 'I was refused and didn't have anywhere to stay. That's when I became homeless, and I got a job working as a care assistant. I worked [...] because I had a daughter to look after.' Frank also urgently needed to remit money to his family back home, but his Section 4 voucher support meant he could not send cash:

> I had to do something to help them survive, and to feel really that yes – I am here for them. Although I didn't have, you know, papers, nothing and I didn't even think of getting one at that particular moment, I had to find something. [...] It was really, really hard, but I had to do it, to make my family survive.

The push into undocumented work is evidently different between individuals and may involve a combination of direct and indirect practical and psychological pressures. What was more commonly experienced by the refused asylum seekers in our sample, however, were the various types of exploitation encountered when creative ways to survive were sought in the absence of the right to work or access to welfare. We turn now to these experiences.

The interaction between risk of destitution, 'illegality' and labour market position

How exactly do refused asylum seekers access employment when legally denied the right to work? There are overlaps here with research on the undocumented migrant population (Bloch et al., 2009; Mckay et al., 2009; Valentine, 2010; Sigona, 2012) of which refused asylum seekers are a significant part. Echoing others' findings, we found refused asylum seekers often have a greater dependence on co-ethnic/co-language employers when seeking work (Bloch, 2013). This is partly due to limited English-language ability and the greater likelihood of finding work where this is not a factor. It is also related to the higher chances of finding work from within known kinship, language or faith group networks. We found refused asylum seekers working in a variety of low-paid jobs such as making or serving fast food, factory packing, care work, cleaning and food processing. Some individuals in our sample, out of fear of denunciation, felt unable to search for jobs from within their co-ethnic/co-language circles and instead often turned to trudging the streets in order to access work. We see here how Rose took her chances and began tidying rubbish outside a pub:

> Because in Africa if you [...] want to find a work, you do it and then they will pay you money. [...] He called me in his pub [...]

I explained to him why I was trying to clear his garden to get a bit of money to eat [...] He told me when there is anything to do, cleaning or sweeping I can come and they will give me some money.

Routes into work frequently rely on informal channels within known networks and workplaces willing to take on workers without requisite papers. Situations where the employer knew the worker was unauthorised were exceptionally risky. Common experiences of exploitation, such as the imposition of excessive working hours, withheld pay or various abusive working and living conditions, were achieved by the employer's instrumental use of the worker's precarious socio-legal status. This was a predominant tool of coercion used to discipline workers who had 'no real and acceptable alternative' but to comply. Jay, who worked intermittently for an agency, describes violence, abuse and employer impunity:

A big bloke who used to drive the van, if you complain, you get one slap you know ... Most of the time he say to me 'You are a foreigner, there is nothing you can do here' [...] What will I say? If I don't work and money to pay my accommodation I'm going to end up living in the streets.

Our interviewees consistently linked their exploitation directly to two aspects of their compromised socio-legal status: the 'doctrine of illegality' that makes it near impossible for those working without authorisation to exercise any employment rights[2] and the risk of deportation and broader experiences of 'deportability in everyday life' (De Genova, 2002) that operate to constrain choices and discipline workers within labour relations. All of those who worked without authorisation either assumed or knew that their 'illegal' status left them without the power to challenge their employers if exploitative practices arose. If workers did attempt to negotiate better pay or conditions, they were swiftly reminded of their expendability in a context of other undocumented workers waiting in the wings. Individuals were told they could leave if they were not willing to accept existing terms:

We have a deal £30 a day and when he cut my £10 it was, £10 is big money for me ... But I couldn't talk about it. I couldn't ask him about that £10 and I was always afraid that if I said ... no more job, that's it go find somewhere else.

(Dedem)

These experiences point to common employer practices of deliberately employing unauthorised workers for the worst and most underpaid tasks. Refused asylum seekers' desire to continue in work that might be considered severely exploitative must be understood in the wider perspective of survival through seeking a livelihood. The fear of losing work and the associated risks of homelessness, destitution or inability to support family members routinely operated as an effective barrier to leaving exploitative labouring situations. In many cases, the refused asylum seekers in our study worked hard to access work and were terrified of losing their job.

Faced with the treatment handed out to those who engaged in undocumented working, a small number of interviewees in our research acquired false papers to access employment. Such decisions were never taken lightly due to the substantial expense involved and fears that being discovered could have catastrophic consequences on any pending appeal or new asylum claim. False papers were therefore only acquired as a last resort when all other avenues to accessing work had been exhausted:

> One of them told me, I can help you to find work you see. And I ask him how he can help me to find work, I have no papers. I don't want to break the law. But he say, 'brother you have [to] – how cannot you break the law? You have nothing, if you don't break the law you will not live'.
>
> (Pascual)

In many ways, current policy encourages the criminalisation of refused asylum seekers and stimulates an environment in which fraudulent papers, fake identities and shared national insurance numbers (NINos) are used by some to access paid work to survive. In these situations, our interviewees were usually paid at legal rates by their employers, and not necessarily badly treated in the workplace, but crucially they did not have control of their earnings as a friend, relative or partner would retain them.

Nanda experienced such withholding of pay when her then-partner procured a NINo for her to use and helped her to open a bank account which he then controlled. When Nanda got an agency job in a packing factory, her partner took all her wages, telling her that it would pay for her rent, food and clothes: 'And I didn't get that money in my hand also.' Gregory also became embroiled in third-party webs of coercion. He began doing agency work via contacts who were working as informal gangmasters. They registered themselves with various agencies but then sent Gregory and others like him who did not have permission to work in their place for 50 per cent of their pay. This was possible because the agencies were not cross-checking the individuals who turned up against the documentation they held.

This section is couched in a broader understanding of how the increasingly normalised techniques of state power such as detention and deportation discipline refused asylum seekers, among a broader target group of undocumented migrants (Bloch and Schuster, 2005). Peutz and De Genova (2010) suggest that the threat of such state power (if not the actuality) leads to irregularity becoming a 'deeply interiorised mode of being' that inscribes migrants' everyday lives and is utilised by state actors as disciplining mechanisms. Yet we do not want to construct migrants as entirely passive. The next section therefore focuses on the less frequent cases in our research of individuals resisting or contesting workplace exploitation.

Contesting exploitation

As noted, severely exploitative labour situations were a common experience for refused asylum seekers in our research. However, although the partial closing down of space for the negotiation of work conditions was common to all of these situations, here we explore how workers *did* actively manage to resist poor treatment at work (Waite et al., 2015, in press).

Such resistance was enacted in varied ways. Some refused asylum seekers spoke of moments of solidarity at work – albeit nascent – that allowed for fleeting forms of effective organising against exploitation. Dedem achieved success in recouping wages, not for himself, but for a friend, through direct, collective confrontation with an unscrupulous employer:

> So, I had to put a knife under his ear, I said 'I'm going to cut your ear'. So this kind of things. [. . .] Then on Saturday we had a meeting, so about, we had five cars and all the people they come with baton, like baseballs and cricket bats and you know.

Direct negotiations were also sometimes entered into by workers. Tino, Gojo and Rose, for example, attempted to apply moral pressure to persuade employers to honour agreed payments. They each revealed their caring responsibilities for children to their employers, but this information was turned back on them as a tool of coercion as employers realised their desperation. Delicate negotiations were always juggled with the pressure to please employers in a bid to secure ongoing work. John describes how the £90 he was eventually paid for two weeks' cleaning work came as a result of repeated, gentle persuasion to elicit hoped-for empathy:

> The way I was asking, I didn't say (shouts) 'where is my money?' [...] The way to ask her, you know, I'm using transport to come to work, so I'll be late that day. [...] I was doing this in a gentle way, so that maybe she could feel for me.

The attempt to negotiate improved working conditions is one way of enacting resistance. Another way of resisting workplace exploitation is to 'exit' the situation. Such exit, however, is far from straightforward. Some refused asylum seekers in our research dramatically 'escaped' confined labour situations only after the gradual building of resilience eventually led to a 'tipping point'. Jay, who we earlier encountered, was living in domestic servitude, absorbing the abuses of his partner until it became 'too much'. Yet, feeling he had 'had enough' did not spark his exit; this only occurred after he re-established contact with a trusted friend who offered him an alternative means of support:

> I just say one day that's it I'm going to move. And luckily I met this guy in (nearby city) who know me back home and he said 'oh, man, come live with me'. [...] I just said 'oh, I'm going for a walk' and I jump on a bus.

Another mode of exiting exploitation was through 'walking away' from more formal workplaces after the progression of worsening exploitation triggered exit. For Assanne, the sudden 'tipping point' came after months of working with irregular or no pay:

> Basically that week, I had worked all week and then on the Friday I had worked till three in the morning, 3am and I went to get my money the next day and there was no money and I just exploded and I thought, I can't! That's why I left.

The threat of being reported to the Home Office further triggered exit in several cases for refused asylum seekers. Workers' attempts to negotiate in the face of deteriorating conditions by, for example, refusing to take on additional tasks or stay excessively long hours often meant leaving without pay. In Frank's case, his exploitation was at the hands of his 'friend' from whom he rented papers. Frank describes how several things came together in his mind so that he no longer felt the risk of working with false papers was worth it:

> I'm working for nothing and that pressure pushed me also to think that [...] if the police come they will just ask me to put a finger on the machine, and they find a different identity, then I'm gone [...] And I realised, it was time for me to back off. [...] I told them that I'm sick and I want to have some time off, and that was it.

In other cases, exit for refused asylum seekers was facilitated not through workers rejecting conditions but as a consequence of being 'pushed away'. Such dismissal sometimes followed resistance, as illustrated here by Parviz, a delivery driver, who was dismissed without pay following his refusal to take on additional cleaning tasks:

> The owner came and asked me to broom outside the shop. I told them that I was your driver not a cleaner and we agreed that I would do whatever you asked me for but not the cleaning. That's why I told them I gave them notice that I wouldn't be working with them the following week.

A final important point is that 'exit' from a particular exploitative labour situation can bring temporary respite, but this is often short-lived as the pressures to earn cash continue. Exploitation is too often a process rather than a perfunctory event for undocumented migrants, meaning exit from one damaging job may be swiftly followed by entering another. Indeed, periods within exploitative informal labour make a shift away from the 'track' of exploitation extremely difficult. This is illustrated by Assanne who, when first refused asylum, found work sorting recycled clothes and received only intermittent wages. After leaving, he managed to launch a fresh asylum claim and access Section 4 support, but this was again refused and his support removed. Following a month staying with friends, facing homelessness and destitution, and lacking any viable alternative he returned to the same employer despite knowing how appalling conditions were: 'at this stage I'm really only working to get some bread basically'.

Conclusions

This chapter has focused on refused asylum seekers as a highly vulnerable sub-set of the UK's undocumented migrant population. They are subject to state-sanctioned enforced destitution, such that their lives following refusal swiftly become survival-oriented to avoid life on the street. Individuals in our research accessed vital support through informal networks, often – but not exclusively – through co-ethnic and co-language communities. These forms of support are frequently 'transactional' as food/housing is provided in exchange for either an explicit or implicit expectation of return services. Although sometimes portrayed as positive by the refused asylum seekers in our research, we also encountered many grey areas of so-called mutuality whereby relations start to slide into coerciveness and abuse.

At this point, or sometimes earlier, individuals will frequently attempt to access the paid labour market. This decision may be crisis-driven ('the end of the road' type scenarios), but it may also be due to the swirling constellation of competing pressures such as remittances, legal costs and desire to contribute cash to host families. Working while undocumented, however, carries many risks. Refused asylum seekers in employment are routinely subject to the worst conditions in the lower echelons of the labour market. Their compromised socio-legal status is often used by unscrupulous employers to maintain exploitative working conditions and/or to close down opportunities for contestation through reminders of expendability or threats of denunciation to the authorities. It is for these reasons that some refused asylum seekers in our research chose to acquire false papers to access employment – a path not devoid of risk either as individuals often become embroiled in highly exploitative third-party relationships.

Refused asylum seekers, however, do not passively accept exploitation. Work 'offers' that are deemed exploitative are sometimes refused at the outset. Work conditions can occasionally be improved from *within* through delicate negotiation and nascent solidarity among fellow-workers to exert pressure on employers. We also acknowledge worker resilience through the very *act of working itself* within an oppressive politico-economic context that denies the right to work and enshrines state-enforced poverty and destitution (Lewis et al., 2014). Exit *from* exploitative labour relations was also seen to occur in our research through a variety of modes of resistance, such as escaping, 'walking away' from exploitation or being 'pushed away' through the job ending or dismissal. Although this may indeed result in exit from particular situations of exploitation, an awareness of processes (and not just events) leads us to conclude by noting the 'sticky web' character (Goldring and Landolt, 2011) of refused asylum seekers' exploitation. Webs of exploitation are difficult to dismantle, and compounding this in the UK are current attacks on labour regulation and labour rights that enhance the impunity of employers and other third-party individuals. It is for all of these reasons that we are terming refused asylum seekers' labouring experiences as too frequently ones of *hyperexploitation*.

Notes

1. Balanced against this are the government 'removals' and 'persons leaving detention' figures; for the same last quarter in 2013, these figures show that including dependants, 1,952 asylum seekers were removed or departed voluntarily from the UK, and 1,476 asylum detainees were recorded as removed from the UK upon leaving detention (35 per cent of the total detainees removed having left detention). It is important to note that many of the individuals in these 'removal' categories may have been in the UK for some time. Sources: http://www.refugeecouncil.org.uk/assets/0003/1356/Asylum_Statistics_Feb_2014.pdf, https://www.gov.uk/government/publications/immigration-statistics-october-to-december-2013
2. Those working without permission are judged to be in illegal employment contracts and are thus deprived of fundamental labour rights or formal routes to legal redress. Nevertheless, recent legal developments might offer some hope. In *Hounga v Allen* July 2014, the UK Supreme Court judged that a domestic worker *could* claim race discrimination despite working illegally (see www.supremecourt.uk/decided-cases/docs/UKSC_2012_0188_PressSummary.pdf). Another measure about to be introduced in the UK that might assist undocumented workers is the EU Victims' Directive that contains legally binding minimum standards which apply to all victims of crime *irrespective of residence status.*

References

Anderson B and Rogaly B (2005) *Forced Labour and Migration to the UK*. London: Trades Union Congress.
Blitz BK and Otero-Iglesias M (2011) Stateless by Any Other Name: Refused Asylum-Seekers in the United Kingdom. *Journal of Ethnic and Migration Studies* 37(4): 657–673.
Bloch A (2013) Living in Fear: Rejected Asylum Seekers Living as Irregular Migrants in England. *Journal of Ethnic and Migration Studies*: 1–19.
Bloch A and Schuster L (2002) Asylum and Welfare: Contemporary Debates. *Critical Social Policy* 22: 393–414.

Bloch A and Schuster L (2005) At the Extremes of Exclusion: Deportation, Detention and Dispersal. *Ethnic and Racial Studies* 28: 491–512.

Bloch A, Sigona N and Zetter R (2009) *'No Right to Dream'. The Social and Economic Lives of Young Undocumented Migrants in Britain*. London: Paul Hamlyn Foundation.

Craig G, Gaus A, Wilkinson M, Skrivankova K and Mcquade A (2007) *Contemporary Slavery in the UK: Overview and Key Issues*. York: Joseph Rowntree Foundation.

Crawley H, Hemmings J and Price N (2011) *Coping with Destitution. Survival and Livelihood Strategies of Refused Asylum Seekers Living in the UK*. Swansea: Swansea University and Oxfam.

Cross H (2013) Labour and Underdevelopment? Migration, Dispossession and Accumulation in West Africa and Europe. *Review of African Political Economy* 40: 202–218.

De Genova NP (2002) Migrant 'Illegality' and Deportability in Everyday Life. *Annual Review of Anthropology* 31: 419–447.

Dwyer P and Brown D (2005) Meeting Basic Needs? Forced Migrants and Welfare. *Social Policy and Society* 4(4): 369–380.

Goldring L and Landolt P (2011) Caught in the Work–Citizenship Matrix: The Lasting Effects of Precarious Legal Status on Work for Toronto Immigrants. *Globalizations* 8: 325–341.

Gupta R (2007) *Enslaved: The New British Slavery*. London: Portobello Books.

Lewis H (2007) *Destitution in Leeds: The Experiences of People Seeking Asylum and Supporting Agencies*. York: Joseph Rowntree Charitable Trust.

Lewis H (2009) *Still Destitute: A Worsening Problem for Refused Asylum Seekers*. York: Joseph Rowntree Charitable Trust.

Lewis H, Dwyer P, Hodkinson S and Waite L (2014) *Precarious Lives: Forced Labour, Exploitation and Asylum*. Bristol: The Policy Press.

McIntyre P and Mogire E (2012) *Between a Rock and a Hard Place: The Dilemma Facing Refused Asylum Seekers*. London: Refugee Council.

McKay S, Markova E, Paraskevopoulou A and Wright T (2009) *The Relationship between Migration Status and Employment Outcomes*. Undocumented Worker Transitions.

Morgan J and Olsen W (2009) Unfreedom as the Shadow of Freedom: An Initial Contribution to the Meaning of Unfree Labour. *Manchester Papers in Political Economy* Working Paper.

Peutz N and De Genova N (2010) Introduction. In N. Peutz and N. De Genova (eds), *The Deportation Regime*. Durham: Duke University Press, 1–32.

Sigona N (2012) 'I Have Too Much Baggage': The Impacts of Legal Status on the Social Worlds of Irregular Migrants. *Social Anthropology* 20: 50–65.

Sigona N and Hughes V (2012) *No Way Out, No Way In. Irregular Migrant Children and Families in the UK*. Oxford: Centre on Migration, Policy and Society, University of Oxford.

Vine J (2012) *An Inspection of the UK Border Agency's Handling of Legacy Asylum and Migration Cases*. March–July 2012. London: Independent Chief Inspector of Borders and Immigration.

Valentine R (2010) *Hope Costs Nothing: The Lives of Undocumented Migrants in the UK*. London: Migrants Resource Centre and Barrow Cadbury Trust.

Van den Anker C (2009) Rights and Responsibilities in Trafficking for Forced Labour: Migration Regimes, Labour Law and Welfare States. *Web Journal of Current Legal Issues*. Available at: http://webjcli.ncl.ac.uk/2009/issue1/vandenanker1.html

Waite L, Lewis H, Dwyer P and Hodkinson S (2015, in press) Precarious Lives: Refugees and Asylum Seekers' Resistance within Unfree Labouring. *ACME*.

Part IV

Hidden from View: The Most Exploited Workers

11
Sweatshop Workers in Buenos Aires: The Political Economy of Human Trafficking in a Peripheral Country

Jerónimo Montero Bressán and Eliana Ferradás Abalo

Introduction

In March 2006, a fire broke out in a medium-sized garment workshop in the working-class Caballito neighbourhood of Buenos Aires, Argentina, leading to the death of two Bolivian workers and four children. All of them were living in the place with another 60 people. They could not escape from the sweatshop because the doors were locked. The tragedy triggered the disclosure of thousands of 'local sweatshops' (Montero y Arcos, unpublished) that supply small, medium and large local and international brands. In 2010, the Under-Secretariat of Labour calculated that in Buenos Aires city alone there were about 5,000 sweatshops (Lieutier, 2010), and at least double that number in Greater Buenos Aires.[1]

The overwhelming majority of the workers in these sweatshops are immigrants from Bolivia. Declarations from workers in court cases have revealed that usually they are approached in their home country and offered a job in Buenos Aires. On arrival, as they have a debt to pay back, they have to live in the place where they work and their salary is significantly below what they had been offered. This movement of workers involving deception, debt-bondage and payments significantly below the agreed baseline salary is tantamount to the mechanism of human trafficking. Furthermore, working conditions are analogous to what the International Labour Organization (ILO) identifies as key elements of forced labour, since it 'is exacted under the menace of a penalty and it is undertaken involuntarily' (ILO, 2005: 5).

This sweatshop economy flourished in Buenos Aires since the mid-1980s, alongside the strong difficulties faced by factory production in view of the global economic stagnation and instability. In the early 1990s, trade liberalisation and an over-valued currency posed further challenges to garment manufacturers. During that decade, the sector experienced a sharp reorganisation, with radical shifts in the labour process: thousands of factories closed their gates and subcontracting to small inner-city workshops became widespread. As cut-throat competition between sweatshops broke out during the 1998–2001 political and economic crises, the companies gained full control over contracting prices. The sharp recovery of the sector since 2003 did not put an end to sweatshop exploitation. On the contrary, this recovery was partly based on the use of sweatshop labour (Montero, 2014).

Local sweatshops are not exclusive to Buenos Aires. These workplaces have burgeoned in large cities in both peripheral and core countries since the late 1970s (Morokvasic et al., 1986; Phizacklea, 1990; Ross, 2004; Montero, 2012). This is linked to changes in the labour process in the global garment industry, as well as to broader changes in the international political economy – namely the shift from Fordism to neoliberalism.

This chapter presents results from a number of research projects carried out in Buenos Aires between 2007 and 2014 (Ferradás, 2011; Montero, 2011, 2014). Over 75 semi-structured interviews were carried out. We also draw on our experience of anti-sweatshop activism in a grassroots organisation (*La Alameda*) since 2008. We start by describing the sweatshops and the recruiting process. In the third and fourth section we analyse the origin and evolution of the vast sweatshop economy of Buenos Aires. In so doing, we follow Peck (1996), who argues that in order to understand labour flexibility and precarity we must consider both changes in the labour process and the institutional conditions of the local labour markets. In the fifth section, we deal with the apparently contradictory expansion of the sweatshop economy during times of sharp economic recovery (2003–09). We then analyse the combination of progress and retreat in the state regulation of sweatshops and state responses to political pressure from grassroots organisations. In the sixth section, we briefly highlight the atypical nature of Argentina's case as a country with an extremely progressive immigration law but which completely fails to enforce the rights of migrants. In conclusion, we argue that the lack of a solid decision of the government to defend migrant workers' rights might render – very welcome – permissive immigration legislation into an institutional device that ends up facilitating trafficking.

Local sweatshops in Buenos Aires

Local sweatshops in Buenos Aires typically operate in private family houses located in working-class neighbourhoods that are rented for these purposes and employ the sweatshop's owner and his family, plus 4–20 workers (Lieutier, 2010). These sweatshops work to the order of large brands, both national and international, supplying to their local markets. The overwhelming majority of workers and owners are migrants, mostly from Bolivia. The managers are usually also migrants with several years of residence in the country, whereas the workforce is mostly made up of newcomers. On the whole, the Ministry of Economy (Instituto Nacional de Estadísticas y Censos (INDEC), 2006) recognises the existence of about 30,000 Bolivian immigrants being subjected to forced labour (understood through the ILO definition) in these inner-city sweatshops.

In her study of the global apparel industry, Collins explains that immigrant communities are often in an especially beneficial position to cover a growing demand of workers in informal activities in garment production:

[E]ntrepreneurs wishing to set up an apparel factory have needed only to rent a space and buy sewing machines (. . .) This has made the industry especially attractive for immigrant entrepreneurs, who could get started with only small loans and tap kin and community networks to recruit workers.

(Collins, 2003: 7)

From time to time, high levels of unemployment and poverty in Bolivia have triggered emigration towards countries such as Chile, Argentina and Brazil. During the 1990s, the strength of the Argentinian currency allowed migrants in this country to send significant remittances to their families back home and attracted a new wave of immigrants from neighbouring countries. The 1991 Census revealed the presence of 143,735 Bolivian citizens. Ten years later, this number had reached 233,464 people, representing an increase of 62.4 per cent, as Argentina became the main destination for Bolivian emigrants (INDEC, 2003). At present, citizens from Bolivia engage in two main activities: intensive agriculture and sewing sweatshops.

Lieutier (2010) quotes declarations from former sweatshop workers to the office of the Public Prosecutor, showing the usual recruitment mechanism of trafficked victims for exploitation in sweatshops: workers either approach informal 'employment agencies' or are approached directly by an employee of the *tallerista* (sweatshop owner) or by the *tallerista* himself in the main Bolivian cities (La Paz, Cochabamba and others). They are offered a stable job in Buenos Aires for a fair wage, including housing and meals. Their transportation is paid by the *tallerista*, and once they reach Buenos Aires bus station, they are taken to the sweatshops. At times the *talleristas* also retain their passports and tell the workers not to leave the workplace, as the police would – allegedly – deport them.

Declarations from workers quoted in Lieutier (2010) and the cases of four of the former sweatshop workers interviewed for this research indicate that while the working and living conditions vary from one sweatshop to another, the most typical situation can be described as follows: workers live in the sweatshops in cramped conditions with improper ventilation and a complete lack of health and safety provisions. They work approximately from 8 am until midnight from Monday to Saturday, are given two meals a day, are not paid until the third or fourth month of work (supposedly, they are told, as repayment for their bus ticket), and earn between 40 per cent and 50 per cent of the agreed baseline salary for the industry. In the worst cases, the doors are locked all day long. Isolated from the broader society, these workers have no access to information about their rights (see following sections).

Similarly to the sweatshop systems present in large cities in the Global North (Aguiar, 2006) and South, the emergence of this phenomenon in Buenos Aires is related not only to changes in the labour process in the clothing industry worldwide and their context-specific repercussions in Argentina but also to the increasing adoption of a neoliberal path in political economy in the country. We now analyse these developments.

From Fordism to neoliberalism in garment manufacturing

The garment industry is a textbook example of the strategies developed by capital to fight its way out of the crisis of Fordism in the early 1970s. Garment manufacturers were strongly affected by increasing international competition, economic stagnation and the instability caused by the growing financialisation, due to the high elasticity demand of what they sell. Faced with the need to rationalise production, the leading firms of the sector, especially the high-end fashion houses, adopted *en masse* a strategy previously developed by sports apparel companies: becoming branded manufacturers. In doing so, they fostered a return to the widespread use of subcontracting, in order to cut labour costs and convey the risks to their subcontractors (see also Smith, Chapter 2, this volume). International outsourcing served these objectives, whereas the incorporation of vulnerable migrant workers through subcontracting to sweatshops located in the proximities of the companies' headquarters allowed these to 'keep one foot at home' at very low costs (Montero, 2011).

Furthermore, in seeking to expand their markets, these companies invested more resources in marketing and design. By the mid-1980s, the expansion of fashion marketing had created a growing demand for more fashion-sensitive clothes (fashionwear), but at lower prices than those offered by the high-end fashion houses. This new market of fashionwear became massive very quickly and a myriad of factory-less companies emerged during the 1980s to supply this flourishing market. It is precisely the kind of garment manufacturing developed to cover this demand for fashionwear that led to the emergence of sweatshop systems in several large cities, because this segment is ruled by the requirement for small batches, quick response and low costs.

Despite certain local specificities, these developments can be seen across Argentina since the mid-1980s, when numerous factories shut down and sewing workshops started to populate working-class neighbourhoods. The effects of changes in international political economy, coupled with a deliberate policy of deindustrialisation from 1976 to 2001 (Schorr, 2005; Basualdo, 2006), strongly affected garment production in factories. This process deepened in the 1990s, with a strong local currency and trade liberalisation. As a consequence of the closure of several factories, from 1984 to 1993 formal employment in the sector experienced a drop of 72 per cent (Ministerio de Trabajo, 2006). This trend continued until 2003. The legacy of such a dreadful experience has a long-standing impact on the industry: the fear of a return to such a crisis is used by entrepreneurs in their bargaining rhetoric as a reason for the continued suppression of salaries, and the main workers' union, which saw its membership shatter in those years, shares this fear with the firms (interview with Ramiro[2] [15/2/08]).

While 'commodity garments' produced in factories were progressively substituted by cheap imports, local firms shut down their factories and shifted to branded manufacturing, subcontracting to homeworkers and informal urban workshops. Therefore, despite the loss of about 29,000 formal jobs during the 1990s (INDEC, 2001), thousands of jobs were created in informal workshops in the same period, entailing an overall process of informalisation of the workforce (Montero, 2012; Monzón, 2001).

The economic growth in the first half of the 1990s had a positive impact on the brands' sales, therefore expanding the labour demand.

With their community links, migrants were in an unbeatable position to supply this workforce. However, when the supply overtook demand in the midst of the 1998–2002 crisis, fierce competition between *talleristas* broke out, giving the brands absolute control to set the contracting prices. In only about a decade, a strategy adopted by garment companies as a response to structural changes had created a vast sweatshop economy.

Nowadays, sweatshops in Buenos Aires also manufacture garments commercialised through informal outdoor markets. The largest illegal outdoor market in Latin America, called La Salada, operates in Greater Buenos Aires. Born as a survival strategy of a few Bolivian families in 1987 (Libchaber and Pogliaghi, 2008), the market exploded during the 1998–2002 crisis and continued to grow until today, that is, during both times of crisis and times of sharp economic growth. Today, it is supplied by thousands of sweatshops operating under the tacit support of municipal authorities.

Widespread precarity as the prelude to forced labour

The emergence of a sweatshop system in Buenos Aires has to be understood in a general context of deindustrialisation, growing unemployment and labour informality, deregulation of the labour market and regressive social policies (see Schorr, 2000, 2005; Arceo and Basualdo, 2006; Basualdo, 2006). The process started in 1976, when a military dictatorship took power and imposed 'a new social regime of accumulation based on financial valorisation' that lasted until 2002 (Basualdo, 2006: 138). During those years, the open repression of unions through state terrorism (1976–83) and, later on, the co-optation of union leaders paved the way to the implementation of an 'increasingly unequal and regressive path of redistribution of wealth' (Schorr, 2000: 156). Labour inspections divisions were scrapped, whereas court decisions favoured irresponsible subcontracting. The widespread adoption of subcontracting arrangements in a context of rife unemployment and weakened unions led to higher levels of informality. Between 1989 and 2002, informal labour increased from 28 per cent to 44 per cent (ILO, 2013).

The combination of these phenomena with the crisis towards the late 1990s led to high levels of tolerance towards deficient working conditions, pushing down the socially acceptable bottom line of labour standards. A labour lawyer from the union Asociación Obrera Textil (Roberto, interviewed on 19/October/09) stated that 'in Argentina labour informality is a direct consequence of unemployment'. His words recall an ILO report on 'The world of work' (2008), which concluded that labour flexibility/precarity in the Global South is expressed as labour informality. Given the pressure from growing unemployment and lack of state support in case of unemployment, flexibility is exercised de facto, no matter what the legislation states. Furthermore, when the state does not combat labour exploitation, a door is opened for the spread of illegal practices. It is in this context that an economic niche supplying formal and informal economies and based on the forced labour of trafficked migrants developed in Argentina.

With the economic recovery since 2003 there have been substantial improvements in employment indicators (Palomino, 2008). However, informal labour remains very high at 34 per cent (SSPTyEL, 2013), progress for informal workers has been less notable and the wage gap between formal and informal workers amounts to 43 per cent (SSPTyEL, 2014). Furthermore, there are 'critical sectors' where forced labour suffered by migrants is rife. Although action has been taken to protect rural and domestic workers, migrant garment workers in sweatshops have only received limited attention.

Nevertheless, a factory fire in 2006 triggered a quick reaction from the City in the form of numerous factory inspections. Further lobbying from civil society, in particular the militancy of *La Alameda* and its strategic alliance with the City's Under-Secretariat of Labour (until 2008), put more pressure on the state to stop sweatshops. Alongside this, the renowned sexual exploitation case of Marita Veron the following year[3] finally led the state to approve the first anti-trafficking law in 2008, six years after ratifying the UN Palermo Protocol to Prevent, Suppress and Punish Trafficking (2000), and only in response to growing popular demand.

Progress and retreat: The anti-trafficking struggle and the State

The government's policy towards sweatshops shows a number of contradictory steps. The introduction of the anti-trafficking law in 2008 allowed significant progress and created a number of bodies in charge of assisting victims and designing legal instruments to support attorneys leading court cases countrywide. Nevertheless, all progress has been mostly triggered by political pressure from grassroots organisations.[4] Moreover, informality in the sector remains at a historical high: 70 per cent (INDEC, 2014). In visiting the country in 2010, the UN Special Rapporteur on Human Trafficking pointed to a number of 'challenges' that the state must address effectively to combat human trafficking and to protect the victims:

> [S]uch challenges include, but are not limited to, the lack of comprehensive data on the trend of trafficking in persons; the weak coordination of anti-trafficking activities; the lack of identification and referral mechanisms for trafficked persons; and the insufficient availability of facilities and services specifically designed to provide trafficked persons with direct assistance.
>
> (OHCHR, 2010: 1)

In her report, the Rapporteur also pointed to the weak capacity of the labour inspections divisions to detect and control sweatshop exploitation and to corruption as a main difficulty in this regard (OHCHR, 2010: 5).

Efforts to control sweatshop exploitation seem to be rather isolated actions from seriously concerned and prominent officials in response to social pressure from campaigners. Evidence suggests that the long-term approach of the executive to this matter is that of letting these highly profitable activities based on the extreme exploitation of migrant labour develop. Two critical actions taken by the government point in this direction. First, in 2008, the Ministry of Labour proposed a modification to the legislation regulating subcontracting. The main change it proposed was to release the brands from shared responsibility. This modification finally failed due to opposition by *La Alameda* and by progressive MPs, but the proposal had been originally designed by one of the clothing chambers (Sanguinetto, 2014). That is, the Ministry of Labour had taken as its own a project developed by the chamber whose members systematically violate labour legislation.

Secondly, in 2012, Jorge Castillo, the most prominent leader of *La Salada* outdoor textile market, was invited by the Ministry of Economy to take part in an official commercial mission to Angola and SE Asia.[5] According to Daniel (from the Ministry of Production, Science and Technology of the Province of Buenos Aires, interviewed on 15/5/12), the plan was to explore the possibility to open a similar market in Luanda, ideally to be supplied by Argentinian exports, therefore opening up an export market for Argentinian manufacturers. In return, Castillo would cooperate in negotiating a plan to upgrade the status of the market towards full registration and formalisation.

This deliberate policy of tolerance towards the firms' labour practices is a way to support the sector. This support is partially explained by the fact that entrepreneurs have successfully managed to present themselves as one of the main victims of the neoliberal era, when the policy of deindustrialisation led to the closure of numerous factories and the loss of thousands of jobs. Any mention of the experience of the 1990s grants entrepreneurs a high level of tolerance towards exploitative labour practices. Members of *La Alameda* assert a further reason: that the ruling party uses this tolerance to ask for support from the sector during electoral campaigns.

Open borders, isolated workers: The atypical case of Argentina's progressive immigration legislation

There is a growing literature on the links between socio-legal status and the vulnerability of migrants to forced labour (Anderson and Rogaly, 2005; Skrivankova, 2006; Gordolan and Lalani, 2009; van den Anker, 2009; Dwyer et al., 2011). Argentina is an atypical case for exploring this issue. Although legislation has changed over time, in practice the country has historically followed an open border policy. The immigration law in force since 2004 is considered a 'worldwide example' by the International Organization for Migration (IOM),[6] especially because it recognises migration as a human right. According to it, migrants are entitled to the rights of health, education, welfare and housing regardless of their status. In addition, when a migrant citizen is found to be in an irregular situation, authorities are not entitled to deport him/her and are instead required to provide him/her with guidance on how to regularise his/her status.

However, as we demonstrate in this chapter, there is a considerable gap between the law and the reality, since migrants are victims of severely exploitative work. This case illustrates that, as pointed out by Dwyer et al. (2011: 27), the vulnerability of migrants to abusive labour is not exclusively linked to their socio-legal status, which is, in the end, only 'an added vulnerability factor'. Indeed, in reviewing a large number of court cases, Pacceca (2011) concluded that a broad variety of migratory statuses can be found in sweatshops. In her own words, 'there (are) people with a valid residence – be it permanent or temporary; people with an expired tourist visa; (and) people with a valid tourist visa but working' (164). In this regard, Dwyer et al. (2011) point to a series of facts that have a critical influence on shaping migrants' work experiences. Among these, there are 'lack of knowledge of rights; lack of access to information; isolation from society; multiple dependence on employer; loss of, or change in, employment; debt accrued in migration;

pressures to remit; and "loss of face" in country of origin' (26). It is precisely in relation to these points that the country's migration policy is failing to ensure the human rights of migrants.

In this context, a permissive immigration status that is not accompanied by a thorough policy aimed at enforcing the rights of migrants may indeed have negative consequences for migrant workers. In several points of entry, the open border policy has translated into the lack of proper control by the border authorities, therefore facilitating trafficking instead of helping to detect it. Furthermore, sometimes the fact that workers are entitled to rights leads the traffickers and sweatshop owners to increase the isolation of workers from the broader society. This could be indeed one of the reasons behind the decision to lock down the newcomers in sweatshops. In sum, as pointed out by the IOM (2008), the Argentinian state must make 'decisions exceeding the strictly migratory and oriented to the creation and consolidation of appropriate conditions for immigrants to integrate in the country, assuring for themselves and their families access to the goods and livelihoods needed to have a decent and healthy life' (42).

Conclusions

During neoliberal times, limited economic growth and economic instability, on the one hand, and the growing 'economic domination' of the state (Jessop, 2002), on the other, have created a high level of tolerance towards informality and other labour rights violations, especially when it involves migrants. The argument that states must ensure market opportunities and create good business environments has reached a level in which states allow the systematic violation of workers' rights to take place, in order not to disrupt capital accumulation. Indeed, the growing occurrence of human trafficking and forced labour is often happening in the sight of states, not only in peripheral countries like Argentina and Brazil, but also in Italy, Spain and the US (El País, 23/6/09; Kwong, 2001; Bernhardt, McGrath and DeFilippis, 2008; Montero, 2011). In this context, the emergence of sweatshop economies might in some cases be seen as a blessing for regional or local economies experiencing economic troubles (see Montero, 2011, 2012).

In Argentina, small inner-city clothing workshops emerged from the mid-1980s as a response to the growing demand of homeworkers from well-known clothing companies. The implementation of neoliberal policies during the 1990s created, towards the end of that decade, a context of rife unemployment and rising labour informality. In the midst of the deepest crisis in the country's history (1998–2002), forced labour and human trafficking became widespread in garment manufacturing. However, the sharp economic recovery since 2003 did not put an end to sweatshop exploitation. On the contrary, the growing demand for garments was supplied by sweatshops where working conditions did not improve after the crisis, partly in virtue of the cut-throat competition between these myriad subcontractors. The lack of state control in this area allowed clothing brands to keep labour costs to a minimum.

Argentina's case shows that permissive immigration legislation is necessary but not sufficient to secure a decent life for migrants. Since 2006, progress to stop human trafficking and forced labour has been made, but high state tolerance towards sweatshop exploitation confines progress to some important but isolated actions taken in response to growing social pressure. In the end, making legal status accessible for immigrants is an immense open door to real progress, provided that grassroots organisations and NGOs prove successful in compelling the state to enforce migrants' rights.

Notes

1. There have not been official estimations since then.
2. All names are pseudonyms.
3. See http://www.bbc.com/news/world-latin-america-26948962
4. The law on 'prevention and punishment of human trafficking and assistance to victims' was passed in April 2008 and modified in 2012 following pressure from social movements. The law of 2008 allowed little progress in combatting trafficking, especially because no punishments applied if the victims were not able to prove that they had been forced to do the jobs.
5. See http://www.lanacion.com.ar/1664576-la-salada-el-negocio-al-filo-de-la-ilegalidad-que-se-beneficia-con-la-inflacion. This was publicly recognised by Castillo himself (see https://www.youtube.com/watch?v=8NpZCaQVf5U).
6. See http://www.infobae.com/2006/11/11/285790-un-plan-migratorio-argen tino-es-ejemplo-mundial

References

Aguiar L (2006) Janitors and Sweatshop Citizenship in Canada. *Antipode* 38(3): 440–461.

Anderson B and Rogaly B (2005) *Forced Labour and Migration to the UK*. London: TUC.

Arceo E and Basualdo E (2006) Los cambios de los sectores dominantes en América Latina bajo el neoliberalismo. In E. Basualdo and E. Arceo (eds), *Neoliberalismo y sectores dominantes*. Buenos Aires: CLACSO, 15–26.

Azpiazu D and Schorr M (2010) *Hecho en Argentina. Industria y Economía, 1976–2007*. Buenos Aires: Siglo XXI Editores.

Basualdo E (2006) La reestructuración de la economía argentina durante las últi-mas décadas. In E Basualdo y E Arceo (eds), *Neoliberalismo y sectores dominantes*. Buenos Aires: CLACSO, 123–177.

Bernhardt A, McGrath S and DeFilippis J (2008) The State of Worker Protections in the United States: Unregulated Work in New York City. *International Labour Review* 147(2–3): 135–162.

Bertranou F and Casanova L (2013) *Informalidad laboral en Argentina: Segmentos críticos y políticas para la formalización*. Buenos Aires: Argentina Country Office, International Labour Organization.

Bonacich E and Appelbaum R (2000) *Behind the Label: Inequality in the Los Angeles Apparel Industry*. Berkeley, CA: California University Press.

Collins J (2003) *Threads: Gender, Labour and Power in the Global Apparel Industry*. London: The University of Chicago Press.

Dirección General de Estudios y Estadísticas Laborales (2006) *Sector textil, indi-cadores productivos*. Buenos Aires: Ministerio de Trabajo, Empleo y Seguridad Social de la Nación.

Dwyer P, Lewis H, Scullion L and Waite L (2011) *Forced Labour and UK Immigration Policy: Status Matters?* York: Joseph Rowntree Foundation.

Ferradás E (2011) *Sobre el consentimiento y la prostitución en sociedades patri-arcales. Primeras Jornadas Regionales Abolicionistas sobre Prostitución y Trata*. Unpublished.

Gordolan L and Lalani M (2009) *Care and Immigration: Migrant Care Workers in Private Households*. London: Kalayaan.

Green N (1997) *Ready-to-Wear and Ready-to-Work*. London: Duke University Press.

Instituto Nacional de Estadísticas y Censos (2006). *Anuario Estadístico*. Buenos Aires: Ministerio de Economía.

International Labour Organization (2005) *A Global Alliance against Forced Labour*. Geneva: International Labour Office.

International Labour Organization (2008) *World of Work Report 2008: Income Inequalities in the Age of Financial Globalization*. Geneva: International Labour Office, International Institute for Labour Studies.

International Labour Organization (2013) *Labour Overview*. Geneve. Available at: http://ilo.org/wcmsp5/groups/public/—americas/—rolima/documents/publication/wcms_242634.pdf (accessed on 1 September 2014).

Kwong P (2001) The Politics of Labour Migration: Chinese Workers in New York. *Socialist Register* 2001: 293–313.

Libchaber M and Pogliaghi L (2008) *La informalidad laboral en confecciones con especial referencia a la comercialización en ferias de la Salada*. Buenos Aires: Unpublished.

Lieutier A (2010) *Esclavos*. Buenos Aires: Retórica.

Montero J (2011) *Neoliberal Fashion: The Political Economy of Sweatshops in Europe and Latin America*. PhD thesis, Department of Geography, University of Durham. Available at: http://etheses.dur.ac.uk/3205/1/Montero._PhD_THESIS_FINAL.pdf?DDD14.

Montero J (2012) La moda neoliberal: El retorno de los talleres clandestinos de costura. *Geograficando* 8(8): 19–37.

Montero J (2014) Discursos de moda ¿Cómo justificar la explotación de inmigrantes en talleres de costura? *Trabajo y Sociedad* 23. Available at: http://www.unse.edu.ar/trabajoysociedad/23%20MONTERO%20Discursos%20de%20moda.pdf.

Montero J and Arcos A (2015) *Migrants as Workers and Workers as Migrants: Why Is Collective Organisation so Low amongst Workers in 'Local Sweatshops'.* Unpublished.

Monzón I (2001) *Transformaciones en la industria de la confección en la década del '90.* Centro de Estudios de la Estructura Económica, Facultad de Ciencias Económicas, Universidad de Buenos Aires.

Morokvasic M, Phizacklea A and Rudolph H (1986) Small Firms and Minority Groups: Contradictory Trends in the French, German and British Clothing industries. *International Sociology* 1(4): 397–419.

Office of the High Commissioner for Human Rights (2011) *Report of the Special Rapporteur on Trafficking in Persons, Especially in Women and Children.* New York: United Nations.

Organización Internacional para las Migraciones (2008) *Perfil migratorio de Argentina.* Buenos Aires: Organización Internacional para las Migraciones.

Pacceca MI (2011) Trabajo, explotación laboral, trata de personas. *Revista Interdisciplinar da Mobilidade Humana* 19(37): 147–174.

Palomino H (2008) La instalación de un nuevo régimen de empleo en Argentina. *Revista Latinoamericana de Estudios del Trabajo* 19: 121–144.

Peck J (1996) *Work-Place: The Social Regulation of Labor Markets.* New York: Guilford.

Phizacklea A (1990) *Unpacking the Fashion Industry.* London: Routledge.

Ross R (2004) *Slaves to Fashion: Poverty and Abuse in the New Sweatshops.* Ann Arbor: The University of Michigan Press.

Sanguinetto MH (2014) La gestión gremial empresaria en primera persona. *MAIByN* 53.

Schorr, M (2000) Principales rasgos de la industria argentina tras una década de ajuste estructural. *Realidad Económica* 170: 123–158.

Schorr M (2005) *Modelo Nacional Industrial.* Buenos Aires: Capital Intelectual.

Skrivankova K (2006) *Trafficking for Forced Labour in the UK.* London: Anti-Slavery International.

Van den Anker C (2009) Rights and Responsibilities in Trafficking for Forced Labour: Migration Regimes, Labour Law and Welfare States. *Journal of Current Legal Issues* 15(1), Available at: http://eprints.uwe.ac.uk/12725/1/vandenankerlegalissues.pdf.

Sources

Instituto Nacional de Estadísticas y Censos. *Encuesta Permanente de Hogares.* Ministerio de Economía y Finanzas Públicas. Available at: http://www.indec.gob.ar/bases-de-datos.asp

Subsecretaría de Programación Técnica y Estudios Laborales. *Boletín de Estadísticas Laborales.* Ministerio de Trabajo, Empleo y Seguridad Social de la Nación. Available at: http://www.trabajo.gob.ar/left/estadisticas/bel/index.asp

12
Experiences of Forced Labour among UK-Based Chinese Migrant Workers: Exploring Vulnerability and Protection in Times of Empire

Rebecca Lawthom, Carolyn Kagan, Sue Baines, Sandy Lo, Sylvia Sham, Lisa Mok, Mark Greenwood and Scott Gaule

Introduction

In this chapter, we use the work of Hardt and Negri (2000, 2004, 2009) to explore experiences of labour as embedded in networks. First, we outline the project briefly. Secondly, we highlight Hardt and Negri's theoretical concepts. Thirdly, we present excerpts from the data, which illustrate the networked nature of the workers. We argue that analysis needs to look beyond seeing workers as vulnerable and individualised units. Families are central to ways in which workers enact work decisions and community practices. The data we present here are based on qualitative interviews with Chinese workers. There is much debate about the status and definitions ascribed to this group of workers, and our sample contained undocumented, 'unauthorised' workers, including student visa and work permit overstayers. The methodology and partnership between the university and the social enterprise Wai Yin, who helped to define the research and carry out the work, are reported elsewhere (Kagan et al., 2011). Our partnership approach, working with a social enterprise, is seemingly in line with the position of the intellectual as advocated by Hardt and Negri:

> The intellectual is and only can be a militant, engaged as a singularity among others, embarked on the project of co-research aimed at making the multitude. The intellectual is thus not 'out in front' to determine the movements of history or 'on the sidelines' to critique them but rather completely 'inside'. (2004: 118)

The research

Working from an explicit critical community psychology base (Kagan et al., 2011), the project team designed a research project to explore experiences of forced labour.[1] Funded by the Joseph Rowntree Foundation as part of a Programme on Forced Labour, the overall aim of the project was to gain an in-depth understanding of the experiences of forced labour among Chinese migrant workers in the north-west of England, the role of family and social relationships, and the extent to which workers were able to exercise control over their lives. Qualitative interviews were undertaken in Mandarin or Cantonese with 37 Chinese individuals who were working in the UK during 2009–11, all referred to by pseudonyms in this chapter. Accounts of the workers were analysed collectively by a writing team across academics and partners in the social enterprise. Keen not to position potential participants as lacking agency and in line with critical community psychology, we positioned workers as individuals embedded in wider networks and contexts (familial, geographic and economic). We were keen to explore how forced labour intersects with other spheres of life beyond the sole focus on labour conditions. Drawing on our previous work, we understand working lives as interlocked with family and social relationships, wider social forces, life events and individual goals and ambitions. We knew little about how these different dimensions of life experience contribute to the choices Chinese migrant workers make and their experiences of forced labour. Family relationships and community ties influence decision-making, and while they lie outside the forced labour continuum (Skrivankova, 2010), they can render workers more or less vulnerable to exploitation. Workers may, for example, take personal risks in order to reach a destination through arrangements made by family and friends; they may tolerate appalling work conditions in order to keep providing for family members; they may become deeper in debt in order to reunify their families; they may not resist abusive working relationships because they are perpetrated by family members; and they may cease to retain hope of returning to China as UK-formed families grow.

Empire, Multitude and *Commonwealth*

Hardt and Negri published a trilogy of books: *Empire* (2000), *Multitude* (2004) and *Commonwealth* (2009). Positioned as autonomous Marxists, their contribution to social theory has been to reconceptualise empire and capital as present and material. Here, economic relations seem more distant from political controls but possibly not. The work is vast and space precludes a full discussion. Rather, we draw upon some of the key ideas articulated to enable theorising of our work. Hardt and Negri conceive of empire as a new global order – a new form of sovereignty, meaning something different from imperialism. They see empire now as decentred and deterritorialised:

> [T]he construction of the paths and limits of these new global flows has been accompanied by a transformation of the dominant productive processes themselves, with the results that the role of the industrial factory labour has been reduced and priority given to communicative, cooperative and affective labour.
>
> (Hardt and Negri, 2000: 2)

In *Empire*, they position Marxist ideas of the bourgeoisie as a powerful yet faceless network of transnational companies, international organisations and the nation-states that act as recipients. In response to empire and as a form of resistance against global systems of power, they use the term 'multitude'. *Multitude* (2004) re-appropriates the Marxist notion of the proletariat as a heterogeneous web of workers, migrants, social movements and non-governmental organisations – potentially as diverse figures of social production. If *Empire* seemed to focus on the problems of globalisation, *Multitude* perhaps aims to propose a solution to those problems – the creation of a truly pluralistic democracy for all mankind. What *Multitude* does is not easily summarised, but its basic idea is around networks. The multitude is not '*the* people' but rather many people acting in networked concert. As a result of its plurality, the multitude can be argued to contain the genus of true democracy. The multitude is further enabled by its ability to communicate and collaborate – often through the very capitalist networks that oppress it, thereby potentially allowing it to produce a common body of knowledge and ideas ('the common'). It is this common that can serve as a platform for democratic resistance to empire.

One may question how the multitude possesses any democratic potential. For Hardt and Negri, the sheer diversity of this network and its mode of dynamic reciprocal exchange are enabling factors. Indeed, these capacities can be argued to grow from the very nature of contemporary social life and economic production, which they see resting on two pillars. The first is a new model of labour, which Hardt and Negri describe as 'biopolitical production'. This label tries to capture the particular dynamic of the production of 'ideas', 'images', 'affects' and 'relationships' in the information economy. These are immaterial rather than material goods. They can spread quickly throughout the world, creating a 'common' that touches on all aspects of social life. The second pillar is the mode of political organisation embraced by the multitude. In place of centralised forms of revolutionary dictatorship and command, the multitude organises resistance to globalisation through networks, which substitute 'collaborative relationships' for hierarchical authority. In this account, then the multitude can be a movement of resistance, which is spontaneous and potentially powerful.

The multitude, positioned in this way alongside the concept of empire, is developed as a post-imperialist entity with no fixed boundaries. Empire promises the making of hybrid identities, flexible hierarchies and plural exchanges of information and communication. It is comprised of self-legitimating discourses and structures, the production of human and social capital, the biopolitical production of self, community, national and global. In short, it is a globalised biopolitical machine (Hardt and Negri, 2000: 40). Using these theoretical concepts, we may question how biopower manifests itself in everyday lives. How do workers (the Chinese workers in our study, for instance) participate in biopower?

The labour and work we engage in – whether manual or bodily (agricultural, factory) mental/intellectual (knowledge work, immaterial labour) and affective labour (emotional, service, self-maintenance, family, community (see Lawthom et al., 2013, for further discussion)) can be said to be an expression or product of biopower. Hardt and Negri see the role of productive labour changing in this new contemporary society – all labour depends on communication and information. They argue that all three kinds of labour implicitly involve social cooperation (networking, communication, teamwork, assembly lines) built into the nature of the labour itself. In this mechanistic mayhem of biopower, Hardt and Negri argue that resistance occurs in the multitude. To resist, the multitude becomes machine-like itself, using access to and control over knowledge, information, communication and affects. While biopower continues to create wealth unequally (Wilkinson and Pickett, 2009; Piketty, 2014), there is space within these new conditions of work and life for empire to resist. The new conditions of work and life in empire are already calling forth new forms of resistance everywhere. We turn now to the analysis of the Chinese workers' accounts. Family, travel and work networks were evident as both protective and vulnerable forces.

Family networks

At the heart of most of our interviewees' decisions to work abroad was the intention to better family lives, doing manual labour for affective labour. Family ties and family networks continued to exert influence over the workers throughout their migratory experience: in decision-making regarding with whom and how to travel; in raising the money to pay travel facilitators; in enabling a point of contact on arrival; in the determination to endure arduous working and living conditions in order to earn to send money home; in decisions about what is best for children; in the emotional ties of family and the continued obligation to pay back monies and to enable families remaining in China to maintain 'face' due to the success of the overseas worker. Decisions were made often in concert with a network of others. This echoes work, which urges us not to see vulnerable workers as contained in isolated labour situations but to consider migration trajectories across time and space involving extensive transnational social relationships (Bastia and McGrath, 2011; Mai, 2011).

The decision to leave was usually made with family members. Liu's initial choice of destination was strongly influenced by the links her family had with the UK. She was involved in Falun Gong[2] and her family thought it best she move abroad. Family members had the idea and made all the travel arrangements, raised the money needed and paid the money owing. They used their contacts and networks to achieve this.

> My aunt knew a snakehead[3] that helped to arrange me to come here for seeking asylum. [All the arrangements] were dealt with by other senior family members because I was only 21 at that time ... My aunt and parents arranged everything for me.

Family hardship catalysed some people's decisions to leave. Mei's father had debts in China and had left the family in difficulties. She felt strong obligations to help and her mother supported the idea that she and some of her cousins find work abroad.

> I came when I was 18.... my family owed some people money, and then my Daddy was not in China: he went to another place as he owed people money.... I wanted to help ease the burden as my family were not able to pay off the debts. At that time I've got several other family members to go with me, like cousins, and we came here together.... My mother agreed I should go. I left my little brother and sister. I was quite ignorant and believed what the others said, so

I went abroad to work and sent money back home. I had no idea how hard it was to earn money abroad.

Evident in this account, we see the fragmented family, each plugged and plunged into a network of capital and people. Most workers made hard decisions to leave their parents, brothers and sisters behind. Some even left their wives and children in China. Here, we see the multitude as positive and protective while also rendering workers vulnerable as unauthorised workers distant from families. Resistance is apparent in the determination to secure employment but often at personal cost. Zhu, a fisherman off the south west coast of China, left his family in China and joined a brother and other relatives in the UK who helped him work.

> My wife, my parents [they] definitely supported me to come here to earn money....my business had failed and I had debts. I came to my older brother [who was already here]. My family gathered several hundreds of money. [That] worried me as I got my wife and children back home and I borrowed so much money [when I arrived in Manchester] from my elder brother, cousin, many of them. Anyway a few of them were waiting for me to pick me up. I worked in my elder brother's workplace, in the kitchen, washing dishes. I lived with my brother – many people, we lived together. When we lived together it was cheap.

During the eight years he had been working in the UK, he supported his children through their education with his earnings. One of his daughters, a university graduate, had recently joined him in the UK to work. Commitments to his family helped him endure the hard working conditions of his life in the UK. Lewis et al. (2014) talk of the 'migrant project' as a period of time, being an 'apprentice' and enduring hardship in pursuance of an imagined future. This commitment to work, at a price, can be seen as resistance and being part of a multitude or interpreted as having choices constrained under the power of neoliberal capital or familial ties. The network maintenance – the affect labour – eventually reconnects Zhu to his daughter once more, as she had recently joined him in the UK.

Migration often leads to family separation, with older generations sharing caring responsibilities, as Ping experienced.

> My oldest daughter was just several months old when I left China...[When I decided to come to the UK] my child was a bit older and we had nearly paid back all the money [for his travel]. I wanted

to come here to work and I wouldn't be able to do that if I needed to take care of a child. She is now a teenager. My mother raised her.

Ping had two more children in the UK and her aspirations are now to settle here. However, she still yearns to see her parents and daughter again, but she cannot travel as she has no right of residence and cannot obtain travel documents. As she says:

> I would be lying if I tell you I don't want to go back. I have parents and my daughter in my hometown. How would I not want to go back? Our biggest wish is for the government to give us right of residence. We would like to go back home for travelling, even if we would need to borrow money from friends.

Ping's account shows the power of the state working variously to restrict her movement, to enable her to provide for her family and to create a new one, albeit with constraints. To travel clandestinely, a major way for people to travel from China to the UK, was by paying a travel facilitator fee. Family members were the ones often to find the facilitators and raise the money. They did not resent paying the fee, recognising this cost as a penalty of overseas work and knowing that the first few years would be spent repaying the fee.

> I had to pay [the snakehead] about 100 thousand RMBs.[4] ... I borrowed it from others....[5] My parents borrowed from their friends and family... My Family in China paid the snakeheads: I called my family in China when I was in the asylum seeker centre.... Then my Mum knew I had arrived in the UK safely but got locked up. When I was released I called my family again to tell them I was released. Then they paid the snakehead's money.
>
> (Wing)

Obligations to family become more than ties of affiliation and love; they are ties of debt. As family members paid off the fee on arrival, migrants thereafter owed money to their family, who often were already living in hardship. These accounts position workers as citizens subjected to biopower, recognising and resourcing this, through networks, even if this was impossible at times to change.

Family in China was never far from migrant workers' minds. They sent money home to help with the education of siblings, to help parents build a new house and to help with the health needs of older members.

The responsibility felt to family was strong, and workers talked of the pressure to be seen to be successful. This meant that even if they were in regular telephone contact, they did not reveal the hardships they lived under. Once migrants had children in the UK, their thoughts about returning home and family allegiances shifted. Family ties provided workers with a way of resisting the Chinese nation-state. For those families who had more than one child in the UK, returning home became an impossible goal as they would never be able to pay the 'one child' tax that would be due on their return.

> I still owe my friends and family money – now it becomes more difficult to pay them back as I have kids (3).... If I go back with 3 kids and no job I do not know when I can pay them back. I would have to pay a fine for more than one kid ... if you do not pay them in China then everyday they will come back to your house and ask for money. There is no way I can live in China.
>
> (Ling)

Overall, family networks both sustained and pressurised migrant workers. Every decision they made about moving, working or staying was influenced by their ties and obligations to family. There were no workers in our study whose experiences were not intricately tied up with family networks.

Travel networks

Migrant workers from China to the UK could only succeed if they tapped into and paid the extensive network of agents, guides and brokers who found them travel routes, provided them with the necessary documents and gave advice about what to do on arrival. Family and friends paid this once travellers had arrived in the UK. After this, workers owed the money to family, the services of the travel facilitators having ended (Pieke, 2010; Minghuan, 2010).

Until relatively recently, Chinese migrants used family and networks of contacts from their local area to travel and find work overseas. However, as Minghuan (2011) notes, it is now a market-driven practice with the introduction of brokerage fees, requiring money to buy every step of emigration. She suggests the 'big snakeheads' may hold multiple nationalities and have a legal status outside China. With large amounts of money at their disposal, snakeheads provide services to potential migrants by linking China with their destination country through the organisation of transnational networks, taking care of documents or facilities for clients and even bribing officials in China and other countries where necessary. Local agents are at the bottom of the hierarchy, operating on an individual basis, with connections to authorised agents and the snakeheads who pay them a commission for recruiting potential migrants. For our migrants, these local, unauthorised agents were sometimes friends of the family, or local people, known to have successfully secured emigration for others. The travel facilitator network is an explicit manifestation of biopower – workers are required to use it for protection, yet their labour (affective and physical) entraps individuals and families into a precarious network.

Most journeys to the UK involved workers being smuggled by chains of travel facilitators or snakeheads across several national borders, reflecting accounts given elsewhere (e.g. Pieke, 2010). Travellers were frequently held up in the middle of their journeys and prevented from leaving a house or talking to people. The majority of people we spoke to were frightened at some point on the journey. These routes usually involved using real or false documentation on early stages of the journey. If the last leg was to be completed by plane or ferry, travellers were instructed to destroy documentation before landing, ensuring that on arrival to the UK they held no means of identification. They were advised (or understood from others) that on arrival they should claim asylum. Most did this and after a short period of detention were released, sometimes with the instruction to report to a police station regularly. Relationships with the authorities relied upon the efficacy of the information network – the collaboration within the multitude. Xiao Hai had been trained to answer questions at immigration.

> [Immigration officers] asked me a lot of things like what school I enrolled at and what course, and I could answer correctly. We were trained for a whole month. The snakeheads were very professional as they even got their own teachers to tell you how to cope with the situations, answer specific questions, a list of questions that would come – really professional. If you could not pass the training they wouldn't let you go. The teachers would give you a final test.

In this account, Xiao is utilising knowledge transmitted through networks to hone her 'story'. A different pattern of travel involved several legs to the journey, with stays, being harboured, sometimes for several weeks or months in one country, usually in a house of other travelling migrants, before moving on to another. For some, the journey was so complicated it was difficult to remember all the details – indeed, some people did not know where they were at some stages, even which country they were in. One described the journey facilitated at each stage by a different agent, guide or harbourer.

> We went by a lot of countries. We went by Moscow, Ukraine, Czech Republic, Germany, Belgium then finally UK. We travelled by plane, ship and walking during the journey. We took a plane to Moscow. I had my passport but when I got to Moscow the snakeheads took it away. Since then I have had no passport, not even a fake one. And carried on from there. We walked to Ukraine. Sometimes we took a bus, sometimes we walked but sometimes we climbed up a mountain. From Belgium we went to London by the ship. In the journey we stayed a while in different places. For example, we stayed in Germany for a few days and we stayed in another place for a month. They just told us to wait there and they would have to plan a good route. We had to stay with a lot of people together in a house. They did let us out sometimes but it rarely happened. In most cases it was impossible for them to let us out. Sometimes we had to leave the next day, sometimes we had to wait another month. It was dangerous but I had no other choice. I knew it was going to be dangerous. When I got off the ship [in the UK] ... the police caught us, took fingerprints from us and notes. They put us in a hotel but we escaped in the night. I don't know how they knew but the snakeheads were there to pick us up after the hotel.

Information flows and contacts between snakeheads are clearly evident here, although the role of travel facilitators is nuanced. Gao (2010) suggests some differentiation in terms – for example, the term 'smugglers' was never used by respondents, who referred to facilitators, agents or 'snakeheads', constituting a network that is established in various countries and includes some form of cooperation. They operate in pyramid-like structures with vertical hierarchy drawing on solidarity networks, are extremely well organised and are established on sound structures involving recruiters, gang leaders, harbourers and guides. This transnational form of empire enables the passage of workers while allowing workers to resist national employment difficulties back in China: deterritorialised (across different settings) but present in the linkages.

For the minority, authorised routes of entry were found. Authorised routes to the UK involved the issuing of work permits and visas by an agency. Three of our sample all had work permits of between 1 and 5 years. Two participants travelled on six-month business visitor visas, which they overstayed, rendering their status irregular thereon. The rest of the participants entered the UK as undocumented and unauthorised migrants, usually claiming asylum on entry (see also Bloch, Sager and Waite et al. in this volume for discussion of the relationship between labour exploitation and irregular migrant status).

Work networks

Once in the UK, the Chinese migrant workers were quickly inserted into the Chinese economy, informally and regardless of work permits. For travellers who had no friends or family in the UK, their strategy was to find a Chinese person who then invariably pointed them to other Chinese people who would be able to get them work. The manual work undertaken by participants in the study was predominantly in the hospitality sector – restaurants and takeaways. Workers started in the lowest-paid, hardest physical jobs. Through discussions with friends they got to hear about possibilities for other work and higher pay. One describes finding out about her low salary.

> I was paid 160 pounds per week. At that time I had no idea whether 160 was considered high pay. All I thought of was earn as much money as I could. Later I got to know that it was very low pay...., another friend of mine also worked as a waitress, the pay was not much higher, 170 per week, so I decided to work as a waitress. Later I got more friends and I knew from them that it was not high pay.

Jobs were often changed on hearing about salary differentials. The networks of friends and relations and friends of friends not only helped people find out about jobs but also entailed moving from city to city for work – all facilitated by word of mouth. Some of these work moves included, for example:

> London–York–London–Reading–Stanley–Reading–Manchester
> London–Leeds–Doncaster–Newcastle–Manchester

The networks outlined above show how accounts of migrant labour can be theorised using the social theories of Hardt and Negri.

Conclusion

In global pancapitalism, individuals live in a society of control rather than a society of discipline. In the society of control, biopolitical power comprises the whole of society; it produces the social body and our individual bodies. Networks in the data gathered offered protection at times but risk at others. The accounts show biopolitical power and affective labour as workers manage complex networks of travel, work and family, while engaging (here) in service work. The resistance potential of being a member of the multitude was framed by workers as enabling work and payment for families both proximal and distant. While Hardt and Negri are rather celebratory around networks, the work also shows the darker side of network participation. Here, sacrifices, distant families and precarious journeys render workers as vulnerable and life as less emancipatory. Protective forces enabled movement, finding work and existing often in the informal UK economy. Hardt and Negri's theorisation of empire and the multitude affords a rich, complicated lens with which to understand how hidden migrant workers view exploitation and opportunity.

Notes

1. The International Labour Organization defines forced labour as '[...] all work which is extracted from any person under the menace of any penalty for which the person has not offered himself voluntarily' (ILO, 1930).
2. Falun Gong or Falun Dafa (Great Law of the Falun) is a Chinese organisation based on traditional qi gong practices that was founded in 1992. The Chinese government's attempts to suppress the movement they see as a cult have resulted in the group becoming known among human rights groups.
3. Snakehead is the term often used for those who facilitated travel from China through different countries to the UK. While in the West the term has negative connotations, participants in the study appreciated the service given to enable them to move.
4. This is the unit of Chinese currency – Yuan Renminbi and at the time of writing equated to c. 13,000 thousand pounds for this journey.
5. Ellipsis refers to omitted sentences in accounts.

References

Bastia T and McGrath S (2011) Temporality, Migration and Unfree Labour: Migrant Garment Workers. *Manchester Papers in Political Economy*. eScholarID: 146037.

Gao Y (2010) Introduction. In Y. Gao (ed), *Concealed Chains: Labour Exploitation and Chinese Migrants in Europe*. Geneva: International Labour Office, 1–4.

Hardt M and Negri A (2000) *Empire*. Cambridge, MA: Harvard University Press

Hardt M and Negri A (2004) *Multitude: War and Democracy in the Age of Empire*. London: Penguin.

Hardt M and Negri A (2009) *Commonwealth*. Cambridge, MA: Harvard University Press.

Kagan C, Lo S, Mok L, Lawthom R, Sham S, Greenwood M. and Baines S (2011) *Experiences of Forced Labour among Chinese Migrant Workers.* Report to Joseph Rowntree Foundation: York Available at: (http://www.jrf.org.uk/sites/files/jrf/Chinese-migrants-forced-labour-full.pdf).

Lawthom R, Kagan C, Baines S, Lo S, Sham S, Mok L, Greenwood M and Gaule S (2013) Experiences of Forced Labour amongst Chinese Migrant Workers: Exploring the Context of Vulnerability and Protection. *International Journal of Work Organisation and Emotion* 5(3): 261–280.

Lewis H, Dwyer P, Hodkinson S and Waite L (2014) *Precarious Lives. Forced Labour, Exploitation and Asylum.* Bristol: Policy Press.

Minghuan, L. (2010) The Chinese in Europe: Population, Economy and Links with China in the Early 21st Century. Paper presented to *China in the World Conference*, 22–23 September Conference, Monash Prato Centre.

Mai N (2011) Tampering with the Sex of 'Angels': Migrant Male Minors and Young Adults Selling Sex in the EU. *Journal of Ethnic and Migration Studies* 3(8): 1237–1252.

Pieke F (2010) Migration Journeys and Working Conditions of Chinese Irregular Immigrants in the United Kingdom. In Y. Gao (ed), *Concealed Chains: Labour Exploitation and Chinese Migrants in Europe.* Geneva: International Labour Office, 139–168.

Piketty T (2014) *Capital in the 21st Century.* Cambridge, MA: Harvard University Press.

Skřivánková K (2010) *Between Decent Work and Forced Labour: Examining the Continuum of Exploitation.* JRF Programme Paper: Forced Labour. York: Joseph Rowntree Foundation.

Wilkinson R and Pickett K (2009) *The Spirit Level: Why More Equal Societies Almost Always Do Better.* York: Allen Lane.

13
The Working Lives of Undocumented Migrants: Social Capital, Individual Agency and Mobility

Alice Bloch, Leena Kumarappan and Sonia McKay

Undocumented migration has occupied a central place in the UK government's migration policy, one symbol being the Coalition government's controversial decision, in July 2013, to send white vans around the country carrying the slogan 'In the country illegally? Go home or face arrest'. Migrants generally, but those without documents in particular, are now demonised as the harbingers of all the ills that society faces, including rising and youth unemployment, a declining health service, a housing crisis and as the rationale for attacking welfare benefits. The Immigration Act 2014 increases the sanctions on employers who hire those without documents, by imprisonment or a fine of up to £20,000, while service providers, such as landlords, are also to be held culpable if they rent accommodation to an undocumented migrant. Yet all these measures are being taken in response to a matter about which little is actually known. Policymakers cannot provide statistical data showing how many undocumented migrants there are, where they come from or why they have migrated, with estimates varying widely between 300,000 and 850,000, and too little is known about their working and personal lives. UndocNet, our two-year study into undocumented migrants and their employers, has tried to cast a spotlight on some of these issues through a focus on three minority ethnic communities in London.

Research with undocumented migrants whose ethnicity makes them visibly different clearly illustrates a group of marginalised workers, most often located in precarious jobs, working long hours for low pay, with poor terms and conditions and little or nothing in the way of formal workers' rights. Job mobility is mainly characterised by horizontal movement between jobs within the ethnic enclave. Job search is most often through word-of-mouth informal contacts, resulting in ethnic clustering within workplaces and sectors. In short, undocumented migrants are thought for the most part to use their networks to find work within what are considered the more likely and safer spaces of ethnic enclave and ethnic minority workers niches (Cobb et al., 2009; Mackenzie and Forde, 2009; Nakhaie et al., 2009; Gomberg-Muñoz, 2010).

In this chapter, we draw on research data from an Economic and Social Research Council project[1] carried out between September 2011 and January 2014. The research involved qualitative interviews with 55 undocumented migrants and 24 employers from China, Bangladesh and Turkey (including Kurds from Turkey and Northern Cypriots) living in London. Among the undocumented migrants interviewed, 40 were male and 15 were female; 12 had entered clandestinely; 17 by using a visitor's visa; and 13 with false documents. Just two had applied for asylum on entry, while others had made asylum claims subsequent to entry, and in all 24 had been refused asylum and had remained in the UK clandestinely. The remainder (11) had entered either with student visas, business visas or transit visas. Here we focus on the working lives of undocumented migrants and in particular on the networks they utilise in their search for work; elsewhere we have written about the employer experiences (Bloch and McKay, 2015). We found that there was a reliance on social networks to obtain work, but these networks could bind individuals into low-paid and highly exploitative labour.

Sectors of work and terms and conditions

Undocumented migrants have different initial reasons for migration that include economic and livelihood opportunities, to seek asylum, family reunion, as an adventure and as a rite of passage (Hagan, 2008; Bloch et al., 2011; Schuster, 2011). Regardless of the initial migratory motive or motives, once in the country of migration undocumented migrants are excluded from statutory welfare provision. As a consequence, the imperative is to find work unless informal exchanges and/or support structures like family members or alternative forms of income, such as savings, are available. The need to find work often leads undocumented migrants, like many other new migrants, directly to social networks, comprised often of family members and friends or acquaintances from the same ethnic or linguistic group. For undocumented migrants, there is an additional issue of trust and these pre-established networks may be understood as more dependable (Ryan, 2008) or accessible, although always in a context where status and the risk of deportation produce mistrust. Locating work through social networks can result in workplaces that are ethnically homogenous (Waldinger and Lichter, 2003: 115). Our research found sectoral clustering and workplaces largely comprised of the same ethnic group. At the time of interview, 45 were working of which half were employed in either restaurants or take-away shops. Restaurants and take-away shops tended to be male-dominated workplaces. This was partly due to stereotypes about what constitutes a good worker and perceptions of the necessary attributes within certain environments (Anderson and Ruhs, 2010). Our analysis of the interviews with employers found racialised and gendered notions of workers and a clear preference for certain characteristics (Dyer et al., 2010; Bloch and McKay, 2015).

The other main sectors of employment were construction (seven interviewees), retail and services (five interviewees), manufacturing (four interviewees) and hair and beauty (three interviewees). Like restaurants and take-away shops, these sectors of employment are those associated most often with informality, low pay and poor terms and conditions of work (Burnett and Whyte, 2010; Lewis et al., 2014). Among our interviewees, conditions of work and pay were often expressed in relation to workers with a regular status. There was an understanding of their disadvantaged position relative to other workers, as a consequence of status. In the following quote, Qasim, a 63-year-old male from Bangladesh, who was working in a laundry that caters specifically for the Indian restaurant business, describes his experiences:

> [E]verybody treats us badly because we do not have papers. They pay us less, look for faults, and make sly comments. What can we do? We have to listen to these moans and complaints and just stay put.

Although undocumented migrants reported earning less than those with documents, there were some variations. However, for the most part there were established rates of pay for certain jobs in certain sectors and these rates were known and understood (Bloch and McKay, 2013), although they were generally set at below the national minimum wage and involved working hours generally above the 48 hours set under the Working Time Regulations (1998).

Within the restaurants employing Bangladeshi workers for unskilled kitchen work, rates of pay were lowest. Hanif, a 40-year-old from

Bangladesh, was earning just £90 a week for his work in an Indian restaurant kitchen though he had earned slightly more in previous jobs. Qasim reported earning £100 when working 'at the sink' and this went up to £200 when he moved to working as a tandoori chef. The pay in Chinese restaurants could be slightly better as Bobby's experiences, which we profile later, show. The use of social networks to find jobs meant that information about pay, employers and workplaces was exchanged and this in turn helped to regulate pay. In the next section we focus on networks in relation to job search among undocumented migrants.

Job search within the context of being an undocumented migrant

The academic literature focusing on ethnic enclaves – which are geographical clusters of people from the same ethnic group residentially and within workplaces (Portes, 1981) – emphasises the role of micro-social networks on arrival and prior to the development of wider and more diverse networks, or bridging capital, that allow for vertical mobility into secondary sector jobs, rather than horizontal movement between enclave jobs (Nee and Sanders, 2001; Lancee, 2012). Among our interviewees, these networks either existed or were quickly developed on arrival and provided information and advice on a range of issues relating to life in the UK, including employment. Network formation is affected by a number of factors including socio-economic status and English language (Gill and Bialski, 2011). However, among undocumented migrants, trust also impacts network formation because choosing the wrong network or confiding in the wrong people could result in deportation, and consequently there is little scope or desire to expand networks beyond the immediate social group based mostly on ethnicity but in some cases on a shared undocumented status (Ryan et al., 2008; Bloch et al., 2014). The narrow networks used in the search for work, alongside the limitations imposed by being undocumented, result in the replication of jobs and sectors, with little scope for movement into new work domains. Among our interviewees there were three main methods of job search: through informal networks of friends and acquaintances; through family members; and through job agencies.

Using networks of friendship and acquaintances

Interviewees were asked about how they had found their current and previous jobs, and among all three groups informal networks of people from the same ethnic group, region and even village dominated.

On arrival networks were not only UK-based; in some instances, people used their transnational connections, though over time, as they established contacts in the UK, those transnational networks were no longer needed. Jiang, from China, had used contacts passed on to him by his family when he rang to confirm he had arrived safely. Informal networks were seen by most as the best way to find work. First, friends do not have to be paid and, secondly, friends and the networks of other undocumented migrants and past employers who knew the situation could be trusted. Having networks was therefore important as the following explanation by Bik, a 23-year-old woman from China, who had worked in restaurants and take-away shops, explains by describing the process of finding work.

> My husband asked his friends to watch out for job vacancies for me and eventually they found the job for me. That friend actually got the information about that vacancy through their friends. So this is rather like a chain reaction. The vacancy was passed on from one person to the next, until eventually I got the job. This for us is a common way to locate job vacancies.

New arrivals found help among those who had been in the UK longer. Hanif, a 40-year-old man from Bangladesh, said that he found work in Britain after two weeks because, 'Someone from my village helped me get it' (see also Park Chapter 9, this volume, for discussion of social networks for accessing work among Bangladeshi fruit vendors in Paris). Fung, a 25-year-old woman from China, who had worked in take-away shops and restaurants, reported a similar experience, saying she found work 'through friends and *tong-xiang* [fellow country-people]'. Drawing on the network of people from the same village, region or country who had been in the UK longer seemed the normal approach on arrival.

Using informal networks meant that others, who were already trusted, gave potential workers a recommendation. This informal network of references and trust was something generally valued by workers and employers alike. In the following quote, Fung, from China, who had found work in restaurants previously through friends, talks from the worker perspective; employers also highlighted the importance of personal references (Bloch and McKay, 2015).

> When introducing you to the [potential] employer, your friend may have already told them something about you. So when you make the call, the boss would know who you are and if you are experienced or not.

Trust of informal networks in the ethnic enclave labour market is bi-directional. Employers benefit from gaining access to a flexible labour force and a pool of available workers and value the knowledge of workers prior to taking them, which, from their perspective, can reduce the risks that they may otherwise face through employing those without documents, while also providing them with workers who have been vouched for (Waldinger and Lichter, 2003; Jones et al., 2006; Bloch and McKay, 2015). Workers are able to tap into these networks to find jobs and employers that are likely to offer them work. Thus networks act as a form of social capital for both groups. More than this, they provide relatively 'safe' channels to work, in contexts where their undocumented status is acknowledged (even if not referred to) and the risks that are taken are understood.

The fear of deportation, which results in a loss of any gains the migrant might have hoped to obtain through migration, dominates over all other factors in relation to work and social life. Thus work that is underpaid and exploitative is balanced against risks. However, this context also keeps workers located within narrow sectors of work from which only a small minority appear able to move by using constructed documents, being willing to take risks and having language and other skills necessary to enter the more formal parts of the economy (Bloch, 2013). It thus may offer short-term advantage but longer-term disadvantage. While the benefits of these networks were evident, there was also a sense among a minority that they could be problematic and so were not the ideal way to find work. Naser, for example, a 30-year-old man from Bangladesh, highlights the possible problems of using relatives and friends for job search in the following quote.

> It is best for friends and relatives not to organise work for people like us. This is because if there is any trouble then they could be accused of setting us up if we get caught, etc. If anything went wrong, then friends and relatives would get the blame. If you go through an agency then you are knowingly going and the agency also knows.

Family support in locating jobs

Despite views of some, like Naser quoted above, a minority of our interviewees had found their first job (and subsequent jobs) through their family networks. Having relatives was seen, in some cases, to be a good route into a job. As Hasan a 34-year-old Turkish man observes, 'you can find a job easily when you have relatives here' even if it could put a strain on relationships due to what were considered unrealistic expectations and a sense of obligation. However, for others, family employment offered a job, but not one that was unproblematic. Ferhat, also from Turkey, had been in the UK since he was 23, which was almost 10 years before the time of his interview. On arrival he started working as a mechanic in his cousin's garage, where he also lives. He works six days a week for between 60 and 70 hours earning £300; Sunday was his day off.

> My cousin already had the shop when I came. It was kind of obligatory for me to work with him. My cousin often goes on long holidays, up to 6–8 weeks, and I manage the whole shop on my own. He thinks I cannot leave him, as I cannot find a job without papers. I am also very sentimental about family relations. He also misuses this.

While for Ferhat, working at his cousin's business provided a living, he desperately wanted to leave and described himself as 'living in an open prison', trapped by his circumstances, including the political landscape, hostility to foreigners as well as obligations of family ties (Ambrosini, 2012; Barrientos et al., 2013; Délanoand Nienass, 2014; Morgan and Olsen, 2014).

Job search through job agencies

Not all had used networks of friends or family. Among Chinese interviewees, in particular, a minority had used 'middle-men' or job agents. These agents advertise their services in newspapers and for a fee will put people in touch with potential employers. According to Fang, a 40-year-old woman from China, who paid £300 to a middle-man to find her first job in a restaurant, this was one of the ways to find work among that ethnic group. Using agents did not always result in a job and tended to be used by those without established networks and who had more limited choices. While for some the outcome was a job, for others the experience was not positive and did not lead to work. Chao, who was 46 and from China, tried to find work through an agent. He describes his experiences thus.

> It was difficult for me to find work. I had no network who could give me real help; what hurts me most is that being Chinese myself, I was cheated by my own people; I was deceived by a fellow-countryman. All this was because someone had suggested that I should contact a job-agent to find work. I found a *zhongjie* [middleman] and I asked him to help me find work. He told me to make a payment of £100

into his bank account and I did. You know, I didn't realize that was a scam. I paid in £100 to his bank account and went straight to the restaurant with the address he gave me. I met the boss but the boss said he didn't need anyone; he said the job-agent had already sent another person there earlier and the vacancy was filled. I was furious.

Some Bangladeshi undocumented migrants had also found work by paying job agencies. These agencies were also able to provide constructed documents that demonstrated a national insurance number (official evidence of a right to work in the UK), and for those who could not find work this could be invaluable.

Job searches were fluid and changeable depending on circumstances. Most of those who had obtained work through agents or agencies had used them as new arrivals prior to developing networks. Jian, a 32-year-old man from China, explains how things had changed for him over time.

> I have got quite a few friends who had been working on building sites already, they sort of knew where might need new workers. I didn't need to pay anyone for this one. Over the years since I came here, I have got to know a lot more people working on building sites. So I have got a network of people who all work in this [sector]; we just recommend work to each other.

Cheung, who was 48 and from China, had been in the UK for three years and found his first job through agents but no longer required their assistance, due to the formation of home country networks, as he describes below.

> When I first came I didn't know how things go. I was new and there were lots of things I didn't know. But I won't go through the middleman anymore. After all these years I have met some *laoxiang* [people from the same region] and we help each other finding work.

A case study: The working life of an undocumented migrant in Britain

Bobby is from China and came to Britain at the age of 19, with the help of snakeheads, 'to work to earn some money'. At the time of his interview, he had been in Britain for 12 years working in different restaurants and take-away shops. He has managed to obtain some skills and achieve some pay rises, though pay cuts too, and had moved between jobs and locations when it made sense for him. Without family ties he has been geographically mobile. Most of his jobs, though not all, had been found through social networks.

On arrival he worked as a kitchen porter at a restaurant in a small town in Yorkshire earning £150 per week; meals and board were included. A charge for finding the job was built-in to the fee paid to the snakeheads to make his journey to the UK, and he remained there for one year during which time he learned how to stir fry food. He managed to use his new skills at his second job, for which his boss' friend, who was looking for workers, recruited him. In the second job he earned £180 per week plus around £20 in tips, using his new skills by stir frying rice and noodles. Bobby stayed for eight months and moved when the chef at his first restaurant in Yorkshire opened a business in the east Midlands and recruited him to chop meats. For Bobby this was a promotion as there were kitchen porters and stir fryers working below him. Moreover, the pay was better too, £280 a week, and he remained there for more than five years until the business began to decline. To find his next job, Bobby used a middleman that had advertised in a Chinese-language newspaper and paid £100 for the job recommendation. Bobby describes:

> When the business was beginning to show signs of slowing down, he [the boss] told me to look for another job. I then began to pay attention to newspaper adverts and later found some telephones to contact. Before too long I made my way to London... to meet that *zhongjie* [middleman].

Through the middleman Bobby found a job in the kitchen of a restaurant, stir-frying rice and noodles for £250 per week. He stayed there for around eight months and left because the atmosphere at work was not good and the boss was verbally abusive, as he describes below.

> Most of the new recruits didn't stay for too long. At one point the restaurant had to replace one newcomer per week; the boss was rather loud mouthed. New recruits couldn't stand the way s/he shouted at people. I found it hard to take it too, but I knew I had to put up with it, because I needed the job, because I had no residential status.

The next job was at a Vietnamese-owned fish and chip shop, through referral from a chain of friends, in the North West. The job was supposed to be that of a chef and he was paid £300 a week, but he left after only a month:

> The reason I left there because earlier they had said that they would hire me as a chef, but actually apart from me, there was only another worker in the kitchen, a *daza* worker [kitchen labourer].... We had to get up at 7 O'clock in the morning to get things done and work through the day until 12 O'clock. It really was a back-breaking job.

Bobby's next job was stir-frying rice and noodles at £280 per week at a restaurant in London. He found the job through the *Wangniao* (Bird) web site and stayed for nearly a year. The boss questioned if he had residential status but still took him on without papers. According to Bobby, the boss said:

> if you didn't have residential status, you'd get a lower wage...They paid me £280 [a week]. I would have gotten £320 had I got status.

It was a fairly large restaurant with five kitchen workers, of which Bobby and the kitchen porter were undocumented. There was a degree of camaraderie between Bobby and the other undocumented migrant due to status.

At the time of the interview Bobby had moved to a different restaurant in London at a job found through a friend who knew of the vacancy. He was earning £280 a week stir-frying rice and noodles, but described the job as 'not stable at all'. However, Bobby has never been out of work and has managed to move seamlessly between jobs using different job search methods. He was, however, very conscious of the ways in which his status affected his job search and his work.

> If you had residential status, you can find a job more easily, and you may even find a job that you really like doing. But without status, even if you may find work without a lot of difficulty, it's inevitably always the kind of job that you didn't want to do, had you had an alternative.

Nevertheless, Bobby in some ways represents a positive outcome for an undocumented migrant. He has acquired new skills, managed to increase his pay and control his labour and geographical mobility through being pro-active in the use of social networks but also websites and a middleman when needed. He was aware of the limitations of his status, noting the glass ceiling, which according to him means that 'I may work in a restaurant, but I can't be the chef'.

Conclusion

In this chapter we have shown that undocumented migrants may cluster in a few sectors; that their work may be mostly for co-ethnic employers; and that most, though not all jobs, were found through informal social networks. Using networks replicated jobs and sectors and was an effective strategy for both workers and employers. Occasionally middlemen, websites, community-language newspapers and agencies were used to find work. Jobs were often short-term and movement between jobs was mainly horizontal, but for some, such as Bobby, there had been an element of skills' acquisition and slight vertical mobility but with a glass ceiling. The disparity between workers with and without documents, in terms of wages and conditions, as a consequence of status, was keenly felt, understood but accepted. The lack of documents can and does leave many in work that is precarious, unable to contest their circumstances, but this alone does not convey the complete experiences of working life for those without documents. As we have tried to show there are counter-balancing circumstances allowing workers' agency to be exercised to mitigate the otherwise harsh environment which immigration law imposes.

Note

1. Undocumented Migrants, Ethnic Enclaves and Networks: Opportunities, traps or class-based constructs? Research funded by the Economic and Social Research Council (ES/I037490/2).

References

Ambrosini M (2012) Surviving Underground: Irregular Migrants, Italian Families, Invisible Welfare. *International Journal of Social Welfare* 21: 361–371.

Anderson B and Ruhs M (2010) Migrant Workers: Who Needs Them? A Framework for the Analysis of Staff Shortages, Immigration, and Public Policy. In M. Ruhs and B. Anderson (eds), *Who Needs Migrant Workers?: Labour Shortages, Immigration, and Public Policy*. Oxford: Oxford University Press, 15–52.

Barrientos S, Kothari U and Phillips N (2013) Dynamics of Unfree Labour in the Contemporary Global Economy. *Journal of Development Studies* 49(8): 1037–1041.

Bloch A (2013) The Labour Market Experiences and Strategies of Young Undocumented Migrants. *Work, Employment and Society* 27(2): 272–287.

Bloch A, Sigona N and Zetter R (2011) Migration Routes and Strategies of Young Undocumented Migrants in England: A Qualitative Perspective. *Ethnic and Racial Studies* 34(8): 1286–302.

Bloch A, Sigona N and Zetter R (2014) *Sans Papiers: The Social and Economic Lives of Undocumented Migrants in the UK.* London: Pluto Press.

Bloch A and McKay S (2013) Hidden Dishes – How Food Gets on to Our Plates: Undocumented Migrants and the Restaurant and Takeaway Sector. *Journal of Workplace Rights* 17(1): 69–91.

Bloch A and McKay S (2015) Employment, Social Networks and Undocumented Migrants: The Employer Perspective. *Sociology* 49(1): 38–55.

Burnett J and Whyte D (2010) *The Wages of Fear: Risk, Safety and Undocumented Work.* Liverpool: University of Liverpool.

Cobb CL, King MC and Rodriguez L (2009) Betwixt and Between: The Spectrum of Formality Revealed in the Labour Market Experiences of Mexican Migrant Workers in the United States. *Review of Radical Political Economics* 41: 365–371.

Délano A and Nienass B (2014) Invisible Victims: Undocumented Migrants and the Aftermath of September 11. *Politics & Society* 42(3): 399–421.

Dyer S, McDowell L, and Batnitzky A (2010) The Impact of Migration on the Gendering of Service Work: The Case of a West London Hotel. *Work, Employment and Society* 17(6): 635–657.

Gill N and Bialski P (2011) New Friends in New Places: Network Formation during the Migration Process among Poles in the UK. *Geoforum* 42: 241–249.

Gomberg-Muñoz R (2010) Willing to Work: Agency and Vulnerability in an Undocumented Immigrant Network. *American Anthropologist* 112: 295–307.

Hagan J (2008) *The Migration Miracle: Faith, Hope and Meaning of the Undocumented Journey.* Cambridge, London: Harvard University Press.

Jones T, Ram M and Edwards P (2006) Ethnic Minority Business and the Employment of Illegal Immigrants. *Entrepreneurship and Regional Development: An International Journal* 18(2): 133–150.

Lancee B (2012) The Economic Returns of Bonding and Bridging Social Capital for Immigrant Men in Germany. *Ethnic and Racial Studies* 34(4): 664–683.

Lewis H, Dwyer P, Hodkinson S and Waite L (2014) Hyper-Precarious Lives: Migrants, Work and Forced Labour in the Global North. *Progress in Human Geography* doi: 10.1177/0309132514548303.

MacKenzie R and Forde C (2009) The Rhetoric of the 'Good Worker' versus the Realities of Employers' Use and the Experiences of Migrant Workers. *Work, Employment and Society* 23(1): 142–159.

Morgan J and Olsen W (2014) Forced and Unfree Labour: An Analysis. *International Critical Thought* 4(1): 21–37.

Nakhaie R, Lin X and Guan J (2009) Social Capital and the Myth of Minority Self-Employment: Evidence from Canada. *Journal of Ethnic and Migration Studies* 35(4): 625–644.

Portes A (1981) Modes of Structural Incorporation and Present Theories of Labour Immigration. In M. Kritz, CB. Kelly and SM. Tomasi (eds), *Global Trends in Migration: Theory and Research on International Population Movements.* Staten Island, New York: Centre for Migration Studies, 279–297.

Nee V and Sanders J (2001) Understanding the Diversity of Immigrant Incorporation: A Forms-of-Capital Model. *Ethnic and Racial Studies* 24(3): 386–411.

Ryan L, Sales R, Tilki M and Siarra B (2008) Social Networks, Social Support and Social Capital: The Experiences of Recent Polish Migrants. *Sociology* 42(4): 672–690.

Schuster L (2011) Turning Refugees into 'Illegal Migrants': Afghan Asylum Seekers in Europe. *Ethnic and Racial Studies* 34(8): 1392–407.

Waldinger R and Lichter M (2003) *How the Other Half Works: Immigration and the Social Organisation of Labour* Berkeley. California: University of California Press.

14
Slavery in the Twenty-First Century: A Review of Domestic Work in the UK

Ismail Idowu Salih

Introduction

Domestic work is difficult to define because it includes a range of household activities (ILO, 1990). Nevertheless, domestic workers have been referred to as 'wage earners working in a private household under whatever method and period of remuneration, who may be employed by one or several employers' (ILO, 1951: no page number). This definition differentiates those who perform their own family tasks from those who perform other people's chores for a fee. Thus, domestic workers may include nannies, cleaners, chauffeurs, gardeners, cooks and those carrying out personal care in the households (UKBA, 2011).

There has been an increase in the call for domestic work to be regulated and standardised and for domestic workers' rights to be properly enshrined in law (HRW, 2014; ILO, 2014) to improve their visibility to the public and alleviate their problems. Central to the issues of domestic workers is the argument that they are a vulnerable group (Salih, 2013) performing precarious work (Sargeant, 2014) in 'hidden' or 'private' workplaces (Lutz, 2008). While both migrants and non-migrants workers in the private and diplomatic households are prone to having their workplace entitlement denied, immigration constraints could worsen the experience of the migrant workers (Iredale et al., 2003). The link between immigration and employment is such that workers' immigration status will determine their employment- and non-employment-related rights (Spencer and Pobjoy, 2012), reduce their job preferences, restrict their access to justice and exclude them from the entitlement to public funds in the case of loss of job (Rechel et al., 2011).

Further, the individual's nationality could determine the chance s/he would take on precarious employment (Wills et al., 2008) and/or would be vulnerable to exploitation and abuses (Fevre et al., 2009). Thus, immigration status and nationality remain a key factor of vulnerability in the labour market.

In most countries, including the UK, different groups of migrant workers do not enjoy the same rights and protection in the host country (Anderson, 2012). There is evidence to suggest that those who are engaged in households are often subjected to more stringent, limiting or invasive visa regulations than other migrant workers (Cox, 2012). Overseas domestic workers (ODW) who are engaged in private and diplomatic households are often excluded from the host country's national laws that protect workers (ILO, 2013) and are therefore among the most vulnerable to exploitation and abuses (Evans et al., 2005; D'Souza, 2010).

On 6 April 2012, the Home Office introduced a new visa regime for the ODW. Unlike the pre-6 April 2012 ODW visa ('old visa') that was renewable in the UK and allowed a change of employers, the new ODW visa restricts the maximum length of stay of newly admitted ODWs to six months, gives no right of renewal and prevents the bearers from changing employers (Gower, 2012). These restrictions put the ODWs at the mercy of their employers, diminish their visibility to the public and reduce their ability to protect themselves, thereby promoting domestic servitude and exploitation that are equivalent to modern-day slavery (Kalayaan, 2014). Further, irrespective of the reason, any ODW who refused to leave the UK at the termination of his/her job, or at the expiration of the visa, would be treated as an over-stayer in contravention of the immigration law.[1] Further to the possible criminal sanction for over-staying visa, under the doctrine of illegality,[2] which is followed by the UK courts, anyone who is employed without the right to work in the UK forfeits the right to challenge the employer(s) under the contract.

Most countries, including the UK, do not share the ILO interpretation that Article 24 of the Universal Declaration of Human Rights (1948) recognises that everyone has the right to rest and leisure, including reasonable limitation of working hours and periodic holidays with pay and that signatory states are obliged to give migrant workers the same employment rights as their national/native workers. Further to some differences in the employment rights of migrants and non-migrants, most national laws continue to differentiate between workers who are documented from those who are undocumented. Undocumented migrants who take on domestic work role in the UK are more likely to be exposed to abuses and exploitation than those who are documented. The restrictions imposed on the newly admitted ODWs by the current ODW visa potentially puts them in a highly precarious immigration status that could easily change from being legal to being undocumented (Clark and Kumarappan, 2012).

In addition, the UK law on unfair dismissal does not support the plight of domestic workers. Within Section 108 of the Employment Rights Act 1996, a qualifying period of 2 years of continuous service is required to bring an unfair dismissal claim against the employer. This requirement cannot be met by the newly admitted ODWs, who are allowed a maximum of 6 months in the UK. Furthermore, Section 51 of the Health and Safety at Work Act 1974 excludes ODWs from health and safety protections. While, Regulation 2 (2) of the National Minimum Wage Regulation 1999 allows the ODWs to be denied the minimum wage if the employer could argue that they have been treated as family member. Thus, it may be argued, what makes domestic workers' experience unique in the labour market is the lack of legal protection.[3]

This chapter examines the reasons for domestic workers' invisibility, attempts to contextualise domestic workers' problems and concludes that in addition to the UK's immigration and employment law, and the health and safety regime that do not provide any or adequate protection for the workers, employers are either unaware of domestic workers' enforceable rights (however limited) or are more comfortable ignoring them.

Context

International and national policies on domestic workers

The private nature of the households contributes to the workers' invisibility to the public (ILO, 2013; UNDP, 2014) and hinders the regulation of domestic work (Gower, 2012). Globalisation and cross-border migration have changed the dynamics of the household workforce in the developed world in particular (Salih, 2013). In addition to indigenous workers, migrants, especially women (ILO, 2010) from the developing countries, are taking on the role of domestic workers in European households. ODW are employed mainly as live-in workers to sort out care deficit (Ehrenreich and Hochschild, 2003), and they do the 'dirty work', which the families are unable/unwilling to do themselves (Anderson, 2000).

Over the years, one aspect of domestic work that has remained unchanged is the employment rights and legal protection of the workers

(Davidoff, 1974). Modern-day domestic workers are no better than their counterparts in the early nineteenth-century England, who were often undervalued, disrespected, abused and exploited (Delap, 2011). Immigration constraints also complicate the experience of ODWs (Piper, 2005). In the UK, politics influences public perception of migrants (Jayaweera and Anderson, 2008). The UK immigration policy, which is elite-led (Statham et al., 2006; Mulvey, 2010), changes according to shifting political agendas of the ruling party. However, it appears that there is a cross-party preference for the admission of highly skilled migrants over low-skilled migrants (Devitt, 2012). The latter category, which includes domestic workers, is often not considered as essential to the economy. Not coincidentally, the plight of domestic workers is often considered less important by policymakers (Schwenken, 2005).

Domestic workers first gained international attention when the ILO (1936) voiced concern that the Convention (No. 52) adopted by the International Labour Conference (ILC) gives workers in manufacturing and a range of other industries the right to six days of paid leave but excludes domestic workers. More recently, in 2011, the 100th annual session of the ILC adopted Convention 189, a framework that is aimed at regulating domestic work worldwide, ensuring decent work for domestic workers, alleviating the workers' problems and providing them with better legal protection. The convention has been ratified by several countries, including Italy and Germany,[4] but the UK government has so far refused to implement it, thereby denying benefits of the framework to ODWs in the UK.

One of the reasons the UK government has refused to ratify ILO Convention 189 is the possible impact it may have on the UK health and safety law that currently excludes domestic workers from its protections. In the view of the government, the implementation of the convention 'would impose disproportionate burdens on businesses and raise issues of privacy [that] could have serious social consequences' (Ministry of Justice, 2014: 29). Nevertheless, a review of Convention 189 shows that signatory states are not obliged immediately to implement its Article 13, which relates to health and safety protection. The implementation of this aspect is expected to be incremental, and through consultation with relevant trade unions.

Notably, the UK government has consistently maintained that it 'supports the principles behind the convention' but 'it does not think that ratification of [it] is appropriate for the UK' (Ministry of Justice, 2014: 28), because domestic workers in the UK are well protected. However, the government stance appears to have ignored the fact that domestic workers are excluded from vital employment law protections such as the minimum wage. In *Nambalat v Taher & Anor: Udin v Pasha & Ors* [2012] EWCA Civ 1249, the Court of Appeal, in determining if a domestic worker has been treated as the employer's family member for the purpose of minimum wage exclusion, stated that the question is whether the employer shared 'any' activity with the worker. This narrow interpretation allows employers to get away without paying the minimum wage. While the recent Modern Day Slavery Act[5] that aims to deal robustly with traffickers and 'slave masters' is welcome, further amendments would have been necessary during the passage of the Bill to be able to protect domestic workers from servitude and modern-day slavery (Kalayaan, 2014).

Given that Italy and Germany are bound by the same EU health and safety law – Directive 89/391/EEC OSH 'Framework Directive' that binds the UK – and have had no problem in implementing the convention, the health and safety argument of the UK government appears weak. Ironically, the UK has previously been credited in a Human Rights Report for its immigration policy on ODWs (HRW, 2001: 39), but now it appears to have missed the opportunity to convince the world that it is committed to protecting the rights of vulnerable workers such as ODW.

Employee/employer relationship

Employment relationships in the UK are historically built on a master (employer) and servant (employee) relationship (Delap, 2011). The advancement in democratic organisations, the evolution of employment laws (Deakin and Morris, 2005) and the enactment of the Trade Union Act 1871 (34 & 35 Vict c 31) that legalised the trade union movement (Mill, 1871; Willman and Bryson, 2007) have helped in balancing the power between employers and employees, thereby improving the socio-economic conditions and employment rights of most workers in Britain (Marmot, 2004). Despite these improvements, because household workers were excluded from the vast majority of measures that protect other workers, employment relationships in the households have remained essentially unbalanced, with the employers retaining absolute or near absolute power over workers (Davidoff, 1974). The power imbalance between the employers of domestic workers and the workers is facilitated and/or precipitated by the UK government policy on domestic workers. A domestic worker position is weak because their employers often have no regard for their residual employment rights. Echoing the government turning a blind eye on what goes on in private households (Clark and Kumarappan, 2012), most employers of domestic workers in the UK do not see themselves as legal employers to the extent that the few employment rights that are available to the workers are conveniently ignored (Anderson, 2001). In some European countries like Italy and Spain, domestic workers are covered by collective agreements.[6] However, domestic work in the UK is not regulated and the workers are not covered under any form of collective agreement, leaving them vulnerable to non-favourable employment contracts.

ODWs in the UK are often not issued with any/or a correct employment contract or statement of terms and conditions.[7] Currently, most agreements between employers and ODWs tend to be verbal (Triandafyllidou, 2013). As a result, employers may arbitrarily change the terms of the agreement, and/or dismiss the worker without any warning and/or any benefit. While some domestic workers work part-time and do not live with their employers, many others are employed as live-in workers. The societal assumption that a unique employer–employee relationship operates in the households, such that live-in domestic workers are presumed as family members of their employers,[8] is highly problematic. There is evidence to suggest that the majority of ODW receive salaries that are well below the national minimum wage (Kalayaan, 2014). There is also evidence of wage theft[9] by bad employers.

The problems of ODWs range from exploitation to abuse and discrimination (ILO, 2013). Although men and women engage in domestic work, where men are domestic workers they normally have different, better-paid tasks, such as gardening or chauffeuring. Similarly, while men partake in household chores, there is evidence to suggest that women continue to do the larger proportion of it (Del Boca and Locatelli, 2008). Given pervasive gender divisions of labour, it is not surprising that the vast majority of domestic workers around the world are women (ILO, 2013).[10] This opens the debate whether the lack of legal protection for domestic workers could be argued as gender discrimination, at least on a moral ground. In *Onu v Akwiwu, Taiwo v Olaigbe* and another [2014] EWCA Civ 279, an attempt by some ODW to argue that the maltreatment of them by their employers constitute discrimination on nationality grounds was unsuccessful. The court held that their experience of discrimination has nothing to do with their nationality or immigration status but is purely a result of their vulnerability. This decision as it stands remains problematic because it is difficult to disassociate vulnerability and immigration status, as a person's nationality could determine his/her level of vulnerability in the labour market.

The invisibility of domestic workers

The invisibility of domestic workers is primarily to do with working behind closed doors, typically isolated from other workers, and often from any social networks, due to very long working hours. This invisibility is augmented by an indication that the job receives less priority from policymakers; those who perform it are often regarded by the public as unimportant, underrated and underappreciated (Cox, 1997); and very little or no attention is focused on their economic importance (Budlender, 2011). Consequently, the workers are often unnoticed (Blofield, 2008: 159). Domestic workers are not the only workers in precarious employment 'which gives rise to instability, lack of protection, insecurity, and social and economic vulnerability' (Tompa et al., 2007: 209). However, domestic workers, especially those from the 'developing countries', are more vulnerable in the labour market because of their inherent attributes, such as very poor socio-economic status, lack of opportunity in their homeland and immigration status in the host country (ILO, 2013). Further, the lack of or inadequate support from policymakers makes the plight of domestic workers different from those of other vulnerable workers and/or those in precarious employment generally (Fevre et al., 2009). The immigration status of domestic workers in the private households is different from the status of their counterparts in the diplomatic households in terms of duration, entitlement and restrictions.

While the ODW visa of those in the private household falls within the immigration rules,[11] the visas issued to those in the diplomatic households fall within the UK obligation under the Vienna Convention on Diplomatic Relations.[12] Further, whereas those in private households are allowed a maximum of 6 months stay and are unable to change employers in the UK, those in diplomatic households could stay up to 5 years, provided they remain employed by their sponsor or any other diplomat (Gower, 2012). However, common to the experiences of the ODWs in the private and diplomatic households is that of servitude, abuses and exploitation. A Kalayaan (2014) report on the impact of the current ODW visa has suggested that between April 2012 and April 2014 it registered a total of 402 domestic workers seeking the organisation's assistance. Although, only 102 of the registrants were on the new visa, while the remaining 300 were on the old visa, the complaints lodged by those on the new visa outnumbered the complaints of those on the old visa. Almost three-quarters of those on the new visa reported never being allowed out of the house unsupervised (71 per cent), compared to under half on the old visa (43 per cent). Further, 65 per cent of those on the new visa did not have their own rooms, shared a room with the children or slept in the kitchen or lounge, compared with 34 per cent of those on the old visa. Fifty-three per cent of those on the new visa worked more than 16 hours a day compared to 32 per cent of those on the old visa; 60 per cent of those on the new visa were paid less than £50 a week, compared with 36 per cent on the old visa.

The recognition that previous ILO conventions and recommendations[13] have failed to improve the working condition of domestic workers worldwide enhances the need to adopt ILO Convention 189. The unwillingness of the current government to extend health and safety laws to protect household workers and the drive towards reducing net migration continue to impact the experience of domestic workers in the UK. Notably, at the Labour Party conference in September 2013, the then Shadow Minister for Borders and Immigration, Chris Bryant promised that the Labour Party would re-instate the ODW visa to its pre-6th April 2012 quality if successful in the 2015 general election (Ramesh, 2013). The Labour Party introduced the old ODW visa as a concession in 1998 and further incorporated it into the immigration rules in 2000 (Gower, 2012). However, given the poor performance of the Labour Party in the May 2015 general election and the return of a Conservative majority government, the hope of having the ODW visa restored to its pre-2012 status remains highly unlikely in the near future.

Conclusion

Households as workplaces provide precarious jobs for vulnerable workers. Even though the majority of these workers are women, government policies that affect them are yet to take gender into consideration. Globalisation and cross-border migration have changed the structure of households' workforce in the UK and around the world. It is therefore the case that 'the plight of migrants is complicated by challenges that labour-based migration poses to policy-makers in the twenty-first century' (IOM, 2002: 2). Many consequently agree that in a civilised world, demographic, economic and security issues make the effective control of immigration quintessential. However, this chapter argues that UK government policies subject ODWs to precarious immigration statuses and strips them of the employment protections that are available to other workers. It is further suggested that this has significantly contributed to domestic workers' invisibility to the public, encouraged employers to exploit, abuse and subject them to servitude at a magnitude equivalent to modern-day slavery. This situation for domestic workers in the UK is incompatible with the UK's international obligation to protect workers, and falls short of the standards expected in a twenty-first-century democratic society. A simple removal of the clauses in the employment law that deny the minimum wage, working condition rights and health and safety protection to the ODWs, and a review of the current ODW visa that ties them to their employers, would make the workers more visible to the public, mitigate their vulnerability and protect them from modern-day slavery.

Notes

1. See the Immigration Act 1971 c77, Section 24(1)(b)(i).
2. This principle that applies to contract, tort and trust is an established defence in English law. In *Holman v Johnson* (1775) 1 Cowp 341, 343, Lord Mansfield CJ related that the doctrine is a public policy of *ex dolo malo non oritur actio* which means no court will lend its aid to a man who founds his cause of action upon an immoral or an illegal act.
3. This is why the issue of ODW visa has become the most contested issue within the debates on the 2014 Modern Slavery Bill.
4. The German government did not introduce any new measures to assist the country's domestic workers. The government only issued a statement confirming the implementation and a declaration that the existing German law is compatible with the convention. For more, see Schwenken (2013) *Speedy Latin America, Slow Europe? – Regional Implementation Processes of the ILO Convention on Decent Work for Domestic Workers*, Draft paper prepared for the United Nations Research Institute for Social Development Conference, 14–15 January 2013, Geneva: Switzerland.
5. See http://www.legislation.gov.uk/ukpga/2015/30/pdfs/ukpga_20150030_en .pdf.
6. ILO – *Domestic workers negotiate new collective agreements in Uruguay and Italy*, Document 02 May 2013.
7. Although employers do issue some form of contract to enable the worker to apply for ODW visa and in the case of those on the old visa, to enable them renew their visas, contracts submitted to the Home Office do not always represent the actual agreement between the parties. See *Taiwo v Olaigbe* [2013] ICR 770.
8. See, for instance, (a) Keklik, H.T (2006) '*As if she is family' the marginalisation of unpaid household workers in Turkey*, Gender and Development, 14(2); (b) Graunke, K.L (2003) *Just Like One of the Family: Domestic Violence Paradigms and Combating on-the-job Violence against Household Workers in the United States*, Michigan Journal of Gender and Law, 131 (2002–03).
9. The term 'wage theft' is commonly used in the US to mean an unauthorised deduction of wages. See United State Government Account Office (GAO), *Wage and Hour Division's Complaint Intake and Investigative Processes Leave Low Wage Workers Vulnerable to Wage Theft*, Testimony before the Committee on Education and Labour, House of Representatives, USA: Department of Labour 2009.

10. And many of course are children: see Craig 2009.
11. https://www.gov.uk/government/collections/immigration-rules last accessed 2 February 2015.
12. United Nations, Treaty Series, vol. 500, p. 95.
13. See ILO – *Relevant ILO Instruments on Domestic Work* – Key ILO instruments, Document 11 December 2009.

References

Anderson B (2000) *Doing the Dirty Work? The Global Politics of Domestic Labour.* London: Zed Books.

Anderson B (2001) Why Madam Has so Many Bathrobes? Demography and Demand for Migrants in the EU. *Journal of Economic and Social Geography* 92(4): 18–26.

Anderson B (2012) Where's the Harm in That? Immigration Enforcement, Trafficking, and the Protection of Migrants' Rights. *American Behavioral Scientist* 56(9): 1241–1257.

Budlender D (2011) *Measuring the Economic and Social Value of Domestic Work: Conceptual and Methodological Framework. Conditions of Work and Employment Series No. 30.* Geneva: ILO.

Clark N and Kumarappan L (2012) *Turning a Blind Eye: The British State and Migrant Domestic Workers' Employment Rights.* London: Working Lives research Institute.

Cox R (2007) The AU Pair Body: Sex Object, Sister or Student? *European Journal of Women's Studies* 14(3): 281–296.

Cox R (2012) Gendered Work and Migration Regimes. In Ragnhild Aslaug Sollund (ed), *Transnational Migration, Gender and Rights (Advances in Ecopolitics)* 10: 33–52.

Craig G (2009) *Child Slavery Now*, Bristol: Policy Press.

D'Souza A (2010) *Moving towards Decent Work for Domestic Workers: An Overview of the ILO's Work.* ILO Bureau for Gender Equality Working Paper 2, Geneva: ILO.

Davidoff L (1974) Mastered for Life: Servant and Wife in Victorian and Edwardian England. *Journal of Economic and Social History* 7(4): 406–28.

Deakin S and Morris G (2005) *Labour Law.* Oxford: Hart.

Del Boca D and Locatelli M (2008) Motherhood and Participation. In D. Del Boca and C. Wetzels (eds), *Social Policies, Labour Markets and Motherhood.* Cambridge University Press, 155–180.

Delap L (2011) *Knowing Their Place: Domestic Service in Twentieth-Century Britain*, Oxford: Oxford University Press.

Devitt C (2012) *Labour Migration Governance in Contemporary Europe – The UK case.* Country Report for the LAB-MIG-GOV Project 'Which labour migration governance for a more dynamic and inclusive Europe?' FIERI Working Paper.

Ehrenreich B and Hochschild AR (eds) (2003) *Global Women: Nannies, Maids and Sex Workers in the New Economy.* London: Granta.

Evans Y, Herbert J, Datta D, May J, McIlwaine C and Wills J (2005) *Making the City Work: Low Paid Employment in London.* Queen Mary University of London. A November 2005 Report.

Fevre R, Nichols T, Prior G and Rutherford I (2009) *Fair Treatment at Work Report: Findings from the 2008 Survey*, Employment Relations Research Report No. 103, London: Department for Business Innovation and Skills.

Gower M (2012) *Immigration: Migrant Domestic Workers*, Commons Library Standard Note, Standard notes SN04786.

Gower M and Hawkins O (2013) *Immigration and Asylum Policy: Government Plans and Progress Made*. House of Commons Library Standard Note (SN05829).

Home Office (2012) *Damian Green's Speech on Making Immigration Work for Britain*, Speech delivered at the Policy Exchange on Thursday 2 February 2012.

Human Rights Watch (2001) *Hidden in the Home: Abuse of Domestic Workers with Special Visas in the United States*, June 2001, 13(2G).

Human Rights Watch (2014) *Hidden Away Abuses against Migrant Domestic Workers in the UK*. London: Human Rights Watch.

ILO (1936) *Resolution Concerning Holidays with Pay for Domestic Servants, Submitted by the Committee on Holidays with Pay*, International Labour Conference, 20th Session (Geneva, 4–24 June 1936).

ILO (1951) *The Status and Conditions of Employment of Domestic Workers*, Meeting of Experts, Geneva, 2–6 July 1951, Report 3, Document MDW/8.

ILO (1970) *The Employment and Conditions of Domestic Workers in Private Households: An ILO Survey*, International Labour Review, October 1970, 391–401.

ILO (1990) *International Standard Classification of Occupations*, Group 9131, ISCO-88, Geneva: ILO 1990.

ILO (2010) *Decent Work for Domestic Workers*, ILC 99th Session, Report IV (1). Geneva: ILO 2010.

ILO (2013) *Domestic Workers across the World: Global and Regional Statistics and the Extent of Legal Protection/International Labour Office*. Geneva: ILO 2013.

ILO (2013) *Domestic Workers Negotiate New Collective Agreements in Uruguay and Italy*, Document 02 May 2013.

ILO (2011) (NORMLEX): *Ratifications of C189 – Domestic Workers Convention, 2011* (No. 189).

IOM (2002) *Trends in International Migration, Information Documents*, Labour Migration, Eighty-Fourth Session, MC/INF/256, 31 October 2002.

Iredale R, Guo F and Lazario S (eds) (2003) *Return Migration in the Asia Pacific*. Cheltenham, UK: Edward Elgar.

Jayaweera J and Anderson B (2008) *Migrant Workers and Vulnerable Employment: An Analysis of Existing Data*. London: TUC Commission on Vulnerable Employment (CoVE).

Kalayaan (2014) *Still Enslaved: The Migrant Domestic Workers Who Are Trapped by the Immigration Rules*, April 2014.

Lutz H (2008) *When Home Becomes a Workplace: Domestic Work as an Ordinary Job in Germany?* In Helma Lutz (ed), *Migration and Domestic Work: A European Perspective on a Global Theme*. Aldershot: Ashgate, 43–60.

Marmot M (2004) *The Status Syndrome: How Social Standing Affects Our Health and Longevity*. New York: Times Books.

Mill JS (1871) *Principles of Political Economy with Some of Their Applications to Social Philosophy* 1 (7th ed.). London: Longmans, Green, Reader & Dyer.

Ministry of Justice (2014) *United Nations Universal Periodic Review*, Mid Term Report of the United Kingdom of Great Britain and Northern Ireland, and the British Overseas Territories, and Crown Dependencies, 22 August 2014.

Mulvey G (2010) *When Policy Creates Politics: The Problematizing of Immigration and the Consequences for Refugee Integration in the UK*. Journal of Refugee Studies 23(4): 437–462.

Münz R, Straubhaar T, Vadean FP and Vadean N (2007) *What Are the Migrants' Contributions to Employment and Growth? A European Approach*, Research Report, HWWI Policy Paper 3(3): 5–7.

Nassbaum MC and Sen A (1993) *The Quality of Life*. Oxford: Oxford University Press.

Piper N (2005) *Gender and Migration*. Paper prepared for the Global Commission on International.

Ramesh R (2013) Labour Vows to Bring Back Overseas Domestic Worker Visas, *The Guardian*, 23 September 2013.

Rechel B, Mladovsky P, Devillé W, Rijks B, Petrova-Benedict R and McKee M (2011) *Migration and Health in the European Union: An Introduction*. In B. Rechel P. Mladovsky, W. Devillé, B. Rijks, R. Petrova-Benedict and M. McKee (eds), *Migration and Health in the European Union*. Berkshire: Open University Press, 3–13.

Salih II (2013) Domestic Workers in the UK: A Raw Deal for Migrants. *E-Journal of International and Comparative Labour Studies* 2(2): 71–96.

Sargeant M (2014) *Vulnerable Workers in Precarious Work*. E-Journal of International and Comparative Labour Studies 3(1): 1–19.

Schwenken H (2005) The Challenges of Framing Women Migrants' Right in the European Union. *Revue Europeenne des Migrations Internationales* 21(1): 177–194.

Spencer S and Pobjoy J (2012) Equality for All? The Relationship between Immigration Status and the Allocation of Rights in the United Kingdom. *E.H.R.L.R.* 2: 160–175.

Statham P and Geddes A (2006) Elites and the 'Organised Public': Who Drives British Immigration Politics and in Which Direction? *West European Politics* 29(2): 248–269.

Tompa, E, Scott-Marshall H, Dolinschi R, Trevithick S and Bhattacharyya S (2007) *Precarious Employment Experiences and Their Health Consequences: Towards a Theoretical Framework* 28(3): 209–224.

Triandafyllidou A (2013) *Irregular Migrant Domestic Workers in Europe: Who Cares?* Aldershot: Ashgate.

UKBA (2011) *Domestic Workers in Private Households, Border Force Operations Manual*, November 2011.

United Nations Development Programme (UNDP) (2014) *Sustaining Human Progress: Reducing Vulnerabilities and Building Resilience*, Human Development Report 2014, New York: UNDP.

United Nations (1948) *Universal Declaration of Human Rights*, GA res. 217A (III), UN Doc A/810 at 71.

Wills J, Datta K, McIlwaine C, Evans Y, Herbert J and May J (2008) *Global Cities at Work: Migrant Labour in Low Paid Employment in London*, Full Research Report ESRC End of Award Report, RES-000-23-0694. Swindon: ESRC.

Willman P and Bryson (2007) *A Union Organization in Great Britain*. Discussion Paper no 774, Centre for Economic Performance, January 2007.

Part V

Interventions: Tackling Labour Exploitation

15
Global Citizenship: The Need for Dignity and Respect for Migrants

Domenica Urzi

Introduction

This chapter will concentrate on understanding the nexus between immigration status and work precarity, and its effects on feelings of human dignity in informal work within the agricultural sector in Sicily (Italy). According to the International Labour Organization (ILO, 2012), the informal economy is growing across the globe and this rise is strongly connected to the reduction of decent work, defined as the availability of employment in conditions of freedom, equity, human security and dignity (ILO, 2009). For Phillips (2013), the informal economy is part of capitalist production and migrant workers, alongside other workers, are adversely incorporated in the socio-economic system through exploitative and precarious work positions where their vulnerability and poverty tend to be produced and reproduced and prevent people from achieving employment security and accumulation.

In my research, the participants' working conditions were linked to their immigration status (the terms of inclusion) and to their right to reside, work and access to welfare (Dwyer et al., 2011). Specifically, the types of work contract available to European migrants differ from the terms of employment for non-European migrants, resulting in differing opportunities for access to decent work. Inequality in the labour market is also institutionalised through inequitable regulations and policies (Kofman et al., 2000). In the Italian agriculture system this is done through the existence of a secondary type of employment in farming, called 'ingaggio', or engagement position, which is a casual and temporary form of employment based on the actual number of days worked on the farms. Holding an 'ingaggio' does not greatly affect the employer's finances, but it provides the worker with some legal protection and access to unemployment allowances and family benefits. Workers, both local or regular migrants, can have either a contract and an engagement position or only an engagement position. Although it can be considered advantageous, the latter does not guarantee the same social security and juridical protection of a full-time formal contract. Therefore, even those workers are vulnerable to the power of the employer to withdraw from their commitment to the workers.

In everyday life, a stable citizenship status within the EU has, de facto, created more favourable conditions to enter formal employment for Romanian workers. The *engagement* position is the minimum requirement that almost all my Romanian research participants tried and usually succeeded to obtain. However, employers are the main benefactors of a new labour force which is much easier to employ through *ingaggio* with lower labour and administration costs and risks compared to the non-European workers. Meanwhile, other categories of migrant workers as regular and irregular[1] migrants and refugees struggle to gain and maintain formal employment (see Phillips, 2013) and are pushed into evermore exploitative work arrangements (Dwyer et al., 2011).

Although many of the working practices illustrated in this chapter are violations of employment rights and some can be considered as indicators of ILO-defined forced labour (ILO, 2012), I reject a dichotomist tendency to conceptualise labour as a binary of free and forced labour (O'Connell Davidson, 2010; Phillips and Mieres, 2015). It is more appropriate instead to consider a continuum of exploitative work experiences (Shelley, 2007) that progressively describes a spectrum of labour conditions from acceptable to undignified (see also Skrivankova, 2010). Here, the nexus between immigration status and work precarity can be easily targeted and its effects on workers' feelings of having been respected in their human dignity clearly evaluated. The continuum goes from the stretching of the working hours, underpayment and denial of rest to extreme forms of abuse, such as workplace bullying, threats of or the actual use of violence (Shelley, 2007: 7), all experienced by my research participants, as discussed in the following. As immigration status was found to be a key factor shaping the terms of incorporation (Phillips, 2013: see also Dwyer et al., 2011) in the labour market, the chapter first identifies the relation between the work conditions and immigration status of migrant farm workers, then progressively analyses how such conditions affect workers' perceptions of respect and dignity at work. However, before proceeding, it is important to clarify how dignity can be conceptualised.

Dignity in the workplace

Individuals spend the majority of their life in workplaces, where they socially interact with employers and co-workers. Exploring social relationships at work reveals how respect of human dignity is a key element for individual well-being and for a propitious civil society (Hodson, 2001; Holloway, 2002; Calhoun, 2003; Bolton, 2007; Sayer, 2007). The workplace offers a laboratory of social interactions, structured and organised around unequal power relations, where the perception of being treated with dignity significantly affects how people interpret experiences at work.

Employers in the formal sector can use their power to deny dignity of their employees at work in several ways. Based on studies carried out in Western societies, Hodson (2001) has identified four key categories of practices that can contribute to the denial of dignity at work: mismanagement and abuse, overwork, incursions on autonomy and contradictions of employees' employment. In informal employment, these 'un-dignifying' labour conditions can also include abusive communication, missed payment, abrupt layoff, overtime and unpaid overtime and physical abuse, which are indicators of forced labour (ILO, 2012). How can feelings related to human dignity be preserved in asymmetrical power relations typical of the workplace while under the threats of informal employment?

Dignity in the workplace presents itself as bonded to internal and external factors, with mutual and multiple structures. Sayer (2007) shows how recognition, pride, respect and worth are positively correlated with dignity, while humiliation, lack of recognition and being distrusted are usually not. Hence, there is the need to appeal to other sentiments that support human well-being to understand dignity. For Sayer, the notion of dignity involves the perception of self-respect, which in turn refers to the way others with whom we regularly interact treat us. Along the same lines, Hodson (2001: 3) describes dignity as the ability to develop 'a sense of self-worth and self-respect and to appreciate the respect of others'.

Dignity seems to involve three fundamental elements: individual perception of dignity, the actions that we put into practice to defend and support dignity in the external social reality and recognition and confirmation through personal interactions and perceptions in respectful social relations.

Methodology

The data presented in this chapter are based on fieldwork for my PhD undertaken in 2012, exploring mainly the living and working experiences of Tunisian (non-EU) and Romanian (EU) migrants in the agriculture sector of Sicily. For my empirical work I used an ethnographic approach. I conducted 30 semi-structured interviews with migrant farm workers: twelve Romanians (six men and six women); 14 Tunisians (twelve men and two women); two Algerian men and two asylum seekers (one Pakistani man and one Somali man). At the same time, I carried out a period of participant observation in two different settings: at the mobile clinic of Emergency NGO[2] and at the immigration office of one of the main trade unions in the city of Vittoria.

I collected data from four neighbouring locations: Vittoria, Santa Croce Camerina, Scoglitti and Macconi. Because of the hidden nature of migrant populations (Pope, van Royen and Baker, 2002) and the sensitivity of researching informal work (Murphy and Dingwall, 2003), I sourced my participants using a non-probability snowball/opportunity sample method (Silverman, 2010). According to the wishes of my participants, some of the names used are pseudonyms and others are real.

The stratification of farm workers

Among the 30 participants, workers in the most exploitative employment and precarious living conditions also had vulnerable immigration status, including non-European regular and irregular migrants and refugees. On arrival in Italy, non-Europeans need to document their stay with a work visa and an already agreed work contract which conveys social, civil and employment rights. One of the many consequences of this tying of work visas to rights is the fostering of a false business of work contracts between employers and aspiring migrants or irregular migrants. Refugee people on the System for the Protection of Asylum Seekers and Refugees[3] (SPRAR) programme instead must wait until the end of their period on the system (two years) before gaining employment, while undocumented migrants should just not exist on the national territory and should not enter any form of work. As Lewis et al. (2014: 9; see also Waite et al., this volume) have highlighted, 'migration processes and immigration restrictions compound precarity to produce various unfreedoms that can close down any real and acceptable alternative to engage in (severely) exploitative labour'. On the other hand, European citizen workers (Romanians) have rights to work and live within the EU but still experienced exploitation due to their involvement within informal work arrangements. Furthermore, until 2014[4] citizens of the A2 countries (Romania and Bulgaria) had restricted access to the labour market and could only work in highly skilled and managerial roles or in agriculture, construction, tourism, metalwork, domestic, personal services and seasonal work, which substantially limited their labour opportunities. Overall, these restrictions within migration suggest the existence of a stratified system of socio-legal entitlements (Dwyer et al., 2011), which support a 'hierarchy of vulnerability' (Gubbay, 1999) that generates the preconditions of exploitation in the labour market.

Romanian workers

Considering the employment conditions of the research participants along an exploitation continuum (Shelley, 2007), on the more positive end there are the experiences of some Romanian people who worked and lived on the farm. This made their lives heavily dependent on their employers and their families for their access to services such as shopping, medical care or banking. They were also permanently available for any needs of the farm, even at night and during weekends. Furthermore, all of these people were on informal agreements with their employers and accepted lower daily wages than the price established by formal employment. None of them had the *engagement* position, although some of them had succeeded in negotiating certain employment conditions such as a daily wage or paid holiday, but their relationship with their employers remained substantially informal. However, during the interviews they did describe their labour experiences as very good. They felt satisfied with their work and said their relationship with their employer was very friendly. Donna, a 45-year-old single parent of one, said:

> [It] is a friendship relation, honestly. Not only with him but also with his family. Sometimes we even eat together... Sometimes he made homemade pizza and we eat together or sometimes we go out

together. If I need to do something or if I need to go shopping it is not a problem, he will take me to town.

Also Andrey, a 51-year-old father of four, had a similar relationship with his employer:

I can't find the words to describe my employer, they are very good people, very good. He more than respects me . . . let's say that we are friends. Friends as it can be between employer and the worker . . . Always when I needed something he is available . . . But also his brother, wife, mother . . . all of them if I need something they will help me.

Silvia, a 51-year-old mother of two adolescent children, said about her relationship with her employer and her work conditions:

We have got a relation of great friendship and respect. He never has offended me in any way and if there is a misunderstanding between us we talk about it . . . I have succeeded to negotiate my work conditions. I did . . . even if there is still not a contract but soon there will be one. There have been not the [economic] conditions . . . but I am happy. I have got paid holidays and I don't pay any rent. I don't even pay food because we eat what we've got here . . . we are like a family.

These three accounts show that, even in the absence of employment rights guaranteed by formal agreements, when the relationship with the employer is based on friendship and understanding the overall work experience is perceived by the worker as favourable to their well-being. However, living on a farm means being completely dependent on the employer and his family, and creating a sizeable imbalance of power. This raises the question of where the power is within 'familial' working situations. Can a positive relationship with the employer in reality represent a situation of 'multiple dependency' (ILO, 2012) in which the worker's ability to negotiate conditions is constrained by the provision of work, accommodation and food?

The perceptions of work relations experienced by Romanian workers living outside the farm were quite different. They perceived the employment relationship as challenging, making the search for dignity and respect a strong necessity. For those living on the farm, feelings of respect and dignity were more apparent as a result of their intimate and familial setting. Workers living outside felt the need to actively build respect from employers, for example, by negotiating better working conditions in terms of time and wage and by having institutional protection and recognition through an *engagement*. Marin, 31, always negotiates with his employer on the *engagement* position and higher wages to pay for living expenses. By living outside the farm he is also more independent from farm duties, for example during bad weather, at night or during weekends. He underlined the importance of being able to negotiate an *engagement* position with the employer, which guarantees some institutional protection and legal power for the worker:

> With the employer I think there should be respect... But you must attain it, because if you don't do anything to achieve it they will always think about their business first... In fact I have never had problems at work because I always ask for the *'ingaggio'* even if you get less money [compared to the formal contract] ... In fact if I get problems and I am engaged I go and report him. Because it is my money and I am not on my own. I have got my wife and my daughter, so.

Although the engagement position is a form of a casual and temporary work position, it still gives the Romanian people that want to be more independent from their employers some institutional protection and social provisions. However, the quest for respect is perceived as more challenging and cannot be taken for granted.

Regular Tunisian migrants

Work experiences of regular non-European citizens tended to be positioned further along the continuum of exploitation towards severe exploitation. An *engagement* position does not confer residency to non-European migrants; therefore, they tend to arrive with a regular work contract usually pre-arranged by friends or family already in Italy. In the case of the 29-year-old Farhat, he joined his older brother to work at the local agricultural retail market for the same employer:

> I have got a regular contract but in the contract there is written to work only from 6.30 am until 12.30 pm: the same times the market [is open]. But me, when I work until midday he sends me to work in his greenhouses... the Italians [colleagues] go to the beach and he sends me to the countryside. I don't know what he thinks, but he definitely does not think that I should rest... I always work, I am not like the others... here one works like a slave.

A regular work contract is the only way for non-Europeans to secure legal status as a worker; yet this is often used by employers as a form of blackmail to produce overwork. Overworking is a central challenge to dignity at work as it leaves the worker not only physically but also emotionally exhausted (Hodson, 2001). Farhat clearly states that he feels enslaved by his employer, and compared to Italian colleagues found his treatment to be very frustrating. Although he had a regular contract, his life is reduced to one in which even rest is denied.

Another regular Tunisian migrant, Omar, a 56-year-old father of six, has worked for almost two decades in Sicilian agriculture. He describes degrading working conditions:

> Sometimes I cannot breathe because inside the greenhouse the air is too hot. When you always breathe hot air your head spins and you lose your balance. Some employers do not allow you to even get your head out to breathe some fresh air for a minute. He is worried about the illnesses that the tomato plants can get, so the webs are always closed. Let's say that the plant is worth more than a person.

Omar's experience represents a clear example of labour commodification. His account helps us to grasp the idea that for some employers the consideration of their workers does not stray far from the perception of having a mere tool of production, a work instrument to whom they deny even basic human needs. Furthermore, because dignity is an innate characteristic (Lucas et al., 2012), when labour relations reach this point of objectification, re-establishing a sense of self-worth and self-respect in the workplace can be extremely difficult for the worker.

In a more severe case of exploitation, Toufie, a 36-year-old father of three, experienced working for fraudulent employers under forced labour conditions, notwithstanding his legal status in Italy:

> Once, one of the many employers that I had, for two months he only gave me 50 Euros a week and then when at the end [of the harvest] he was supposed to give me the rest he started to say that there was no money because the market did not pay him. I gently asked him to pay me and he promised that he was going to do it a week later... after that week he did not give me either money or the official days [useful to receive the engagement benefits]. Instead, he started to say that he

never worked with me. I said 'ok there is God in life... I left him two or three hundred Euros [short]'.

The withholding of wages is an indicator of forced labour (ILO, 2012).[5] Although regular migrants are in the position to ask for legal help from trade unions or the employment inspectorate, often the fear of losing their work contract and therefore their regular immigration status prevents them from asking for help. In these cases a sense of commodification is added to the feelings of powerlessness, making the establishment of a sense of self-worth and self-respect in the workplace extremely difficult.

Refugee workers

Asylum seekers and refugees also experience labour exploitation. I recorded in my fieldwork the work experiences of two people granted refugee status residing in SPRAR centres. To benefit from the facilities and services offered by the SPRAR programme these people must wait until two years have elapsed before gaining employment. However, because of pressures to support their families in their countries of origin, and having plenty of free time confined in the middle of the countryside, many accept work whenever there is an opportunity. Often, employers recruit them directly from the centres. Gadi, for instance, is a 56-year-old Pakistani English teacher who had to leave his family behind when fleeing his country:

> I go sometimes with those people [employers] and I work with them because I need to work, I have got a big family... Once, I was working harvesting tangerines and the person that I was working for did not want to pay me. We [with other refugees] had to ask the director of our refugee centre where we are living to call him and ask for the money... Finally, after 15 or 20 days he paid us but only 25 Euros a day [rather than the agreed 30 Euros].

Farm employers see men from the refugee centre as a very profitable temporary labour source. As they already have accommodation, food and facilities, employers feel less responsible for the refugees as workers. Furthermore, refugees would be reluctant to ask for help to recoup unpaid wages as they would risk losing their temporary accommodation and support in the SPRAR programme.[6] Undoubtedly, as Amid, a

28-year-old Algerian refugee, highlighted, not all farm employers are the same:

> I have been working even many hours but happy because they were nice people. Some other times instead, I have worked eight hours but not happy at all... The relation depends on the boss... If he is a good person you work well... You work with your heart. But if the person is not nice and he makes fun of you, speaks dialect, insults you... you cannot... Work in the countryside is not good for foreign people... If you go to work for 20 Euros you feel like an animal. I do not want to feel like that anymore.

For Amid, being paid less than a local person was the most humiliating feature of his work. He felt included in employment, but in a negative way, which reinforced his feeling of being an outsider, a foreigner, reduced to the level of a pack animal. The sensation of being treated as sub-human is a form of abuse that has a negative impact on employees and their maintenance of dignity (Lucas et al., 2012). This is the primary consequence for people who are treated as a mere body and therefore struggle to reaffirm their sense of self-worth and self-esteem.

Irregular migrants

Finally, the working conditions experienced by irregular migrants with expired or no documentation were at the most severe end of the exploitation continuum. Irregular migrants are usually not recorded in statistics because it is in their interest to avoid contact with statutory service providers to prevent detention and the risk of removal (Bloch et al., 2011). These research participants inhabit abandoned houses in the countryside during the night or get temporary accommodation with acquaintances. During the day, they congregate around known places of informal recruitment to get any possible farm work that provides a basic income for survival. Irregular workers cannot claim any rights or benefits. This becomes clearer when irregular workers face cases of withheld wages and when employers refuse to pay. In the absence of a legal employment contract, this can happen to any worker, but it is a quite common experience among irregular workers. Samir, 29, for example, had irregularly worked for more than a decade in the sector. On one occasion, Samir attempted to obtain some institutional support for a withheld payment:

Once, I had the problem that I didn't get paid... I went to the employment inspectorate office in Ragusa and they say that without a permit to stay it was better for me to escape or I was risking being arrested. So, I went scared and I left. I let it go ... I left him four months worth of work.

The lack of institutional protection induces irregular migrants in particular to feel powerless against the abuse of their employers (Bloch et al., 2009; Lewis et al., 2014). Furthermore, irregular migrant workers felt that their employers were well aware of their vulnerable immigration status and lack of access to protection.[7] Several participants underlined their situation of defenselessness and described how the withholding of wages was a frequent occurrence. However, I would argue that this was done not to compel the person to remain at work as suggested by the ILO forced indicators (2012) but to obtain cost-free labour.

The abuse of power by an employer can go beyond missed payments and includes forms of super-exploitation (Marini, 1974) in terms of extreme low payment, overwork, unpaid overtime, no day of rest, verbal mistreatment and even physical assault. The most extreme case encountered among my participants involved Terir, a 28-year-old irregular Tunisian man. I met him at the immigration office of one of the most prominent trade unions in the city of Vittoria. Despite his immigration status, Terir was trying to resolve his case. He found a casual work position, working for the same family business for two years under a promise of a legal work contract that would allow him to regularise his migration status. After months of verbal abuse with negative and offensive remarks and menace, the family actually physically assaulted Terir, and the case ended up in the hands of the local police and trade union. He understood their abuse as a form of power which the family felt they had over him because he was an irregular migrant or 'clandestino'[8]:

Do you know what my problem is? It is that I haven't got the documents. When they were beating me they were thinking: he is a clandestine, he cannot do anything!... They think clandestine equals animal. I was treated like an animal. Why? We are not people?... Do they have feelings?... When the police put me inside the car the lady said 'he is a clandestine, send him away' and I said '... before I want to take back my sweat, the money that I have worked for. Without *engagement* and without anything. Actually, you also ate the money that I gave you for my contract' [that was never secured].

Terir's experience features forced labour indicators, including abuse of vulnerability in relation to insecure immigration status, deception and physical violence (ILO, 2012). Under such conditions, having a dignified life in the workplace, where he also lived, is far from achievable.

Conclusion

Migrants are adversely incorporated through their stratified immigration status in socio-economic systems and structures in European economies, resulting, for many, in relegation to exploitative work where their conditions of poverty and vulnerability are produced and reproduced (Phillips, 2013). Immigration status and its consequent 'unfreedoms' and 'restrictions' (Lewis et al., 2014) create a 'hierarchy of vulnerability' (Gubbay, 1999) that exposes migrants to the risk of labour exploitation, particularly in the informal labour market. However, against a dichotomist tendency to conceptualise labour into free and unfree (O'Connell Davidson, 2010; Phillips and Mieres, 2015), it is more accurate to organise labour experiences in a continuum where they can be closely scrutinised and understood for their severe repercussions on peoples' feelings of being respected and treated in a dignified manner. A number of Romanian workers, for instance, lived on site and accepted fully informal employment despite their regular citizenship status. Often, these people live in a condition of 'multiple dependency' with their employers and families, but overall they have described their labour relations as very friendly and rewarding. Romanian workers that want to live off site for reasons of life privacy and independence from farm duties seek on the other hand to obtain higher wages and the *ingaggio* position in order to attain some institutional recognition and social provisions. For these people labour relations tend to be much more challenging and the quest for respect and dignity is a strong necessity. In the cases of documented Tunisian migrants, forms of exploitation from their employers are often accepted in order to maintain a work contract that guarantees them a regular immigration status. Although this category of migrants can access institutional help for their employment problems, often the fear of losing both their regular work contract and immigration status discourages them from appealing. In these cases, a sense of commodification is added to the feelings of powerlessness and obscuring a sense of self-worth and self-respect in the workplace. Labour exploitation is also an experience common among refugee workers who decide to take on informal employment in order to send remittance to their families. Often, employers drastically underpay these workers and forms of verbal mistreatment are not uncommon. Several refugee workers felt they were disregarded as people and treated more as sub-human. This is a form of abuse that has a negative impact on employees and their maintaining of dignity. Finally, undocumented migrants reside on the most exploitative segment of the continuum line. For them the lack of institutional protection is coupled with forms of super-exploitation which in one documented case became physical assault. Under such conditions, having a dignified life in the workplace is far from achievable. As a final point, the material presented in this chapter helps to develop and improve our understanding of how the nexus between immigration status and work precarity generates an array of labour conditions that can be best analysed along a continuum of exploitation which explains the effects that they have on the feelings of respect and recognition of human dignity for the people involved.

Notes

1. In my thesis, the term 'irregular migrant' used is in line with the recommendation of Düvell, Triandafyllidou and Vollmer (2008). It uses the term 'irregular migrant' to specify that migrants are not criminals but they are irregular in consideration of their entry and/or residence status. Similar terms are 'undocumented migrant', a person without the required travel or residence documents, and 'unauthorised migrant', a person without legal permission to enter or reside in that country (Düvell et al., 2008).
2. Emergency is an Italian NGO that operates nationally and internationally, delivering free medical care to populations of people who are victims of poverty and war.
3. Italy decided to end these restrictions in 2012.
4. Available at http://www.ilo.org/wcmsp5/groups/public/—ed_norm/—declaration/documents/publication/wcms_182004.pdf
5. ILO (2012) indicators of forced labour.
6. For a description of the services offered by SPRAR centres see: http://www.serviziocentrale.it/file/server/file/SPRAR%20Description%20-%20Italy.pdf
7. This is an aspect that has emerged more clearly during the interviews with employers which are not included in this chapter. For more information, see D. Urzi (forthcoming) 'Migrant workers, temporary labour and employment in Southern Europe: A case study on migrants working in the agricultural informal economy of Sicily'. PhD Thesis. Hallward Library, University of Nottingham.
8. 'Clandestino' is the legal Italian definition for people who entered the Italian territory without the required documents to live and work in the country.

References

Bolton S (2007) *Dimensions of Dignity at Work*. Oxford: Elsevier.
Bloch A, Sigona N and Zetter R (2009) *'No Right to Dream': The Social and Economic Lives of Young Undocumented Migrants in Britain*. London: Paul Hamlyn Foundation.

Bloch A, Sigona N and Zetter R (2011) Migration Routes and Strategies of Young Undocumented Migrants in England: A Qualitative Perspective. *Ethnic and Racial Studies* 34(8): 1286–1302.

Calhoun C (2003) An Apology for Moral Shame. *The Journal of Political Philosophy* 11(2): 1–20.

Davidson JOC (2010) New Slavery, Old Binaries: Human Trafficking and the Borders of 'Freedom'. *Global Networks* 10(2): 244–261.

Düvell F, Triandafyllidou A and Vollmer B (2008) *Ethical Issues in Irregular Migration Research, Report on Ethical Issues for Research Project CLANDESTINO Undocumented Migration: Counting the Uncountable*. Data and Trends across Europe, European Commission, October. Available at: http://onlinelibrary.wiley.com/doi/10.1002/psp.590.

Dwyer P, Lewis H, Scullion L and Waite L (2011) *Forced Labour and UK Immigration Policy: Status Matters*. York: Joseph Rowntree Foundation.

Gubbay J (1999) The European Union Role in the Formation and, Legitimation and Implementation of Migration Policy. In G. Dale and M. Cole (eds), *The European Union and Migrant Labour*. Oxford: Berg, 23–35.

Hodson R (2001) *Dignity at Work*. Cambridge: Cambridge University Press.

Holloway J (2002) Zapatismo and the Social Sciences. *Capital & Class* 26(3): 153–160.

ILO Indicators of Forced Labour. Available at: http://www.ilo.org/wcmsp5/groups/public/—ed_norm/–declaration/documents/publication/wcms_203832.pdf

ILO (2009) 'World of Work Employment'. Available at: http://www.ilo.org/wcmsp5/groups/public/—dgreports/—dcomm/documents/publication/wcms_118384.pdf

ILO (2012) 'Global Estimate of Forced Labour: Results and Methodology'. Available at: http://www.ilo.org/wcmsp5/groups/public/—ed_norm/–declaration/documents/publication/wcms_182004.pdf

Kofman E, Phizacklea A, Raghuram P and Sales R (2000) *Gender and International migration in Europe*. London: Routledge.

Lewis H, Dwyer P, Hodkinson S and Waite L (2014) Hyper-Precarious Lives Migrants, Work and Forced Labour in the Global North. *Progress in Human Geography*.

Lucas K, Kang D and Li Z (2012) Workplace Dignity in Total Institution: Examining the Experiences of Foxconn's Migrant Workforce. *Journal of Business Ethics* 114(1): 1–16.

Marini RM (1974 [1973]). *Diale'ctica de la dependencia* (2nd ed.). Me'xico: Ediciones Era.

Murphy E and Dingwall R (2003) *Qualitative Methods and Health Policy Research*. New York: Aldine de Gruyter.

Phillips N (2013) Unfree Labour and Adverse Incorporation in the Global Economy: Comparative Perspectives on Brazil and India. *Economy and Society* 42(2): 171–196.

Phillips N and Mieres F (2015) The governance of forced labour in the Global Economy. *Globalizations* 12(2): 2–17.

Pope C, van Royen, P and Baker, R (2002) Qualitative Methods in Research on Healthcare Quality. *Quality and Safety Health Care* 11: 148–152.

Sayer A (2007) Dignity at Work: Broadening the Agenda. *Organisation* 14: 565.

Shelley T (2007) *Exploited: Migrant Labour in the New Global Economy.* London: Zed Books.

Silverman D (2010) *Doing Qualitative Research.* London: Sage Publications Ltd.

Skrivankova K (2010) *Between Decent Work and Forced Labour: Examining the Continuum of Exploitation. JRF Programme Paper: Forced Labour.* York: Joseph Rowntree Foundation.

16
Winning a Living Wage: The Legacy of Living Wage Campaigns

Ana Lopes and Tim Hall

Introduction

There is perhaps no more current high-profile campaign relating to low-paid workers in the UK than the living wage campaign. Since its launch by a broad-based community organisation in 2001, the campaign has secured more than £200m as additional wages to some of society's most insecure and poorly paid workers.[1] This has led to higher tax receipts and savings in in-work benefits. A recent report estimated that net savings to the Treasury from the introduction of the living wage across the UK would be approximately £3.6bn (Lawton and Pennycook, 2013). Campaigns have been led by community organisations, trade unions, student unions and political parties and 'wins' have been secured across the economy in banking and financial services, healthcare, cleaning, hospitality and catering, and latterly retail. Unusually for campaigns of this kind, they enjoy cross-party support. Their success is all the more remarkable given long-term trends towards outsourcing in managerial and organisational practice and the onset in 2008 of the deepest recent global recession. Commentators have accounted for this success in terms of new organisational models adopted by trade unions and community organisations (Wills, 2008; Holgate, 2009; Hearn and Bergos, 2011), particularly highlighting the success of the latter in mobilising communities and non-typical actors in these campaigns.

However, while there is a growing body of research on living wage campaigns and the economic benefits of a living wage, their longer-term impacts have been little researched, especially from the perspective of workers receiving the living wage. Are there lasting benefits for these workers or are these benefits offset by contractors and clients

through increased workloads and reduced hours? Such questions cannot be entirely separated from questions about the benefits accruing
to clients and contractors, end-users and the community at large.
A common finding, for example, is that workers receiving a living
wage often feel more recognition for their work (Wills, 2009). Similarly,
clients and contractors often report increases in productivity as a consequence of increased staff retention and more contented workforces
(Wills and Linneker, 2012). While such questions are linked, the distinction between a workforce struggling to manage increased workloads
as a result of squeezed profit margins and a more productive – because
they are more contented – workforce should be clear.

Here, we draw on research (including our own) undertaken in the
US and the UK to evaluate the impact of introducing the living wage.
By impact, we understand the range of benefits and detriments accruing to workers, clients, contractors, end-users and the community as
a result of the introduction of the living wage. In doing this we leave
to one side the question of whether raising the wage floor has a positive or detrimental effect on the economy and whether the way living
wage is calculated favours some family forms over others.[2] This is not
because such questions are unimportant; it simply reflects our focus on
the possible negative impact of the living wage, in particular increased
job insecurity as a consequence of a reduction in contracted hours and
increased workload. If, as our study suggests, the introduction of the
living wage brings about greater insecurity, then supporters and campaigners need to know. In the conclusion, we discuss possible responses
to this, calling for more research on the impact of introducing the living
wage. We begin with an overview of the campaign for the living wage
at the University of East London (UEL) from where our cohort of cleaners is drawn. We then look at existing research on the impact of living
wage introduction as well as current research. We go on to present and
analyse our data, finally drawing and contextualising our findings.

We note at the outset that we were active as both organisers and supporters and therefore write as academics who were heavily involved in
the campaign. We address issues of bias and the relation between this
research and the campaign in the 'Methods' section.

The living wage campaign at the UEL

The UEL was one of a number of universities in London introducing
the living wage from 2007 onwards. The campaign was led by The East
London Communities Organisation (TELCO), the founding chapter of

Citizens UK,[3] with local branches of Unison and Universities and Colleges Union (UCU), focusing primarily on outsourced cleaning workers at the university. The campaign took place against the backdrop of the outsourcing of security and catering. These workers were also covered by the living wage.

While the UEL has a high percentage of black and minority ethnic students and staff, the cleaning workers as a group were drawn mainly from Spanish-speaking South America and Portuguese-speaking Africa, with very limited levels of English.

The living wage campaign was broad-based, involving many groups and constituencies, including unions, academics, students, administrators, the chaplaincy and neighbouring institutions such as schools and churches as affiliates of TELCO. Organisers and activists began by conducting one-to-one meetings with individual cleaners. After meetings to determine a strategy, a letter was sent to the university's vice-chancellor, requesting a meeting to discuss the living wage. When no meeting was forthcoming, the campaign group undertook a number of actions on campus, attracting media attention. Shortly after this, the vice-chancellor announced that the UEL would sign up to the living wage.

It began to be introduced across the university as contracts came up for re-tendering in 2011. Cleaning workers received the living wage in August 2011 when a new company with a strong ethical track record got the contract. The campaign team wrote a report one year after the implementation. While we were aware, anecdotally, that there were issues with the new contractor, the findings were unexpected. This report was sent to senior managers at the university and eventually formed the basis for a meeting between the campaign team, facilities managers and the contractor. After the meeting a number of issues raised in the report were addressed and union representatives and the contractor now meet regularly.

The living wage: Impact and problems

The London living wage campaign was launched in 2001 by Citizens UK, a coalition of community groups, schools, faith-based groups and trade unions, following similar initiatives in the US. The living wage is intended to respond to in-work poverty; it is above the National Minimum Wage (NMW) and is updated annually in November. While the NMW is set by the government's Low Pay Commission and represents 'what the market will bear' (Wills, 2009: 38), the living wage, set by the Greater London Authority, expresses the costs of living: housing, transport costs and childcare, as well as a basic basket of goods.

There is a significant body of literature evaluating the impact of the living wage, mostly in the US. This research points to small to moderate effects on municipal budgets, increasing less than the rate of inflation in Baltimore and allowing the bidding for municipal contracts to remain competitive or even improving their competitiveness. Moreover, studies show living wage affects mostly adult workers and their families, finding little evidence of diminished employment. Finally, evaluations of the US living wage point to raised productivity and reduced staff turnover, benefitting employers (Thompson and Chapman, 2006).

In the UK, a recent study commissioned by Trust for London[4] focused on costs and benefits of the London Living Wage, using a mixed methodology, including case studies, interviews and survey, as well as statistical data analysis. This research confirms what anecdotal evidence previously suggested: that the wage premium was being managed down by employers and clients in different ways. In some cases, the living wage implementation led to very little increase in overall contract costs and in one case costs went down. In this case the client decided to reduce workers' hours and the frequency of some jobs. The research revealed that the introduction of the living wage meant increased costs 'that were less than might be expected in relation to the headline changes in wages' (Wills and Linneker, 2012: 18). The research also suggests that the move to the living wage 'precipitated an examination of costs and renewed efforts to keep the costs down' (Ibid.). In most cases the initiative to introduce the living wage came from the client or the employer, rather than the contractor. The living wage usually became mandatory in procurement processes, while decisions about differentials were left to the tendering firms. The research concludes that 'costs associated with the living wage have to be considered in light of the power relations between the clients and their contractors, and in regard to the way in which the clients chose to manage their service' (op. cit.: 20). Moreover, the introduction of the living wage was associated with increased staff retention, improved attitudes among workers and the ability to attract better staff, as well as reputational improvement (Ibid.: 21–22).

The impact of the living wage from the workers' perspective was researched via a survey of 416 workers in living wage and non-living wage workplaces. Researchers found a statistically significant association between receipt of the living wage and psychological health, after adjusting for socio-economic factors. They also found that 54 per cent of workers reported experiencing benefits from the living wage in relation to work. This was based on questions about whether they were working harder, feeling happier, more respected, more valued; having more pride in their job; and being more likely to stay in the job. At one particular site, however, workers complained about the association of the living wage with cuts in their number of hours worked, reductions in overtime and bonus payments. Financial benefits were reported by 38 per cent of respondents and family benefits by 32 per cent. The research also found that respondents who earned the living wage claimed fewer state benefits than others and that the move to the living wage is associated with slight household income improvement. If workers are not willing or able to claim benefits, the move to the living wage has more significant positive impact on household disposable income. A surprisingly high percentage of worker respondents (35 per cent) reported experiencing no benefits from the move to the living wage (Ibid.: 22–34).

A recent report on employment practices in the UK cleaning sector commissioned by the Equality and Human Rights Commission similarly focused on benefits and detriments to workers, contractors and clients from paying the living wage (EHRC, 2014: 39). The report interviewed 93 cleaners across the UK and developed six in-depth case studies examining procurement processes for outsourced cleaning services. These case studies were drawn from six different sectors. Three of the organisations had introduced the living wage, enabling researchers to compare conditions and practices in living wage and non-living wage organisations. Clear benefits to workers found by the report included higher pay rates, thereby obviating the need for a second job, and greater visibility and respect in the workplace (Ibid.). Benefits to clients and contractors included a reduced staff turnover (Ibid.: 69, 70), in some cases to as little as 1 per cent (Ibid.: 15); improved service (Ibid.: 72); and higher productivity rates (Ibid.: 15).

However, the report also found evidence of reduced staffing levels and increased workloads, to offset the cost of paying the living wage. According to one worker, the workforce was halved when the living wage was introduced and the remaining workers were each left to do the work previously done by two staff (Ibid.: 36). Despite these negative findings, the report was highly positive about the impact of the living wage campaign on the cleaning sector as whole and encouraged more firms to include it in procurement policies.

We now turn to the research undertaken with cleaners at UEL following living wage implementation in August 2011.

Methods

Our research proceeded in two stages. During the first stage, a questionnaire was distributed among cleaning staff and supervisors prior to the implementation of the living wage. We received 39 responses, a 43 per cent response rate. The questionnaire covered experience of and reasons for migrating, experience of campaigns, and union and faith-group membership. This was followed by semi-structured interviews with eight respondents in which the same issues were explored in greater depth. The respondents were chosen on the basis of their participation in the campaign, balancing gender.

In a second stage, a year after the implementation of the living wage, a questionnaire was distributed, focusing on pay and working conditions, workloads, overtime and hours, payments and grievances. Forty-one responses were received, a 46 per cent response rate. The same themes were further explored in a focus group and through seven semi-structured interviews.

Our positionality as campaign activists influenced our approach, best described as a piece of community-engaged research (Handley et al., 2010) or action research (Wills, 2014). Partnership between the community and the researchers was built and strengthened throughout the research. The community partners collaborated in the research, in activities such as participant recruitment and data collection. Findings were disseminated to the community prior to write-up and submission of the completed article. In a very direct sense, the research was action-oriented, undertaken in the context of a campaign to ensure that the benefits of the living wage were secured. Our findings were published in a report sent to university senior managers and used as the basis for negotiation between the campaign team – comprising TELCO, Unison and other trade union representatives – and the client and the contractor. This accounts for the fact that, unlike the Wills and Linneker study (2012), only cleaning workers participated in this research and not clients, contractors or end-users. A fuller assessment of the costs and benefits of the introduction of the living wage at the UEL would require not only broader participation but also a greater lapse of time to allow for the new contract to bed down. We are currently engaged in writing this evaluation. However, in this study the research is undertaken explicitly to bring about change: to give voice to a marginalised community and ensure that ownership of the campaign translates into lasting control over their work and its impacts on their lives.

Data analysis and findings

A year after the implementation of the living wage, it was clear that some progress had been made. Questionnaire data showed that while in 2011 a majority (62 per cent) of cleaning staff had received incorrect pay, the figure dropped to 44 per cent in 2012. Late payments also happened less frequently: they were reported by 62 per cent of respondents in 2011, but only by 12 per cent in 2012.

Another noticeable change was in the number of respondents who stated being a trade union member: from 46 per cent in 2011 to 51 per cent in 2012. Furthermore, 44 per cent of those who stated union membership also knew who their branch representative was, demonstrating some engagement with the union (Table 16.1).

Benefits from the introduction of the living wage

While just 24 per cent of our respondents said they were better off and only 20 per cent said that their life had changed as a result of receiving the living wage, we did nonetheless find evidence in the interviews that the pay rise had made a difference. One cleaning worker responded as follows:

> Yes I am [better off]. Well, it's astonishing because in other places they pay £6 or £6.30 at most. Not even £7. So it's great that here they pay £8.30. That had a very positive impact because you can really see the difference between this company and other companies. Lots of people want to work here because we earn £2.30 more than most others... It made a big difference.
>
> [Paulo][5]

Table 16.1   Living wage cleaner profiles, one year on

One year on – Summary table	
Experienced increased workload	56%
Experienced problems taking leave	58%
Have a contract	90%
Have always been paid on time	88%
Have always received correct pay	56%
Are no better off as a result of the living wage	61%
Trade union membership	51%
Know their TU representative	44%

Note: n = 41.

Another described its benefits as twofold:

> First, the rise itself. I know I have two more pounds than I had before.
> With those two pounds I can buy things I couldn't afford before and
> I can save up and then buy something for which I wasn't able to save
> up before. And there's a second thing – we are not alone; we have
> support. If we have a problem the union helps us and they stand
> firmly by us. I was very happy with that and I think we should have
> done it before. I believe all cleaning workplaces should be unionised,
> because without the union our voice can't be heard – our cries are
> muted.
>
> [Laura]

Others said they used the additional money to save or purchase additional items that they would not have otherwise been able to afford.

There was evidence that cleaning workers thought the new contract was better managed, with 88 per cent of respondents saying they were paid on time. This contrasts with the previous contractor, who frequently did not pay staff promptly, and often underpaid them. Cleaning staff also appreciated fortnightly payments, with one former supervisor characterising the benefits as follows:

> It's good because it gets easier for one to manage one's money. With
> one payment you pay the rent, with the following payment you pay
> something else ... I think it's good.
>
> [Carmen]

However, cleaning staff were also frustrated that for various reasons, separate from pay, they were not able to perform to their best abilities in their job. The following comment was typical of this frustration:

> If they would treat the cleaners well, this would work very well. We
> could even do twice as much work, without being degraded. We work
> better if we're more relaxed and less ... they don't have to humiliate
> us. I don't get it. If they ask us to do something, we do it. There is no
> need to degrade, mistreat, shout ... It's a very sad situation.
>
> [Jose]

'Evening things out': Negative consequences of living wage introduction

However, we unveiled a range of problems, including workers working without contracts; difficulties in booking leave; and instances of bullying and victimisation of staff that had taken an active role in the campaign. Such problems are not unusual, particularly in a campaign's aftermath and can generally be addressed by building capacity in the trade union branch. What concerned us more was the reported increase in workloads and the reduction in the length of some contracts from 52 to 39 or 29 weeks. Regarding workloads and time allocation, 72 per cent of respondents said they did not have sufficient time to complete their work; 56 per cent said their work had actually increased under the new contractor in contrast to 34 per cent who said it had not.

When we interviewed cleaning staff, many reported that work had become more insecure, workers being sent home when there was not enough work. We explored this further in interviews. The following is a typical response:

> Before [with the previous contractor] the work was normal but now with [the new contractor] one has to do the work of two or three people... One has to clean more rooms, more corridors, you do some work in a certain floor, then you have to go to another floor and do other things.... So it's a lot more work.

In response to the question whether there was enough time to complete the work, one interviewee said:

> No, I don't have enough time. There never is enough time. If you put a little bit more into your work, if you want to do it well... you have to be very fast because there is no time. It's two hours. For example, we have two hours to do all of the toilets in the Ground Floor... So it's fifteen toilets that I have to do in two hours. And if I am to do it well... and I like doing it well because I always said that I do my work well. But often I go past my hours. I never finish at the same time.
>
> [Manuela]

Another described working with a colleague:

> Just recently I was working with a lady called Paula... and that lady, she seems crazy. She runs and runs and runs in despair. She picks up the bags and the rubbish... I asked her: 'Paulita, what's the matter with you? Are you OK?'
> Why, sonny, why do you ask that?
> Because you're running and running...
> I have to run otherwise they say I don't do enough
>
> [Jose]

Moreover, 61 per cent of survey respondents said they were no better off as a result of receiving the living wage. We expected the reduction of in-work benefits to be the central reason for this. While we found some evidence of a reduction of tax credits in some households, a number of interviewees said they were happier to be paid more and receive less in-work benefits. However, the main reason lay elsewhere: with increased workloads and the reduction in the length of contracts. While workers were receiving the living wage – over £2 an hour more than their previous hourly rate – their annual wage was considerably less. This in turn led to increased pressure on workloads as the remaining staff carried the work of those not working and increased job insecurity. One cleaning worker described this as a process of 'evening things out'. While the hourly rate increases the overall contract is reduced and the workload is increased. Another interviewee summed the problem up as follows:

> The problem is that there is no stability. For example, when the lectures are over there is less work and so they lay off some people, so one ends up having to do double the work. The work of that worker, if they lay her off, then you have to do it yourself. But if you have to do it on top of your own, I think they should pay us double. And they pay us the same. So you do double the work and they pay you the same amount. I don't think that's right.
>
> [Manuela]

Another commented on the insecurity of work with the new contractor:

> For example, here in East Building there were permanent cleaners from 6am to 8am and some of them stopped doing that. That's the case of Paula ... they cut her morning hours. So they told her they were going to give her more hours in halls but some days they don't call her! Some days they call her, some days they don't!
>
> [Alfredo]

In response to the question whether the living wage campaign had been worthwhile, one interviewee responded:

> Well ... No, I don't. They do pay more, but with so much work one hardly notices it. It's like ... they just demand more work and that's how they compensate for it. They pay more but now we have to do more work – a lot more actually. I'm having to clean an office, clean a glass panel, put the paper, get the rubbish, to clean

the lamps...things I didn't have to do before. So that's it...they increased the workload.

[Jose]

Another former supervisor and central activist in the campaign commented:

No, I don't. Totally not.... When we started the campaign we thought it was going to be very different. We thought everything would remain the same but we would be earning more. That's all totally gone. Many people have preferred to quit or to look for other jobs. Specifically jobs where they can work all year round. And people have come to understand that...how do they benefit from earning eight fifty per hour if they're going to be out of work for almost half of the year? It's better to earn less but to have security for the year for their bills, their food, their rent, and their needs.

[Camilo]

In short, many cleaning workers had been rendered more precarious as a result of the introduction of the living wage.

Discussion

It was a sobering and humbling moment for us and others who had campaigned for the living wage at the UEL to have to accept some of its negative consequences. The benefits of the campaign were principally economic. Was this a problem with the living wage as such or the way that it had been implemented at the UEL? A comparison of our findings with those of Wills and Linneker (2012) would suggest the latter. While the concept of a living wage is not unproblematic, the UEL experience is, based on the evidence collected, principally a problem of implementation, indicating the need for further attention by researchers and campaign groups. Our findings support those of Wills and Linneker that the experience of implementation can vary according to sector, the existence of a trade union and also the diligence of facilities managers. Universities, like other public sector institutions, have seen a steady loss of operational and strategic expertise in facilities management and are at a significant disadvantage when negotiating and overseeing contracts with large-scale companies. Evidence from Wills and Linneker and the Equality and Human Rights Commission (EHRC) suggests that the best examples of implementation are where contract managers retain responsibility for this process rather than passing it to the contractor – for example, in auditing the total hours needed rather than leave this up to the contractor and industry standards. While we are unable to support this argument directly due to the scope of our study, the likelihood is that something similar occurred at the UEL. A recent positive development in this regard is the creation of the Living Wage Foundation (LWF) in 2010. The purpose of the Foundation, set up by Citizens UK, is to recognise living wage employers through an accreditation system and to function as a resource for best practice for clients and contractors. While the bar for becoming an accredited living wage employer is set quite low, it nonetheless provides a network of clients and contractors to share best practice for implementing the living wage. This goes some way towards addressing the lack of expertise in managing contracts identified at the UEL and other organisations.

With respect to trade unions and campaign groups, our findings suggest that, when possible, campaign groups should remain involved and should not be content with winning the living wage alone. The existence and support of trade unions and the unionisation of the cleaning staff themselves make this more likely. Our findings also support the call by Holgate (2009) and others[6] for better and closer cooperation between community organisations and trade unions to secure the implementation of the living wage and campaign sustainability. While there is undoubtedly a division of labour between community organisations and trade unions, it is not rigid. Workplaces are communities with ample opportunities for practicing good citizenship. On the issue of living wage implementation, lines of responsibility are blurred. Community organisations ought not to wash their hands of organisations that implement living wage irresponsibly, walking off with the 'win' and leaving trade unions to pick up the pieces. Conversely, trade unions should not complain of encroachment onto their terrain as sustained communal relations engendered by broad-based organising will ensure responsible implementation of the living wage.

Conclusion

The experience of the implementation of the living wage at the UEL shows that winning the living wage does not necessarily translate into improved job security. As much research shows, workers can in fact experience detriment through the implementation of the living wage, in the form of reduced contracted hours, increased workloads and redundancy. More is needed beyond the introduction of the living wage, to ensure its benefits to workers are not negated. Community organisations and trade unions each have their part to play in ensuring and recognising the best employment and procurement practices. The establishment of the Living Wage Foundation is a positive development as a resource for ethical implementation of the living wage.

Notes

1. London Living Wage Research, Department of Geography, Queen Mary, University of London. http://www.geog.qmul.ac.uk/livingwage/
2. See, for example, Grover (2008) and Weldon and Targ (2004). Both argue that calculations of the living wage work against single-parent families.
3. Citizens UK is an alliance of over 300 member organisations representing UK civil society in the UK. Founded in the 1990s, it brings together churches, mosques and synagogues; schools, colleges and universities; unions, think-tanks and housing associations; GP surgeries, charities and migrant groups to work together for the common good.
4. Trust for London is an independent charitable foundation, supporting and funding work tackling poverty and inequality in London.
5. All names have been changed.
6. See Symon and Crawshaw (2009).

References

Equality and Human Rights Commission (2014) *Invisible Workforce: Employment Practices in the Cleaning Sector.* Available at: http://www.equalityhumanrights .com/publication/invisible-workforce-employment-practices-cleaning-sector (accessed 11 September 2014).

Grover C (2008) A Living Wage for London? *Benefits* 16(1): 71–9.

Handley K, Pasick R, Potter M, Oliva G, Goldstein, E and Nguyen, T (2010) *Community Engaged Research: A Quick-Start Guide for Researchers.* University of California: San Francisco. Available at: http://accelerate.ucsf.edu/files/CE/ guide_for_researchers.pdf (accessed 20 May 2014).

Hearn J and Bergos M (2011) Latin American Cleaners Fight for Survival: Lessons for Migrant Activism. *Race & Class* 53(1): 65–82.

Holgate J (2009) Contested Terrain: London's Living Wage Campaign and the Tension between Community and Union Organising. In J. McBride and I. Greenwood (eds), *Community Unionism: A Comparative Analysis of Concepts and Contexts.* Basingstoke: Palgrave Macmillan.

Lawton K and Pennycook M (2013) Beyond the Bottom Line: The Challenges andOpportunities of a Living Wage, IPPR & Resolution Foundation.

Symon G and Crawshaw J (2009) Urban Labour, Voice and Legitimacy: Economic Development and the Emergence of Community Unionism. *Industrial Relations Journal* 40(2): 140–155.

Thompson J and Chapman J (2006) *The Economic Impact of Local Living Wages.* Economic Policy Institute, Briefing Paper 170.

Weldon S and Targ H (2004) From Living Wages to Family Wages? *New Political Science* 26(1): 71–98.

Wills J (2008) Making Class Politics Possible: Organising Contract Cleaners in London. *International Journal of Urban and Regional Research* 32(2): 305–324.

Wills J (2009) The Living Wage. *Soundings: A Journal of Politics and Culture* 42(1): 36–46.

Wills J and Linneker B (2012) The Costs and Benefits of the London Living Wage. Trust for London. Available at: http://www.geog.qmul.ac.uk/livingwage/pdf/ Livingwagecostsandbenefits.pdf (last accessed 15 July 2014).

Wills J (2014) Engagement. In R Lee, Noel Castree, Rob Kitchin, Vicky Lawson, Anssi Paasi, Chris Philo, Sarah Radcliffe, Susan M. Roberts and Charles Withers (eds), *The Sage Handbook of Progress in Human Geography*. London: Sage.

17

Forced Labour and Ethical Trade in the Indian Garment Industry

Annie Delaney and Jane Tate

The International Labour Organization (ILO) has acknowledged a focus beyond the state – on the private sector as a major contributor to contemporary forms of forced labour. This can be partly attributed to the recognition of the increase in labour exploitation present in global production networks/chains (ILO, 2013). The chapter examines the case of Sumangali camp workers in the textile garment industry in Tamil Nadu, South India. We explore how key actors, local and international labour rights non-governmental organisations (NGOs), and a multi-stakeholder initiative engage in the issues of bonded and forced labour. Our analysis draws on field research conducted in India between 2011 and 2014 in the garment sector, as part of a broader research project exploring the effectiveness of non-judicial redress mechanisms to human rights grievances. In the case of the garment and textile sector in Tamil Nadu, the power imbalance between the thousands of young women and child workers in garment and textile factories and the employers and global brands is significant. The case explores characteristics of local and international campaign mobilisation and the impact on workers' sense of agency. Further, we seek to understand the responses by corporations through the multi-stakeholder initiative actions on forced labour.

The garment industry has existed in this region for many years, and bonded, forced and child labour is not uncommon, particularly in the handloom and weaving workshops (Carsons and DeNeve, 2013). More recently, the large-scale textile mills and garment factories have sought to employ young women and children in line with a change from producing for national markets to an export focus. The feminisation of the workforce has coincided with the emergence of new forms of institutionalised exploitation (Narayanaswamy and Sachithanandam, 2010). The gendered nature of global production remains an important

site of investigation; feminist scholars have shown that the feminisation of labour and the demand for cheap and productive labour have
not receded (Pearson, 2007; Prieto-Carron, 2008).The global garment
industry is notorious for its treatment of women and child workers,
and numerous examples could be given of exploitative conditions of
employment.[1] Many UK retailers are selling T-shirts, sportswear, children's clothes and nightwear sourced from this region, and we question
the effectiveness of their corporate social responsibility (CSR) responses
to forced labour and other labour exploitation in the garment industry.

The nature of the contemporary global garment production is
described here as a network, rather than a linear supply chain (Coe et al.,
2008; see Phillips, this volume). This raises important questions around
the role of the lead firm or brand, and how they are held accountable
for labour abuses experienced by workers. We are further attracted to
Coe et al.'s (2008) suggestion that global production networks (GPNs)
are relational. The strength of this idea is in its capacity to reflect the
range of relationships between the multiple institutional actors (firm
and non-firm actors), to capture the linkages and influences between
global and local networked relations and to locate and highlight the
diverse power relations within the network. Rather like Lund-Thomsen
and Coe's (2013) focus on CSR and agency in Pakistan, we seek to
explain the experience of women garment workers in forced labour
arrangements, specifically to understand the types of interventions and
outcomes on policies, institutional factors and power relations that can
assist women workers' labour agency; yet we acknowledge that challenges remain in order to understand how workers may develop 'agency
legitimacy' in GPNs (Delaney et al., 2014).

We recognise that a key contributor to forced labour relations in the
Indian garment industry can be explained by neoliberal trends of capitalism (Elias, 2013). Global brands or buyers are able to assert leverage
to secure lower prices and short lead times that necessitate local suppliers to shift the burden onto the most vulnerable workers (Lerche,
2007; Phillips, 2013). This pattern reflects the most common cause of
forced labour and labour exploitation in the supply network/chain (ILO,
2005, 2013). We seek to examine the situation of women workers in
the Indian garment industry in order to understand the factors that
contribute to their vulnerability, such as gender and caste, in relation
to the key indicators of forced labour (ILO, 2013). We evaluate the
actions and responses by the multi-stakeholder initiative – the Ethical
Trading Initiative (ETI) – and initiatives by local and global campaigns
aimed at addressing such labour rights abuses and the effectiveness

of these strategies. We examine the factors that shape key actors' responses to forced labour and everyday labour exploitation. Further, we seek to understand how the varieties of labour exploitation may be conceptualised in a labour exploitation continuum.

The chapter is structured into four sections. The first discusses definitions and indicators of forced labour, the second draws on empirical data to illustrate key characteristics of the Indian garment sector, the third analyses key actors, local and international NGO campaigns and the ETI responses to forced labour, and the final section discusses the implications of these interventions and analyses the various responses to forced labour.

Forced labour and labour exploitation

According to the perspective of the ILO, the definition of forced labour has been consistent since the passage of the ILO Forced Labour Convention, 1930 (No. 29). However, the focus on particular types of forced labour has shifted as new forms of exploitation of labour have emerged; similarly, the indicators of forced labour have evolved over time (ILO, 2005, 2013, 2014). The ILO (2014) indicators of forced labour are aimed at providing guidance in identifying situations of forced labour. These include abuse of vulnerability; deception; restriction of movement; isolation; physical and sexual violence; intimidation and threats; retention of identity documents; withholding wages; debt bondage; abusive working and living conditions; and excessive overtime (ILO, 2005, 2014). These indicators are proffered as a useful means to operationalise the concept of forced labour.

Scott et al. suggest that there are a number of obstacles to operationalising the concept of forced labour, including reconciling areas that may or may not circumvent national labour laws. It is important to bridge 'real-world boundaries' between forced labour and broader exploitation when considering forced labour (Scott et al., 2012: 9). The fluidity and circumstances of forced labour are complex, and the terms 'forced labour' and 'labour exploitation' can be easily interchanged (Skrivankova, 2010). It is therefore useful to encapsulate the multiple experiences of labour exploitation along a continuum; at one end of the spectrum would be decent work and at the other end forced labour (Ibid.). From the perspective of workers affected by forced labour arrangements, it is important to consider how workers understand their circumstances. For example, they may 'tolerate' the everyday exploitative practices they experience in order to maintain ongoing work and access to income (Ibid.). Building on the concept of a labour exploitation continuum may provide a useful approach to conceptualising the causes and resolution of forced labour and where it intersects with and facilitates other forms of labour exploitation.

The textile and garment sector in Tamil Nadu, India

Coimbatore in the western part of Tamil Nadu was one of the traditional areas for the production of cotton and yarn in India. In the past, when most textile production took place in spinning mills and was for national markets, the workforce was mainly male and strongly unionised. The significant increase in the proportion of young women and migrant workers has occurred at the same time as the shift to garments and export-focused production (Tewari, 2004). A key aspect of efforts to gain a greater share of export markets is competition on price.

In general, Tamil Nadu has been industrialising rapidly over the last 20 years and agriculture has declined rapidly. This has led to many of those with small landholdings no longer being able to survive from subsistence work. Sometimes, whole families have responded by migrating to industrialised areas to find work; at other times, just young women go to work in factories and mills while living in provided hostels. The feminisation of the workforce in the sector came about because poor rural women were identified as a potential pool of workers in the late 1990s to meet the textile mill employers' objectives to recruit more 'manageable' workers (Narayanaswamy and Sachithanandam, 2010) – this has become known as the *sumangali* scheme. The term *sumangali* is a Tamil word meaning happily married woman and the employment scheme was portrayed as an opportunity for young single women to earn a living at the same time as saving up for their marriage expenses, while living away from their families in company-controlled hostels. The reality, however, is that thousands of young women and girls, most of whom are between 14 and 20 years of age, have been recruited to work in conditions that amount to forced or bonded labour.

Beginning from the late 1990s, the South Indian Mill Association (SIMA) began to implement a strategy that included a push against unionised labour and a shift to employing young women workers. SIMA reported the strengths of women workers, being 'the aptitude of women workers, being better disciplined, and more passive in regard to union activity' (Kumar, 2009: 1). The details of the different schemes known as *sumangali* vary but the key features are that young women are recruited to work for a fixed employment period, usually as apprentices, for between three and five years. During this period they live in company-controlled hostels, where they have no freedom and are not paid a full wage on the basis that part of the wage is withheld to make up a lump sum, paid at the end of the fixed term as a form of 'marriage assistance'. The lump sum is attractive to many poor families as one way in which they can pay a dowry, which is illegal but widespread in Tamil Nadu. At the same time, another form of forced labour, known as 'camp labour', continues in many mills and factories. This form of employment does not entail a fixed period but still involves forced labour where young women are housed in company-controlled hostels with no freedom of movement or association, and have no option but to work long hours of overtime when required.

The majority of young women and girls are recruited from very poor, rural backgrounds in Tamil Nadu and are from Dalit or low-caste communities. They are vulnerable due to their age, gender and caste background, all of which combine to give them few choices in their family and community. Patriarchal control in the family and community is replaced by similar control in the workplace, by management and supervisors, with little opportunity for support or resistance. The majority of women pay all their wages to their families and have at best small amounts for their own use. Wages are sometimes used for education of their brothers, to save up for a marriage or simply for daily expenses of the family or repayment of loans.

Recruitment to work in mills and factories, located many miles away from the villages, is often informal and through agents based in the villages who are paid a commission for each worker recruited. Employment is portrayed as an opportunity to earn good wages, with safe housing and opportunities for education, training and leisure activities. Without any written contracts, it is difficult for the women or their parents to challenge the actual conditions in the workplace and hostels.

Those living in hostels have no freedom of movement. They are generally not allowed to go outside of the hostel unsupervised, and supervised excursions are usually restricted to once a week or month. Phone calls and visits are limited to parents only. The result is almost complete isolation and lack of any support when faced with difficulties. Many women report verbal and physical abuse, and sometimes different forms of sexual harassment. Trade unions do not exist in these workplaces and there are rarely effective grievance mechanisms of any kind.

There are many complaints about conditions in hostels. Most common are complaints about bad food supplied in canteens and inadequate bathing or toilet facilities. Long hours of work (12-hour shifts), double shifts and working through the night are also frequently reported. Many women have to work seven days a week and are denied a day of rest. There are numerous reports of women being woken in the middle of the night to go and work, and they have few rights to leave to visit their families, apart from those during one or two major festivals.

Seven of the eleven criteria of forced labour recently outlined by the ILO are clearly present in Tamil Nadu: abuse of vulnerability; deception in hiring; restriction of movement; isolation; intimidation and threats; abusive living and working conditions; and excessive overtime. Applying the ILO criteria for the existence of forced labour shows that the situation of many young women workers fits the continuum of new forms of forced labour in modern supply network/chains, even if the form it takes is different from traditional images of slavery. The fixed-term schemes can also be seen as a modern form of bonded labour since part of the wages are withheld; women are not usually free to terminate their employment and when they do manage to leave, usually for reasons of ill-health, they are not paid any part of the lump sum due. The combination of the lack of freedom of movement intersects with and is reinforced by forced overtime, poor health and safety and non-payment of minimum wages.

Interventions on forced labour

Indian campaigns

Within Tamil Nadu there have been strong campaigns against *sumangali* and camp labour for nearly ten years. These campaigns have had limited success. They have extensively documented the abuse of young women workers in the sector and through using national and international lobbying have had some success in limiting the use of *sumangali*, or similar schemes. Camp labour, however, remains widespread and many women and activists report that forced labour continues, let alone other abuses of labour rights along the supply chain.

Local activists estimate that there are about 200,000 employed in situations of bonded or forced labour out of a total workforce of 800,000 in the region. Local campaigns have focused on this section of the workforce, along with employment of children under 14. Campaigns against child labour report frequent rescues of child workers, mainly from Tamil Nadu, but sometimes from other states in India (TPF, 2007).

The Tirupur People's Forum for Protection of Environment and Labour Rights (TPF) is a coordinating body for over 40 NGOs in Tamil

Nadu that has been campaigning around abuses in the sector. The majority of the organisations operate in areas which are sources of recruitment, and they are only able to contact the women outside their workplace in the community. Their activities have included local surveys to document conditions; rehabilitation and counselling of returned workers; awareness-raising among parents and the wider community; and provision of education and alternative employment, in addition to wider lobbying and advocacy work.

There are a number of different trade union federations active in the areas where the mills and factories are based, particularly in Tirupur and Coimbatore. Trade unions have been weakened by their political divisions, and their workplace activities are mainly restricted to the remaining government-run mills. They have, however, lobbied for the implementation of existing labour law and taken key test cases to court. In 2009, they won an important test case at the Madras High Court for the right of apprentices to be paid minimum wages.

Local NGOs work with the Women's Commission in Tamil Nadu to conduct public hearings which have led to recommendations that the *sumangali* schemes be recognised as forms of bonded and forced labour. There have been subsequent calls for the Tamil Nadu government to abolish them. There have also been extensive NGO campaigns and lobbying throughout Tamil Nadu to raise awareness among communities and to build public support for the abolition of *sumangali* and for an end to child labour and other abusive practices at the workplace. Such campaigns have been successful in gaining legal and government institutional bodies to determine *sumangali* and camp labour as bonded and forced labour. The NGOs have limited capacity however to implement the labour organising gap left by unions.

International campaigns

NGOs in Tamil Nadu have over the years built up international contacts to facilitate campaigning. In Europe, the Indian Committee of the Netherlands (ICN) and the Dutch research organisation SOMO (Centre for Research on Multinational Corporations) have produced a series of reports, documenting forced and bonded labour in the sector and linking brands to their suppliers (SOMO/ICN, 2010, 2012; SOMO, 2012). Similarly, Anti-Slavery International produced a report (ASI, 2012) which led to the formation of a working group, involving nearly 20 retailers and brands within the multi-stakeholder ETI in the UK (see the following).

The result of growing publicity and campaigns in both Europe and their equivalents in North America has led to many new initiatives and projects within Tamil Nadu. Some changes have included activities within the workplace aimed at improving management methods and increasing awareness among women workers of their rights. One brand has facilitated a few suppliers to work with a local NGO to develop a training programme, which includes thousands of young women, with an ongoing monitoring programme. Another development at the workplace has been instigated by the Dutch FairWear Foundation which has supported workplace education and awareness-raising around the setting up of a committee against sexual harassment, a legal requirement in India since 2013.

In general, in spite of a proliferation of projects in the area, the impact to date has been limited and there is still a need for a more targeted and comprehensive approach, particularly aimed at workplace representation and grievance procedures. International groups have worked collaboratively with the Indian campaigns, with a focus on tracing supply chains. The publication of reports highlighting the extreme exploitation has arguably contributed to making the brands somewhat more accountable for labour exploitation across the production network.

Ethical Trading Initiative

The ETI is a key Multi-Stakeholder Initiative (MSI) with many notable UK- and European-based garment and textile retailers being members. Given the large number of retailers and brands who have signed up to the ETI code of practice, it has the potential to exert influence across large parts of the sector. However, the responses by the ETI to systemic human rights abuses experienced by young girls and women in textile mills and garment factories in Tamil Nadu have been very limited. To date the ETI has engaged in various discussions on the issue, but little action has resulted. The lack of action, in particular to effect any change at the factory level in Tamil Nadu, remains a major concern. While the ETI depends upon retailers and brands' voluntary commitment to the ETI base code, some individual companies are implementing their own projects in specific factories. The impact of these voluntary measures has been limited and many of the initiatives have been restricted to specific workplaces without making improvements across the sector as a whole.

A number of factors obstruct the quest to improve working conditions. Companies often refuse to take direct responsibility for factory production, and it is easy to shift the blame to another player in the chain. Within the ETI the focus of attention by brands has been on *sumangali* schemes and has failed to address issues of forced labour and associated labour exploitation. The ETI actions appear driven by attention from international NGO reports and media; yet the ETI programmes have not developed strategies to implement the base code through the production network and instead focus on personal hygiene programmes and strategies that do not address the range of documented exploitative practices.

Using the exploitation continuum to inform policy, ethical trade and campaign responses

Our analysis of the Tamil Nadu garment industry suggests a correlation between the labour arrangements of workers in 'camp labour' and the ILO key indicators of forced labour. In addition, it suggests that the various forms of labour exploitation intersect and coexist. Many authors acknowledge the links between poverty, vulnerability and an increased likelihood of people being recruited into forms of forced labour (Lerche, 2007; Phillips, 2013). Our case suggests a complex form of interrelationships between exploitative practices. This points to a need for a broader conceptualisation of forced labour and the linkages to exploitative labour practices as suggested by an exploitation continuum (Skrivankova, 2010). A continuum approach acknowledges everyday labour exploitation and extremes of exploitation that can reinforce each other. For example, the situation of limited freedom of movement and hostel accommodation facilitates forced overtime for the garment workers. It is dependent upon the women workers being drawn from an economically and socially vulnerable group. In order to operationalise ways to address forced labour, it appears critical to situate and address all forms of exploitative labour practices, not one at the expense of the other.

Ethical trade, as demonstrated by the ETI, and other responses to the mounting evidence of forced labour and exploitative practices in Tamil Nadu have been mainly ineffective. The lack of action to ensure the prices paid by brands are sufficient to meet compliance of CSR standards and the few incentives offered to suppliers, such as long-term contracts, illustrates the conflicted interests between global and local firms and workers within the GPN. To date the ETI Tamil Nadu group makes no mention of how or when it will eliminate the circumstances contributing to forced labour in the production network/chain, nor reasons for not addressing the constraints on the workers that deny their freedom of movement and freedom of association and other exploitative practices.

Campaigns in India have had some success in influencing government institutions, instigating legal reform and highlighting the difficulties the women workers experience, in particular child labourers, as well as improving community awareness among communities targeted for recruitment to the mills and factories. While such campaigns are important to create a point of pressure on brands, this alone will not assist the workers to improve their labour agency and collectivism, nor will they act as a means to shift the power imbalance in the GPN. The challenge is to support the women to establish forms of collective organisation as this appears critical to address the power asymmetries in the GPN. This work is slow, however, without the characteristic assistance of a trade union. It takes time to build awareness, confidence and solidarity between the women and for a clear strategy and set of demands to be developed. The views among the key NGO actors and the local and international campaigns are not consistent in how to end forced labour and address the everyday exploitation the workers experience. While the campaigns have tended to focus on the worst abuses and negative features of the sector in Tamil Nadu, campaigns that focus on removing women from the factories and mills and providing alternatives in the community tend to draw the focus away from action around labour rights.

The role of local and international NGOs is significant in documenting the work conditions of women workers and making this known on a national and international platform around labour exploitation and corporate responsibility. The NGO campaigns commonly portray the women as young victims in need of rescue or implicitly suggest that the women should stop going to the factories despite their economic circumstances necessitating this. While it is important to eliminate the worst abuses, such as 'rescues' of child, bonded or forced labour workers, we should not let this detract from a focus on improving conditions in the workplace. The circumstances that contribute to how the various actors in the GPN view the women workers and therefore what opportunities to exist for them to challenge the asymmetries of power seem heavily weighted against them. The failure of an ethical trade response to adhere to local labour laws and international ETI code standards contributes to and undermines workers' potential to shift the power asymmetry.

We need to develop a much fuller understanding of how worker agency is constructed and what spaces of resistance women can carve out with the assistance of support agencies and other interventions (Rainnie et al., 2011). There is a need for a strong solidarity campaign to publicise the conditions in which the clothes that we buy are made and to put pressure on retailers to take decisive action on labour rights. Such a campaign needs to put at its centre the voices of the women workers themselves. The case of women workers in the textile sector in Tamil Nadu suggests that the way to shift structural power in the production network is through supporting the women workers to improve their labour agency and to collectively organise. If this can be done, other actors can act in support of women workers, rather than on their behalf, and ensure that real changes can be made.

Note

1. There have been, for example, several recent high-profile incidents in Bangladesh involving fires and building collapses which have involved hundreds of deaths among the workforce.

References

ASI (2012) *Slavery on the High Street: Forced Labour in the Manufacture of Garments for International Brands*. London: Anti-slavery International (ASI).

Coe N, M Dicken P and Hess M (2008) Global Production Networks: Realizing the Potential. *Journal of Economic Geography* 8: 271–295.

Delaney A, Burchielli R and Connor T (2014) Positioning Women Homeworkers in a Global Footwear Production Network: Identifying Barriers and Enablers to Claiming Rights, available at SSRN 2497381.

Elias J (ed.) (2013) *The Global Political Economy of the Household in Asia*. Basingstoke: Palgrave Macmillan.

Fairwear Foundation (2014) *Country Plan India 2014*. Netherlands: FairWear Foundation.

ILO (2005) Co29- Forced Labour Convention, 1930 (No. 29).

ICN (2013) *Report and Other Documents on Child Labour Published by the India Committee of Netherlands and Stop Child Labour*. The Hague: India Committee of the Netherlands.

ILO (2013) Tripartite Meeting of Experts on Forced Labour and Trafficking for Labour Exploitation. *Report for Discussion at the Tripartite Meeting of Experts Concerning the Possible Adoption of an ILO Instrument to Supplement the Forced Labour Convention, 1930 (No. 29)*. Geneva: International Labour Organization.

ILO (2014) ILO Indicators of Forced Labour. Geneva. International Labour Organization. Available at: http://www.ilo.org/wcmsp5/groups/public/—ed_norm/—declaration/documents/publication/wcms_203832.pdf

Kumar V (2009) Spinners Hike Output to Overcome Losses. Available at: http://expressindia.indianexpress.com/fe/daily/19990927/fco27098.html (accessed 14 July 2014).

Lerche J (2007) A Global Alliance against Forced Labour? Unfree Labour, Neo-Liberal Globalization and the International Labour Organization. *Journal of Agrarian Change* 7: 425–452.

Lund-Thomsen P and Coe N (2013) Corporate Social Responsibility and Labour Agency: The Case of Nike in Pakistan. *Journal of Economic Geography* March 1 15: 275–296.

Narayanaswamy K and Sachithanandam (2010) A Study to Understand the Situation of Arunthathiyars Girls Employed under the 'Sumangali Thittam' Scheme in Erode, Coimbatore, Tirupur, Viruthunagar and Dindigul Districts of Tamil Nadu. Arunthatiyar Human Rights Forum (AHRF).

Pearson R (2007) Beyond Women Workers: Gendering CSR. *Third World Quarterly* 28: 731–749.

Phillips N (2013) Unfree Labour and Adverse Incorporation in the Global Economy: Comparative Perspectives on Brazil and India. *Economy and Society* 42: 171–196.

Prieto-Carron M (2008) Women Workers, Industrialisation, Global Supply Chains and Corporate Codes of Conduct. *Journal of Business Ethics* 83(1): 5–17 10.1007/s10551-007-9650-7.

Rainnie A, Herod A and Mcgrath-Champ S (2011) Review and Positions: Global Production Networks and Labour. *Competition & Change* 15: 155–169.

Scott S, Craig G and Geddes A (2012) *The Experience of Forced Labour in the UK Food Industry*. UK: Joseph Rowntree Foundation.

Skrivankova K (2010) *Between Decent Work and Forced Labour: Examining the Continuum of Exploitation*. UK: Joseph Rowntree Foundation.

SOMO and ICN (2010) 'Captured by Cotton: Exploited Dalit Girls Produce Garments in India for European and US Markets'. Amsterdam: SOMO (Centre for Research on Multinational Corporations) & ICN (India Committee of the Netherlands).

SOMO and ICN (2012) Maid in India: Young Dalit Women Continue to Suffer Exploitative Conditions in India's Garment Industry. Amsterdam: SOMO (Centre for Research on Multinational Corporations) & ICN (India Committee of the Netherlands).

SOMO (2012) Bonded (Child) Labour in the South Indian Garment Industry: An Update of Debate and Action on the 'Sumangali Scheme'. Amsterdam: SOMO (Centre for Research on Multinational Corporations).

Tewari M (2004) The Challenge of Reform: How Tamil Nadu's Textile and Apparel Industry Is Facing the Pressures of Liberalization. Paper produced for the Government of Tamil Nadu, India and the Center for International Development, Cambridge, MA: Harvard University.

TPF (2007) *Women Workers in a Cage: An Investigative Study on Sumangali, Hostel and Camp Labour Schemes for Young Women Workers in the Tirupur Garment Industry*. Tirupur: Tirupur Peoples Forum.

18
The Staff Wanted Initiative: Preventing Exploitation, Forced Labour and Trafficking in the UK Hospitality Industry

Joanna Ewart-James and Neill Wilkins

Introduction

Research and anecdotal evidence suggest that workers in certain industries in the UK are particularly vulnerable to exploitation, forced labour and trafficking. These are commonly agreed to be care, catering, cleaning, construction, agriculture and hospitality (Lalani and Metcalf, 2012). However, legislative and policy response has largely been limited to agriculture and cleaning and mostly limited to addressing low pay or irregularity around wages. Recognising the hospitality sector as a key area of concern, Anti-Slavery International[1] and the Institute for Human Rights and Business (IHRB)[2] have jointly developed The Staff Wanted Initiative,[3] a programme that seeks to raise awareness and challenge situations of abuse and exploitation facing some workers in the UK hotel industry. This intervention has faced many challenges, shedding light on the reality of undertaking efforts to tackle labour exploitation in practice.

The Staff Wanted Initiative has used the United Nations (UN) Guiding Principles on Business and Human Rights as a framework to understand, explain and challenge failings by both the government and business adequately to protect staff and agency workers employed in the UK hotel sector from labour exploitation. With the aim of ending exploitation, Staff Wanted identifies governance gaps in the regulation of staffing agencies in the UK and the subsequent need for increased due diligence by businesses to reduce workers' vulnerability to forced labour. From the business perspective, Staff Wanted provides a risk management tool that, once implemented, reduces the risk that exploited workers will be present in the business's labour supply chains.

UN Special Representative Professor John Ruggie led the development of the Guiding Principles on Business and Human Rights, unanimously endorsed by the UN Human Rights Council in June 2011. The Guiding Principles have subsequently become the key human rights standard and reference for business across all sectors and locations, based on three key pillars:

1. The State duty to protect against human rights abuses by third parties, including business, through effective policies, legislation, regulation, enforcement activity and adjudication.
2. The business responsibility to respect human rights and avoid infringing on the rights of others.
3. The need for effective access to remedy through both judicial and non-judicial means.

Nature of the hotel industry

The hospitality industry is significant to the life of the UK and its economy. It is the fourth largest industry in the country employing (directly, or through agencies) approximately one in ten of the working population of the UK and generating over £39.6 billion annually in tax revenues (British Hospitality Association, 2014). The hotel sector is extremely competitive, with intense pressure on costs and, therefore, labour, which is a major component of a hotel's balance sheet. These pressures can result in the exploitation of some hotel workers, in operations both big and small. Whilst hard to quantify for lack of in-depth research into labour abuse in the sector, anecdotal evidence suggests that exploitation is particularly acute for low-paid, low-skilled migrant workers, where language gaps, lack of access to informed support networks and lack of awareness of their employment rights increase their vulnerability.

Workers in the hotel industry are generally disempowered; trade unions find it difficult to organise effectively in many UK hotel operations and are poorly represented. Whilst some provision is made at a national level, unions frequently lack the resources to overcome language, staff dispersal, the casual and transient nature of employment and other barriers to local organising. This is compounded by the short-term agency and outsourced staffing models common in many hotels.

Use of third parties

A key feature of employment in the UK hotel industry is the ubiquitous use of recruitment and employment agencies as well as the wholesale outsourcing of staffing. The move towards agency working can be found in many sectors employing low-waged and unskilled workers and reflects the changing nature of employment relationships globally towards increased involvement of third parties between the worker and labour user, as explained in the Employment and Recruitment Agencies Sector Guide On Implementing the UN Guiding Principles on Business and Human Rights (IHRB and Shift, 2013).

Originally agency workers were used as a 'buffer' by hotels to overcome peaks and troughs in demand over seasons; however, the flexibility and perceived cost savings on labour has resulted in agency working becoming a dominant model in the industry. Some hotels now outsource all housekeeping functions to agency contractors forming a triangular relationship between the hotel, the employment services agency and the worker. Therefore, a business relationship (between two companies) replaces the employment relationship between a hotel and its staff, severing the direct link between the hotel, the employer and the worker on their premises. This 'hands-off' relationship can mean hotels are unaware of exploitation and abuse – which is frequently hidden. In other cases, hotels might be wilfully blind and 'hide behind their contract', stating that they pay an agreed sum for services to the agency, and it is for the agency to take responsibility for how those services should be delivered. UK law is clear, if still untested, that wilful blindness to exploitation is not an option, as highlighted in the Ministry of Justice leaflet Slavery, Servitude and Forced or Compulsory Labour (Ministry of Justice, 2009).

Low-wage, low-value business model

Much of the modern UK hotel industry is reliant on a large and constantly replaceable supply of cheap labour mostly supplied by agencies. This impacts on perceptions of the industry. It is a sector characterised by the following: poor quality, low-skilled jobs; low wages; high employee turnover; a casual workforce; minimal training; and little opportunity for career progression. This in turn leads to problems recruiting and retaining staff, further entrenching the casual and precarious nature of employment in the industry. This means the hotel industry is reliant on a constant flow of low-paid, frequently migrant, agency labour.

Despite well-documented vulnerabilities, the government has failed to put in place any effective regulation or enforcement systems to ensure that agency staff are protected from exploitation. This has helped facilitate fierce competition among unlicensed, unregulated agencies and individuals to supply staff to hotels. As agencies compete on price to secure hotel contracts, they in turn may squeeze terms and conditions for workers, which can lead to exploitation and forced labour.

Trade union organisers have reported examples of hotel sector labour abuse, including excessive hours and compulsory overtime, with workers coerced into being constantly available under threat of future work being withdrawn; the intensification of work, with unrealistic piecework rates often only achieved through extra hours resulting in pay below the minimum wage (see Lopes and Hall, this volume); the withholding of wages; unjustified or unaccounted deductions from wages; non-payment for holiday and sick pay; excessive charges for services, uniforms, laundry and food, a particular risk where accommodation is provided by the employer; and at worst, threats of violence and sexual harassment. These practices are indicators of forced labour (Geddes et al., 2013). Migrant agency workers may be particularly susceptible to forced labour shown by indicators, including the control of passport and documents; control of bank accounts or ATM cards; illegal fees for finding work; excessive charges for services such as administration and translation services; tied and substandard accommodation; and bogus self-employment.

It is well documented that low-skilled, low-paid migrant workers can find themselves particularly vulnerable to exploitation (Jayaweera and Anderson, 2008), not least because of a lack of English-language skills and so access to accurate information on their rights or mechanisms for redress. Some workers are deliberately dissuaded from learning English so that they might be coerced through unfounded threats, such as denunciation to immigration authorities. Migrant workers frequently lack the support networks which might help them assert their rights.

A further feature facilitating exploitation is self-employment, described as 'endemic' within London hotels (BBC Newsnight, 2012). Agency workers, registered as self-employed (but supplied via an agency) were not operating as bona fide self-employed workers. Instead, their work was managed by the hotel, their self-employed status merely a ruse to keep down costs and restrict their rights.

Some hotels may believe that by outsourcing responsibility for these housekeeping or human resources functions to an agency they are also outsourcing their liability. Evidently, this is not the case, either from the viewpoint of the worker, the customer or the law. All companies have a duty to respect and look after those who work within their operations.

By failing to manage these functions properly, hotels are leaving their staff, including agency staff, liable to exploitation and abuse. If a company has known or should have known about exploitation, it can be considered complicit in abuse. Furthermore, criminality seldom occurs in a vacuum and hotels might find themselves inadvertently exposed to other risks. London's Metropolitan Police are increasingly concerned about the involvement of criminal gangs in a number of industry sectors. The horsemeat scandal across Europe (Food Standards Agency, 2013) has revealed the alacrity with which criminal gangs will become active in sectors where they spot opportunity.

The low-cost/low-value business model adopted by the hospitality industry doesn't just affect individual workers. The UK's hospitality industry, and its trade body the British Hospitality Association (2014), has attempted to position itself as a *super sector*, a vehicle for jobs and growth. In reality, it punches below its weight with negative perceptions of the industry hampering its performance. The sector remains undervalued as a key contributor to the economy, as it fails to command respect or attention from key stakeholders, has few advocates within its own workforce and lacks public support and influence with policymakers. The low-cost/low-value model impedes access to the attention and respect that other equivalently sized industries achieve.

The London 2012 Olympic Games and Glasgow 2014 Commonwealth Games

The London 2012 Olympic Games and Glasgow 2014 Commonwealth Games helped mobilise support for the Staff Wanted Initiative amongst a wide range of stakeholders and provided a useful vehicle to promote its aims to the industry, particularly hotels in London. The increased public scrutiny and media attention on global sporting events increases corporate sensitivity to brand reputation and governmental sensitivity to political impacts. This galvanised governmental bodies and parliamentarians in London and Glasgow to focus attention on the risk to workers in hospitality.

Staff Wanted Initiative at the government level

Although Staff Wanted Initiative aims to influence the hospitality industry directly to protect workers, the initiative also sought to demonstrate that the state authorities could do more in their regulation of the sector. The UN Guiding Principles (op. cit., 2011) make it quite clear that the state has a duty to protect all persons including workers, whatever their employment situation, or industry. Anecdotal evidence of labour exploitation suggests that the state is failing its responsibilities towards workers in the hospitality sector, not least due to weak and ineffective regulation of organisations and individuals supplying agency workers to the hospitality sector.

In 2010, the Department Of Business, Innovation and Skills, in evidence to the Low Pay Commission on the National Minimum Wage (BIS, 2010), showed that complaints in the hospitality sector exceeded other industries. It also noted the Low Pay Commission's concerns around non-payment of the minimum wage in parts of the hospitality industry with recommendations for more targeted enforcement activity. Because exploitation in the UK hotel sector is often at the hands of unregulated labour providers easily set up with little restriction or government oversight, stronger regulation of third parties accompanied by increased and more effective enforcement activity would be a major way that the risks to workers in the sector could be reduced.

At the time of writing, the Employment Agency Standards Inspectorate (EASI) holds responsibility for regulating agencies in sectors in which workers are particularly vulnerable to exploitation, such as construction and care. EASI implements this responsibility with just eight inspectors. Due to such limited resources, it focuses on responding to calls to the *Pay and Work Rights Helpline*, a telephone hotline service for those seeking advice or action regarding exploitation and abuse. However, the helpline is only a reactive measure, and the Initiative's engagement with the police, community organisations and media reports suggests that this may be the tip of an iceberg with many of the most vulnerable workers lacking the confidence, awareness or ability to access this service. Cases that reach the helpline are unlikely to give an accurate picture of where the most egregious abuses take place, as by virtue of being under someone else's control, those in forced labour are likely to be isolated and unable to access such a service.

Indeed, the evidence of exploitation suggests that the hotline is inadequate for the government to meet its responsibility to protect. A hotline should only be used to complement other enforcement activity by the state as it undertakes its duty to protect. This protection must be proactive with a view to deter and prevent abuse before it happens – not simply manage the situation afterwards. Other areas of concern, such as health and safety legislation, rely on wide-ranging enforcement proactive and reactive elements.

In contrast with the hotel sector, agencies supplying workers to the agriculture, horticulture and certain areas of food processing are regulated by the Gangmasters Licensing Authority (GLA), a non-departmental government body. Agencies supplying staff to this sector must be licensed and are subject to proactive checks and inspections by the GLA. For labour users in these sectors, it is illegal to use the services of an unlicensed agency. Whilst the GLA licensing regime is far from perfect, it has been relatively successful – given its very modest resources – in reducing the incidence of both small-scale exploitation and more severe abuses within the sectors in which it operates.

The contrast in effectiveness of the proactive, intelligence-led approach of the GLA to the reactive approach of EASI was plainly revealed in the key findings of the parallel Hampton Implementation Reviews of the two bodies in 2009. In its assessment of the GLA (BIS, 2009), the review reported that the GLA's impact in improving working conditions for some vulnerable workers has been impressive, particularly in view of its relatively small size; that it has a good awareness of the unintended consequences of its operational decisions and takes proactive steps to minimise these, that the GLA has done well in building consensus amongst its diverse stakeholders on the best way forward with regulation and that the GLA has actively sought to minimise any unnecessary additional regulatory burdens that might have followed its licensing regime. In contrast, the Hampton Implementation Review Report of the EASI (Ibid.) found its strategy and operational systems lagging behind changes in the industry. It also comments on the limited sanctioning options, the lack of necessary powers to address rogue businesses (i.e. no 'stop now' orders or administrative penalties available) and the poor capacity of EASI to store, analyse and share data related to business risk and non-compliance.

The lack of effective enforcement activity also contributes to the lack of solid data on the scope and extent of exploitation within the hospitality industry. Unsurprisingly, there have been very few prosecutions, giving the false impression that there are few problems within the industry. This point is well made by Mark Boleat (2009), former chair of the Association of Labour Providers – a trade body for agencies supplying staff into (mostly) the agricultural sector. Boleat stresses that unenforced regulations can be damaging, by giving the impression that there is effective regulation and allowing those engaged in malpractice to operate with a 'false halo of respectability'. Boleat also makes the case for effective and proactive enforcement activity to match regulation, stating that the decision to comply with relevant laws is also influenced by enforcement (Ibid.: 33).

In 2014, EASI was merged into the Her Majesty's Revenue and Customs; at the time of writing, the impact of this shift remains to be seen. Effective supervision is still sadly lacking across a range of sectors outside those under the remit of the GLA. Despite efforts to extend the remit of the GLA to other sectors, government policy is to reduce, rather than extend regulation (UK Government, 2014). The UK government's aim is to encourage business to take more responsibility for issues within their sector, even when of a criminal nature.

The absence of effective regulation has very serious negative consequences for the industry, exposing law-abiding business to unfair competition from those operating illegally and placing workers at direct risk of exploitation. There are clear limits on how far responsible business can or should police their sector. The enforcement of appropriate standards and protection for labour and human rights is the responsibility of government agencies. These agencies should be adequately resourced and organised to deliver the level-playing field law-abiding businesses need to compete fairly within the law.

The Staff Wanted Initiative undertook a range of activities with policymakers and government departments highlighting the anomaly of the UK agency licensing regime and encouraging a more considered and robust response. It worked to secure cross-party support and triggered discussion on the issue in parliament. Pressure on government to do more to combat trafficking and exploitation in all industry sectors enabled Staff Wanted Initiative to engage with government actors to guide action to improve recruitment practice in the hotel sector. The Home Office produced a leaflet entitled 'Human Trafficking Practical Guidance' (Home Office, 2013), a brief but clear guide, which reflects many of the concerns and recommendations for business put forward by Staff Wanted. The Staff Wanted Initiative is endorsed by the Metropolitan Police Human Exploitation Team SCD9, which has been a strong advocate for the Initiative within the police and externally. Staff Wanted Initiative leaflets were included in delegate packs for the National Association of Chief Police Officers conference and sent to all police forces in the UK.

Staff Wanted Initiative's work on business responsibility to respect human rights

The UN Guiding Principles (2011) make clear the duty of all businesses to respect human rights; barring a few exceptions, the hotel industry has failed to engage meaningfully with any sustainability agenda beyond environmental best practice. The Staff Wanted Initiative aimed to show that all hotels, whatever their size, should take full responsibility for staff working on their premises, whether directly employed or supplied by agencies.

Despite new UK legislation (Ministry of Justice, 2009), engaging with the hospitality industry to tackle trafficking and forced labour has however proved challenging. The lack of solid data or regular exposures of cases means the hidden nature of the exploitation induces ignorance or outright denial from the industry and in particular from its trade body, The British Hospitality Association. In common with other sectors, concern for brand reputation means even when businesses become aware of exploitation and address these issues, few hotels, even 'best practice' hotels, are willing to admit to problems within their operations or the steps they are taking to combat the issues.

For these reasons, the approach taken by the Initiative from the outset was non-confrontational. An awareness-raising message was delivered within helpful, business-orientated guidelines for the industry. A key tenet of the UN Guiding Principles is the concept of undertaking an effective due diligence process to identify, prevent, mitigate and account for how a company impacts on human rights. As part of this Initiative, clear guidance to identify operational changes for hotel management to take to protect their workforce was developed. *The SEE formula* encourages hotels to

> Scrutinise – their relationships with their suppliers of labour and contracted out services
>
> Engage – with those working on their premises
>
> Ensure – that they provide a fit and proper workplace, including guidance for those whose job it is to hire or manage agency staff

The acronym SEE also alludes to the hidden nature of exploitation and challenges companies to consider 'What they would SEE if they really looked'. Staff Wanted published and widely distributed to hotels and posted on a dedicated micro-site a simple leaflet setting out specific and practical measures, serving the dual purpose of providing guidance and alerting business to often unrecognised red flags to forced labour and human trafficking (Staff Wanted Initiative, 2012).

Engagement with one major hotel chain was followed by a review of their operating procedures. It must be hoped that the higher profile of trafficking for forced labour in all sectors should encourage increased and better hospitality industry engagement along with the spectre of reputational risk. A critical tipping point with the industry however has yet to be reached.

To encourage and foster business engagement, the Initiative has also established links with other organisations with the similar objectives to end exploitation forced labour and trafficking in the hospitality industry. Staff Wanted Initiative is a key feature in advocacy work undertaken by the Interfaith Centre for Corporate Responsibility (ICCR), which organises substantial shareholder engagement with business regarding human rights. As part of their Celebration without Exploitation Programme around the Olympics, a letter from ICCR and its major investment company partners was sent to all the major hotel chains located in London, explicitly calling for engagement with the Initiative. Staff Wanted also established a good working relationship with the International Tourism Partnership (ITP), following which ITP formulated a position statement and set of guidelines for ethical recruitment used by its hotel members (International Tourism Partnership, 2013). This has given trafficking and exploitation of staff a far higher profile.

The next steps for Staff Wanted Initiative involve concentrating on strengthening the voice of worker. Pillar 3 of the UN Guiding Principles states that victims of human rights abuse must have access to remedy; Staff Wanted Initiative has promoted effective methods of reporting abuse and grievance mechanisms. Hotel industry workers lack knowledge and often access to simple processes to claim their rights. Again, this is partly a symptom of the often precarious nature of the work provided through agencies. Migrant workers represent a significant portion of those employed in the industry and can face language, social and cultural barriers further adding to their vulnerability to exploitation and inability to assert their rights. For the industry, the exploitation remains hidden and there is little pressure on the hotel industry to address workers' vulnerability. Indeed, some hotels are either tacitly complicit or wilfully blind to the exploitation of agency staff on their premises. This remains the least developed of the work undertaken so far, but nevertheless the empowerment of workers to access grievance mechanisms and claim their rights is crucial for the Staff Wanted Initiative to achieve its aims.

Going forward, the Initiative plans to work towards improving workers' awareness of grievance mechanisms, identifying and overcoming barriers to securing redress and empowering vulnerable workers to claim their rights. In particular, it will seek to engage better with organisations with whom agency and particularly migrant workers may be in contact, such as national support networks and faith groups. It is hoped that these groups may serve as an additional conduit to deliver better information to workers in order that they may assert their rights.

Conclusions

The experience of the Staff Wanted illustrates a wider problem in tackling forced labour, the need for an in-depth, comprehensive survey of the situation for hospitality workers, not just to better understand the challenges, or to simply be better equipped to measure impact, but crucially to demonstrate to business and government that this is a real issue and a matter that must be taken seriously. Official statistics, such as those provided by the Pay and Work Helpline, are likely to bear little resemblance to the true picture.

The commitment of most businesses to address forced labour and exploitation is questionable and unlikely to be sufficient without being coupled with effective government regulation. There is little doubt that current regulations are failing to protect workers from labour exploitation. Regulation and enforcement activity must be meaningful, that is, proactive, intelligence based and well resourced to ensure that law-abiding business is able to operate on a level-playing field. In addition, regulations must keep up with ever-changing business practices that leave workers increasingly vulnerable to exploitation, such as bogus self-employment and the use of complex business relationships that obscure or remove labour users' responsibilities towards workers.

None of this will result in meaningful improvements in working conditions and an end to labour exploitation unless workers' voices are heard and they are empowered with access to redress, particularly the most vulnerable. Access to remedy is often thought of as the end of a process but through the experience of Staff Wanted, it is clear that it is best used as the starting point for identifying issues and opportunities for challenge and change.

The greatest impact of the Staff Wanted Initiative to date is its success in raising awareness of the vulnerabilities of hotel workers in the UK. Whilst we do not yet know if raising awareness has been translated to a reduction in vulnerability, it is an important first step for an industry that, thanks to the Initiative and the work of other organisations, is beginning to wake up to the need to put in place measures to protect workers. The Initiative has built momentum amongst a wide group of influential stakeholders, which, combined with action to empower workers, has sown the seed to combat exploitation, human trafficking and forced labour in the UK hotel industry.

Notes

1. Anti-Slavery International (http://www.antislavery.org/english/) is a UK-based non-governmental organisation. It works at local, national and international levels to eliminate all forms of slavery around the world by supporting research to assess the scale of slavery in order to identify measures to end it, working with local organisations to raise public awareness of slavery, educating the public about the realities of slavery and campaigning for its end, lobbying governments and intergovernmental agencies to make slavery a priority issue and developing and implementing plans to eliminate slavery.
2. The Institute for Human Rights and Business (http://www.ihrb.org/) is a UK-based 'think and do' tank dedicated to being a global centre of excellence and expertise on the relationship between business and internationally proclaimed human rights standards. They seek to provide a trusted, impartial space for dialogue and independent analysis to deepen understanding of human rights challenges and issues and the appropriate role of business.
3. Visit http://www.staff-wanted.org/ for more information about the Staff Wanted Initiative.

References

Anti-Slavery International, Institute for Human Rights and Business and Scottish Human Rights Commission (2013) Meeting Report – Responsibility and Rights: The Glasgow Commonwealth Games. Upholding Human Rights. Preventing Forced Labour and Trafficking. Glasgow, UK. 22 October 2013.

British Hospitality Association (2014) Home Page. Available at: http://www.bha.org.uk (accessed 4 August 2014).

British Hospitality Association Media Centre (2014) Industry Facts and Figures. Available at: www.bha.org.uk/media-centre/ (accessed 4 August 2014).

Boleat M (2009) An Agenda for Better Regulation. London, Policy Exchange. Available at: http://www.policyexchange.org.uk/images/publications/an%20agenda%20for%20better%20regulation%20-%20dec%2009.pdf (accessed 4 August 2014).

Department for Business Innovation and Skills (2009) Employment Agency Standards Inspectorate – A Hampton Implementation Review Report. London, Department for Business Innovation and Skills. Available at: http://webarchive.nationalarchives.gov.uk/20121212135622/http://www.bis.gov.uk/files/file53511.pdf (accessed 4 August 2014).

Department for Business Innovation and Skills (2009) Gangmasters Licensing Authority – A Hampton Implementation Review Report. London, Department for Business Innovation and Skills. Available at: http://webarchive.nationalarchives.gov.uk/20121212135622/http://www.bis.gov.uk/files/file52901.pdf (accessed 4 August 2014).

Department for Business Innovation and Skills (2010) Government non-economic evidence to the Low Pay Commission. London, Department for Business Innovation and Skills. Available at: http://webarchive.nationalarchives.gov.uk/20090609003228/http://www.berr.gov.uk/assets/biscore/employment-matters/docs/n/10-1153-national-minimum-wage-non-economic-evidence-2010.pdf (accessed 4 August 2014).

Food Standards Agency Available at: https://www.food.gov.uk/enforcement/ monitoring/horse-meat (accessed 19 January 2015).

Geddes A, Craig G and Scott S (2013) *Forced Labour in the UK*. York: Joseph Rowntree Foundation.

Home Office (2013) Human Trafficking – Practical Guidance Home Office. Available at: https://www.gov.uk/government/uploads/system/uploads/ attachment_data/file/181550/Human_Trafficking_practical_guidance.pdf (accessed 26 August 2014).

Institute for Human Rights and Business and Shift (2013) *Employment and Recruitment Agencies Sector Guide on Implementing the UN Guiding Principles on Business and Human Rights*. Bruxelles: The Institute for Human Rights and Business.

Interfaith Center on Corporate Responsibility (2012) Celebration without Exploitation. Available at: http://www.iccr.org/our-issues/human-rights/ celebration-without-exploitation-ht-large-events (accessed 26 August 2014).

International Tourism Partnership (2013) ITP Position Statement on Human Trafficking. Available at: http://www.tourismpartnership.org/what-we-do/key-issues/human-trafficking (accessed 26 August 2014).

Jayaweera H and Anderson B (2008) *Migrant Workers and Vulnerable Employment: A Review of Existing Data*. TUC Commission on Vulnerable Employment. Oxford: Centre on Migration, Policy and Society (COMPAS).

Lalani M and Metcalf H (2012) *Forced Labour in the UK: The Business Angle*. York: Joseph Rowntree Foundation.

Ministry of Justice (2009) Slavery, Servitude and Forced or Compulsory Labour. Ministry of Justice UK. Available at: http://www.justice.gov.uk/downloads/ protecting-the-vulnerable/forced-labour/slavery-and-Servitude.pdf (accessed 4 August 2014).

Newsnight (2012) Cleaners Anger at Outsourcing in Top London Hotel 2012. BBC BBC2 27 September 2012.

Office of the UN High Commissioner for Human Rights (2011) Guiding Principles on Business and Human Tights. Office of the UN High Commissioner for Human Rights. Available at: http://www.ohchr.org/Documents/Publications/ GuidingPrinciplesBusinessHR_EN.pdf (accessed 4 August 2011).

Staff Wanted Initiative (2012) SEE Formula. Available at: http://www.staff -wanted.org/see-formula.html (accessed 24 August 2014).

Staff Wanted Initiative (2012) Available at: www.staff-wanted.org (accessed 24 August 2014).

UK Government (2014) Response to the Draft UK Modern Slavery Bill. Gov UK Publications. Available at: https://www.gov .uk/government/uploads/system/uploads/attachment_data/file/318771/ CM8889DraftModernSlaveryBill.pdf (accessed 19 January 2015).

UK Parliament EDM 276 Preventing the Exploitation of Staff in UK Hotels (Session 2011–2012) Available at: http://www.parliament.uk/edm/2012-13/276 (accessed 4 August 2014).

Index

Africa, 39, 143, 232
Agenc-y (-ies) (labour/job), 4, 149, 151, 193, 258, 259
Angola, 168
Anti-Slavery International, 93, 250, 256
Apple, 19
arbitrage, 28, 34, 35
Argentina, 34, 161
Asia, 39, 41, 104
    Central, 143
    East, 73
    South, 133, 140, 143
    South East, 74, 168
Association of Chief Police Officers, 263
Association of Labour Providers, 262
asylum/asylum seekers, 6, 7, 87, 101ff., 115ff., 129ff., 143ff
audit, 16, 20
Australasia, 34
Austria, 42

Bangladesh [-i]/Bengali, 7, 10, 21, 32, 34, 36, 37, 42, 129ff., 188, 256
BME (Black and minority ethnic), 51, 52, 53, 60, 187
Bolivia, 8, 161, 165
bonded labour, 249
Brazil, 23, 163
Britain/UK, 34, 44, 48, 49, 50, 51, 53, 65, 67, 86ff., 133, 174ff., 201, 203, 205, 207, 208, 230ff., 244, 250, 256ff
Buenos Aires, 161
Bulgaria, 105, 219

California, 15, 20, 21
Canada, 31, 60ff
capital (-ist/-ism), 5, 7, 28ff., 44ff., 59ff., 71, 101ff., 124, 125, 164, 170, 176, 179, 245
care, 5, 59, 60, 66

casualised, 5
Centre for Social Justice, 21
CGIL (Confederazione Generale Italiana del Lavoro: also CSIL, UIL), 52
child labour/slavery, 244ff
Chile, 163
China/Chinese, 8, 31, 32, 35, 36, 37, 39, 49, 74ff., 87, 174ff., 188
citizenship, 9, 215ff
Citizens UK, 232, 241
Civil Penalty Scheme, 51
civil society/community organisations/NGOs, 9, 18, 21, 171, 218, 230, 241, 242, 244ff
commodification, 5, 46, 59, 222, 223, 226
Commonwealth Games, 260
Council of Europe, 89, 90, 92
CSR (corporate social responsibility), 17, 19, 20, 89, 245, 252
Cuba, 41
Czech Republic, 74

debt(-bondage), 82, 162, 169, 174ff
Denmark, 123
deportation, 118, 143, 151
deregulation, 2
destitution, 7, 33, 111, 143ff
detention, 102, 106, 151, 184
diaspor-a (-ic), 108, 133
dignity, 205ff
dispersal, 106, 108
diversity, 6, 176
domestic (workers/labour/servitude), 8, 59ff., 87, 152, 153, 167, 200ff., 219
Dutch Fairwear Foundation, 251

EASI (Employment Agency Standards Inspectorate), 261, 262
East London Communities Organisation (TELCO), 231ff

Employment Rights Act (1996), 202
enclave (ethnic), 1, 8, 190
Equality and Human Rights
    Commission, 234, 240
Esping-Andersen, 46
Ethical trade, 244ff
    Trading Initiative, 245, 250, 251
EU (European Union
    /Commission/Eurozone), 44, 48,
    50, 73ff., 125, 130
Europe(an), 29, 31, 34, 42, 104, 116,
    123, 129, 130, 134, 140, 144, 202,
    205, 215, 216, 218, 219, 222, 226,
    250, 251, 260
    Eastern/East and Central, 72ff.,
    102ff., 143
European Integration Fund, 79
European Statistics on Income and
    Living Conditions (EU-SILC),
    44, 46
European Trade Union
    Confederation, 3

faith, 145
Falung Gong, 185
FDI (Foreign Direct Investment), 29,
    32, 49, 105
Finland, 42
FLAI-CGIL (Federazione Lavorotori
    Agro-Industria-Confederazione
    Italiana del Lavoro), 51
forced labour, 5, 15ff., 81, 86ff., 105,
    163, 171, 174ff., 217, 244ff., 256ff
Fortress Europe, 28, 48
Foxconn, 19
France, 129ff

Gangmasters Licensing Authority
    (GLA), 88, 91, 92, 262
Gap, 19, 21
GDP (Gross Domestic Product), 35, 36,
    37, 48, 105
gender [-ed] (women), 3, 51, 60ff.,
    108, 125, 244ff
General Motors, 32, 36
Germany, 49, 203
'Global North', 2, 3, 4, 53, 164
'Global South', 2, 4, 5, 47, 53, 164, 166
governance, 15ff

GPN (global production networks),
    245ff
Greater London Authority, 233
Greece, 44, 74

H&M, 32, 36
Hampton Implementation Review,
    262
health and safety, 93, 104, 164, 202,
    203, 204, 207, 208
    Act (1974), 202
    Executive, 91
Her Majesty' Revenue and Customs,
    263
homelessness, 147, 150, 153
housing, 145, 187
Hungary, 74

ICCR (Inter-faith Centre for Corporate
    Responsibility), 265
illegal (irregular [-ity], unauthorised,
    undocumented, *au noir*), 3, 6, 7,
    8, 46, 125, 129ff., 174ff., 187ff.,
    201, 202
ILO (International Labour
    Organization), 2, 30, 33, 37, 39,
    41, 48, 80, 87, 89, 90, 93, 95, 161,
    166, 185, 201, 203, 207, 215, 216,
    244, 246, 249
    fundamental principles, 20
    International Labour Conference,
    203
IMF (International Monetary Fund),
    34, 35, 38
Immigration and Nationality
    Directorate, 107
imperialis-t [-m], 4, 29, 32, 41, 103
Independent Asylum Commission,
    101, 107
India/Indian, 9, 35, 78, 244ff
industry-[-ies]
    agriculture, 163, 215ff., 247, 256
    care, 148, 256
    cleaning, 9, 51, 130, 148, 231ff., 256
    construction, 189, 219, 256
    food services, 130, 148, 189, 256
    fruit vending, 129ff
    garment/clothing, 7, 18, 21, 34, 40,
    162, 244ff

hair and beauty, 189
horsemeat, 20
hospitality, 9, 130, 256ff
logistics, 53
manufacturing, 189
metalwork, 219
textile, 9, 21, 34, 244ff
Ingaggio, 215
Institute for Human Rights and
    Business (IHRB), 256
integration, 48, 61, 77, 79, 106, 107,
    123, 129, 135, 139
International Tourism Partnership,
    265
IOM (International Organization for
    Migration), 34, 72ff., 169
Italy, 44, 48, 49, 50, 51, 53, 133, 170,
    203, 215, 218

Japan/-ese, 28, 29, 31

Kalayaan, 64, 65, 205, 206
Korea, South, 74
Kosovo, 116

Latin America, 39, 41
living wage, 9, 42, 230ff
    Foundation, 241
Low Pay Commission, 233, 261
Low Skill Pilot Programme, 66

Malta, 74
Metropolitan Police Human
    Exploitation Team, 263
Mexico, 28, 30, 36
Middle East, 34, 143
Migrant Integration Policy Index, 77
Migration Advisory Committee
    (MAC), 91, 95
Modern (Day) Slavery Act/Bill, 66, 89,
    92, 94, 203
Morgan Stanley, 35

National Asylum Support Service, 107
National Minimum Wage, 232, 261
    Regulation (1999), 202
National Referral Mechanism, 87
Netherlands, 250

network(s), 8, 29, 89, 101ff., 129ff.,
    143ff., 154, 163, 174ff., 188
NGOs, *see* civil society
Nike, 19, 38
North America, 29, 34, 251
Norway, 123

OECD (Organisation for Economic
    Cooperation and
    Development), 49
Olympic Games, 260, 265
outsourcing/offshoring, 4, 20, 28ff.,
    48, 164

Pakistan(i), 218
Palermo Protocol, 79, 88, 90, 95, 167
Pay and Work Helpline, 266
Philippine Women Centre, 68
Poland, 74
political economy, 3, 4, 5, 21, 28ff.,
    44ff., 61, 68, 101, 161
    feminist, 59ff
Portugal, 44
poverty/impoverishment, 48
Primark, 21, 32
privatisation, 5, 59

'queue-shifting', 120, 121

racism/discrimination, 45, 52, 108,
    127, 138, 155
refugees, 3, 6, 74, 102ff., 115ff., 123,
    135, 193, 218, 223
remittances, 34, 153
resistance, 6, 101, 104, 105, 108, 110,
    151, 152, 153, 154, 176, 177, 179,
    185, 246, 253
Rumania(n)/Romania(n), 74, 105,
    216, 218, 219, 220, 226

Sao Paulo, 23
Saudi Arabia, 34
Schengen, 48, 74
Sicily, 9, 215, 222
SIMA (South Indian Mill Association),
    247
slavery, 6, 15, 20, 24, 67, 86ff., 200ff
Slovakia, 72ff
snakehead (gang), 174ff., 194

Somali(a), 218
SOMO (Centre for Research on
    Multinational Corporations), 250
South Africa, 21
South America, 231
Spain, 44, 170, 205
Staff Wanted Initiative, 256
street work, 129ff
supply chain (s), 1, 4, 9, 15ff., 41, 90,
    95, 241, 245, 251
sweatshops(s), 161ff
Sweden, 7, 42, 115ff., 133
System for the Protection of
    Asylum-Seekers and Refugees
    (SPRAR), 218

TGWU/UNITE
    Justice for Cleaners Campaign, 51
Third World, 30
TNCs (Transnational Corporations),
    29, 36
TPF (Tirupur People's Forum for
    Protection of Environment and
    Labour Rights), 269
Trades Union Congress, 87
    Commission on Vulnerable
        Employment, 51, 87
trades unions, 10, 45, 47, 49, 51, 52,
    53, 78, 79, 120, 123, 165, 166,
    203, 204, 230, 234, 238, 240, 241,
    242, 248, 259
Trade Union Act (1871), 204
traffick-ed [-ing], 3, 4, 15ff., 67, 78,
    86ff., 161ff., 254ff
Trust for London, 233
Tunisia(n), 218, 222, 226
Turkey, 188

UK, *see* Britain
UKIP (United Kingdom Independence
    Party), 52

Ukraine, 73ff
unfreedom/unfree labour, 5, 57ff
Unison, 232, 234
United Nations, 48
    Conference on Trade and
        Development (UNCTAD), 29,
        30, 31, 35, 39, 49
    Guiding Principles on Business and
        Human Rights, 90, 256ff
    Human Rights Council, 257
    Organisation on Drugs and Crime,
        88, 89
    Special Rapporteur on Human
        Trafficking, 167, 168
    Universal Declaration of Human
        Rights, 201
Universities and Colleges Union, 232
University of East London, 231, 232
USA, 28, 38, 104, 170, 231

value chain(s), 17, 19, 21
Vienna Convention on Diplomatic
    Relations, 206
Vietnam, 74ff., 194
violence, 77ff
visa, 8, 10, 61, 64, 65, 66, 69, 123,
    169, 174, 183, 188, 201, 206, 207

Walmart, 21
Werner International, 40
Worker Rights Consortium, 40
Workers Registration Scheme, 105
Working Time Regulations, 189
in-work poverty, 5, 44, 48
World Bank, 34, 38

xenophobia, 28, 52

zero hours, 2

CPSIA information can be obtained
at www.ICGtesting.com
Printed in the USA
LVOW04*0134170116
470966LV00017B/452/P